1972

POSTWAR GERMAN THEATRE

Also by Michael Benedikt
and George E. Wellwarth

MODERN FRENCH THEATRE

POSTWAR GERMAN THEATRE

AN ANTHOLOGY OF PLAYS

EDITED AND TRANSLATED BY

Michael Benedikt AND *George E. Wellwarth*

MACMILLAN · LONDON · MELBOURNE

1968

MACMILLAN AND CO LTD
Little Essex Street London WC2
and also at Bombay Calcutta and Madras
Macmillan South Africa (Publishers) Pty Ltd Johannesburg
The Macmillan Company of Australia Pty Ltd Melbourne
The Macmillan Company of Canada Ltd Toronto

Printed in Great Britain by
Lowe & Brydone (Printers) Ltd., London

Individual Copyrights and Acknowledgments

GEORG KAISER: *The Raft of the Medusa.* English translation copyright © 1966 by George E. Wellwarth. Originally published as *Das Floss der Medusa* by Verlag Kiepenheuer & Witsch, Köln, copyright 1963.

WOLFGANG BORCHERT: *The Outsider.* English translation copyright © 1966 by Michael Benedikt. Originally published as *Draussen Vor Der Tür* in *Draussen Vor Der Tür und Ausgewählte Erzählungen* by Rowohlt Verlag GmbH., Hamburg, copyright 1956.

ERWIN SYLVANUS: *Dr. Korczak and the Children.* English translation copyright © 1966 by George E. Wellwarth. Originally published as *Korczak und die Kinder* by Rowohlt Verlag GmbH., Hamburg, copyright 1957.

FRIEDRICH DÜRRENMATT: *Incident at Twilight.* English translation copyright © 1966 by George E. Wellwarth. Originally published as *Abendstunde im Spätherbst* by Peter Schifferli Verlags AG "Die Arche," Zurich, copyright 1959.

MAX FRISCH: *The Great Fury of Philip Hotz.* English translation copyright © 1966 by Michael Benedikt. Originally published as *Die Grosse Wut des Philipp Hotz* in *Stücke 2* by Suhrkamp Verlag, Frankfurt am Main, copyright 1956.

TANKRED DORST: *Freedom for Clemens.* English translation copyright © 1966 by George E. Wellwarth. Originally published as *Freiheit für Clemens* by Verlag Kiepenheuer & Witsch, Köln, copyright 1962.

CARL LASZLO: *Let's Eat Hair!* and *The Chinese Ice-Box.* English translation copyright © 1966 by George E. Wellwarth. Originally published as *Essen Wir Haare* and *Der Chinesische Kühlschrank* by Verlag H. R. Stauffacher, Limmatquai 72, Zurich, copyright 1956. *Essen Wir Haare* also copyright 1956 as an opera with music by Rolf Fenkart by Verlag H. R. Stauffacher.

GÜNTER GRASS: *Rocking Back and Forth.* English translation copyright © 1966 by Michael Benedikt. Originally published as *Beritten Hin und Zurück* by Gustav Kiepenheuer Bühnenvertriebs GmbH., copyright 1960.

CONTENTS

* The date in parentheses indicates the year in which the play was completed.

A*

INTRODUCTION

CREATIVE DRAMA in Germany ended in 1933 and came to life again in 1945. There is a clear and indeed obvious reason for this. Dramatic form and content are conditioned by the politico-social situation under which the plays are written. Under the dictatorship which existed in Germany during the twelve-year cultural hiatus of the Nazi regime no creative artistic work was possible. Artistically, the Nazi regime was characterized by its maniacal orgies of public book burning. These tremendous hysteria-inducing, latter-day *autos-da-fé* served only to show up with their blackening flames the cultural night which had descended over Germany. It was indeed an insult during the Nazi period, as Georg Grosz complained, not to have one's books handed over to the secular arm by the literary inquisitors. Grosz's works were unjustly neglected. They deserved a nobler fate—that of his friend Bertolt Brecht's works, which were pitched into the conflagration as a matter of course.

Under the complete police-state that Germany was from 1933 to 1945 paintings, novels, essays, and plays were produced to order in accordance with the requirements of the Ministry of Propaganda; and artistic activity was consequently at a standstill. Like France and unlike England and America, Germany had produced a truly enormous amount of interesting and significant drama between the wars. Experimental and intellectual drama can only be produced in a politically permissive society, i.e., in a democracy. The Weimar Republic did not work, to be sure; but it was nevertheless as pure an example of the democratic form of government as the human race has seen since ancient Greece. Ger-

man writers were split between despair at what had happened
and hope for the future embodied in the twin beacons of
Weimar democracy and the starry-eyed, high-minded, and deluded
idealism of intellectual Communism. In England and America,
on the other hand, victory brought an intellectually debilitating
sense of relief and self-satisfaction, leading to a desire for a return to normalcy—in other words, to intellectual and artistic reaction. Only the anomalous efforts of Shaw and O'Neill consistently broke the rule of comfortable mediocrity in English and
American drama. The uninspired monotony of post-World War I
English and American drama is, as always, due to the national
temper. A nation that has won a war labors under the delusion
that it has won what it fought for—to wit, the preservation of the
prewar order. Subconsciously it must realize that that prewar order has been destroyed in the very act of being defended; and it
seeks solace for the disappointments of reality in wistfully viewing
the nostalgia-laden illusions served up on stage and screen. The
drama, which began as an extension of religious ritual, thus
comes full circle and rejoins its origins as a secondary opiate for
the masses.

In France the intellectual climate between the wars was somewhat different. France, to be sure, had also won the war—officially.
Physically, it had suffered more than Germany and bore all the
visible marks of a defeated nation. Spiritually, it was fully conscious of having been defeated and that its so-called victory was
really due to the help of Britain and America. Hemingway aptly
remarked that it was wrong to speak of a French defeat in World
War II, since they had already been defeated in World War I
and had never really recovered. France, then, was a victorious
country which had, in effect, been defeated; its postwar drama
reflected this in the cynicism of the Surrealists and the nihilism
of the Dadaists.

This is not the place to detail the fantastically varied and
lambent efflorescence of dramatic inventiveness which characterized the democratic German theater between the wars. We are
concerned here with the drama that sprang from the pulverized
rubble of Germany's total defeat in 1945. It is, as we shall see,
a drama of criticism, of vituperation, of guilt, and, in its later

stages, of withdrawal from reality through emphasis on technical experimentation.

The earliest of the plays in this book, Georg Kaiser's *The Raft of the Medusa*, like Brecht's plays,[1] actually belongs to the drama written during the war by exiled German writers. It is included here because it provides a link between the prewar German drama, of which Kaiser was one of the most prominent representatives, and the themes of a new generation of writers who became active after the war. Kaiser began his play in 1940, basing it on an actual occurrence which had been reported in the Swiss papers. Completed in 1943, it was first performed in Kaiser's adopted country in 1945, when Robert Pirk, another German exile, produced it at the State Theatre in Basle. German audiences did not see it until 1948, when Reva Holsey produced it at the Hebbel Theatre in Berlin.

The Raft of the Medusa lacks the angry reaction so character- istic of the postwar drama. Kaiser's orientation is more traditional, his effort more to understand and explain than to castigate. The lifeboat on which his thirteen children float to their destiny is a microcosm of the world, a fact which he emphasizes by making the children English rather than German. The germ of bestiality, of which the Nazi torpedoing of the children's ship was only one manifestation, is present in all men at all times. The innate decency of the rare good human being, Allan, is defeated, ironi- cally, by "civilized" society's perversion of Christianity, as per- sonified in Ann. Ann, corrupted by superstition and a perverse misinterpretation of Christ's teachings, singlemindedly pursues evil. Allan explicitly becomes a Christ figure at the end when he falls into a crucified position under the German plane's gunfire. Unable to bear the thought of living in a world where his love is returned with evil, he chooses to sacrifice himself. Allan and Ann represent the extremes of human conduct in the play, but it is the other children, nameless and almost indistinguishable from each other, who are, in a sense, the play's most important characters, because it is they who make Ann's evil intentions possible. They represent the followers and time-servers who, through spineless-

[1] The editors were unfortunately unable to obtain permission to include a later Brecht play in this anthology.

ness and acquiescence, abet evil and carry it out. They are the
gray and faceless masses who abdicated their moral responsibilities
and, with clear consciences, carried out orders as they played the
great game of "follow-the-leader." [2]

Kaiser's protest is mature, urbane, and based on a legend that
has become part of the matrix of universal dramatic themes. It
is angry—yes!; but always cold, incisive, controlled, and essentially
objective. Kaiser had a great deal of Shaw in him; he was an
artist attacking a problem analytically. When he had finished chip-
ping geometrical cracks in the problem, it crumbled—theo-
retically. Wolfgang Borchert's The Outsider had the same effect
but used the opposite method. With an hysterical, Samson-like
fury he exploded the problem from within. Borchert had been part
of the Nazi system. Only twenty-six when he died (with relentess
tragic completeness, on the day before the sensational première
of his great work), he had been forced to spend his whole life
beyond childhood in the grip of the oppressive Nazi system that
sought to mold his mind before it had had a chance to cast out
feelers and choose a path of its own. That Borchert was able to
grow mentally despite this premeditated and efficient attempt to
stunt his intellectual independence is an eternal testimony to his
genius.

If there is one word that could possibly sum up the spirit of
The Outsider, it is outrage. The play is a passionate rejection of
all that young Germans were taught, a graphic and mercilessly
unrestrained excoriation of the sinister and diabolic system that
had destroyed Germany so completely, both morally and physically. Borchert and his compatriots returned to a Germany that
truly reflected the vision of Jarry's nihilistic "Savage God," Père
Ubu: "Nous n'avons point tout démoli si nous ne démolissons
même les ruines!" [3] Even the ruins were razed to the ground.

The form which Borchert used to express his cosmic disgust
was an intensified variation of the Heimkehrer theme. A crippled soldier, obviously an alter ego for the author, comes home

---

[2] Kaiser also seems to have foreshadowed a good many of the elements in
William Golding's novel of a shipwrecked colony of children who descend to
savagery, Lord of the Flies.
[3] "We have not destroyed everything if we do not destroy even the ruins!"

to Hamburg to find his family gone and his house destroyed. The opening scene takes place at night on the banks of the Elbe. Everything is completely dark and silent. Then, faintly, we hear the unmistakable sound of a recently fed man belching. The belching comes nearer, and a spotlight picks out a portly gentleman in evening clothes taking an after-dinner stroll on the banks of the river. Cheerfully and callously he comments on a figure that is standing too close to the edge and seems about to fall or jump in. Jump in the figure does, and the fat man surmises that it is another one of the old soldiers who are constantly seeking the "easy way out" because they cannot find food or work in postwar Germany. An old man enters, and the two explain who they are. The old man is the God whom mankind has forgotten; now doddering and senile, he wanders forlornly over the earth trying to find in what way he has failed. The fat belcher is a member of the only profession that prospers anymore: he is an undertaker. Here we have a confrontation between the old God and the new. The former is now bewildered and old, wondering what he has done wrong; the latter is an obscene symbol of Death. The second scene takes place at the bottom of the Elbe. Borchert gives us a situation here that is at the same time completely expressionistic and completely credible. Beckmann, the soldier who has thrown himself into the river in the previous scene, lies on the riverbed where he has fallen. An old hag, the spirit of the Elbe, comes shuffling along and tells him to get up and get out: she is fed up with having the bottom of her river cluttered up with suicides who haven't the guts to face life. The Elbe, she tells him, is an industrial river and has better things to do than harbor suicides.

The rest of the play concerns Beckmann's futile and despairing attempts to find some place where he belongs after the Elbe has spewed him out again. But everywhere he goes he is unwanted; everywhere he winds up "draussen vor der Tür." The play ends with a tremendously powerful scene in which he curses all the people who have rejected him, including The Little Old Man Who Used To Be God who is still wandering around in his cosmic daze.

That *The Outsider* is to a great extent Borchert's personal protest against German postwar society is fairly obvious. Yet the play is by no means one long complaining wail. Despite the fact that Borchert had been brought up in Nazi society and was only in his twenties when he wrote the play, he was mature enough to realize where to lay the blame for the inhuman conditions of which he wrote. In two magnificent satiric scenes, entirely expressionistic in technique, he exposes the German's love of militarism and his ability to anesthetize his moral sense. In one of them Beckmann goes to visit the colonel of his old regiment. Beckmann has been having nightmares because the colonel once made him responsible for a group of men, eleven of whom were killed. In this nightmare, which is always the same, Beckmann is haunted by the eleven women the soldiers had left behind and by a giant skeletal figure in a general's uniform which plays on an enormous xylophone made of human bones. As Beckmann relates the dream to the colonel, he becomes more and more hysterical; the sound of the frantic xylophone fills the theater, and the colonel turns into the nightmarish figure of the skeleton with broad, blood-red stripes down its trousers. The other scene is very simple. Beckmann has stolen a bottle of liquor from the colonel's table. In his drunkenness he savagely caricatures the army routines which in his youth had enslaved his mind and crippled his body. Almost beside himself with rage, he struts around the stage, his stiff leg forcing him into a grotesque parody of the goosestep, shouting "Heil!" at every step. Borchert could not have written a sharper denunciation of the Nazi ritual than this furious, twisted ridicule.

The play remains important first because it is an excellent drama in itself, the only completed play by one of Germany's greatest modern poetic geniuses; second, because it is the most perfect expression of postwar German youth's disillusionment with the system which had ruined their country and their own best years; and third, because it is the only really successful re-creation of the World War I art form known as Expressionism.

Expressionism is a term that has been so frequently misunderstood that it might be advisable to define it at this point, particularly as it refers to a movement that has had a profound and lasting influence on the twentieth-century German drama. Expressionism is perhaps the most completely self-centred art form ever evolved. The expressionistic writer takes the whole human race and the whole cosmos as his province, but he observes it through the eyes of one character—almost invariably an alter ego for himself. Thus, for the expressionist, the world is crammed into the compass of one man's vision, and, as it is completely subjective, it becomes deliberately and purposefully distorted. This subjective distortion always emerges in the form of protest and rebellion. "Protest" and "rebellion" are, at least, the words that automatically come to mind when one thinks of the German expressionist drama, but perhaps they are somewhat too strong. The German expressionist drama is better characterized as complaint. It is *tua culpa* drama. "Not me, not me," the expressionist hero always screams, "it wasn't my fault—circumstances were to blame." The expressionist hero's eternal question is, "Why was *I* picked out to suffer this horrible fate? What have *I* done?" One would suppose that this endless wailing and cosmic complaining would rapidly become tiresome, but a surprising number of dramatists brought it off because they had enough poetic power to make their heroes' outbursts credible. The expressionist theater has been called an "ecstatic" theater by the critic Felix Emmel, a description that applies most appropriately to the language. In the hands of a master of language like Walter Hasenclever, of the early expressionists, or Wolfgang Borchert of those who came later, this ecstatic language makes the action and point of view of expressionistic drama completely credible and carries the audience along with it.

The most interesting aspect of post World War I expressionism—as compared to its revival after World War II—is the change that has taken place in the object of the rebellion. Originally expressionist drama dealt with rebellion within the family. The battle against the family as a symbol of repression has now been accomplished—indeed, has become out of date. The post World War II expressionist does not write plays of sons struggling against fathers: he faces the conflict directly and writes plays of sons struggling against their country and against God. Society and The Little Old Man Who Used To Be God have become the enemies.

Borchert's typically expressionistic reaction to the barbarism that he had encountered was immediate and instinctive—almost a reflex action. As the years wore on and as Germany rapidly rebuilt her damaged cities—the visible reminders of the depths to which she had sunk—the memory faded. Demonstrating a moral resiliency so extraordinary that it might be called a national characteristic, the Germans lapsed into a comfortable, even self-congratulatory, complacency and adopted a Pilate-like attitude of pseudopious and rather offended innocence. The dramatists and other responsible intellectuals of postwar Germany, many of them returned exiles, were horrified by the rapidity with which their countrymen had succeeded in repressing all consciousness of their guilt or in transferring it to the dead. They felt it their duty to become psychiatrists in reverse—to induce guilt complexes into a people that had all too successfully been practicing autotherapy. For the postwar German burgher, hard work equalled material prosperity equalled innocence. It was this pernicious logic that Erwin Sylvanus, for one, was trying to break down when he wrote *Dr. Korczak and the Children.*

Sylvanus chose to write about the murder of Jewish children in the Warsaw Ghetto. He realized, however, that straightforward narrative would have been useless. The audience would have felt (a) insulted because it was being told something it knew all about already; and/or (b) cheated because it had come to the theater to be entertained, not to be depressed by having old tales which were better left forgotten raked up again; and/or (c) outraged because it felt that the play was trying to place some of the blame on it, whereas everyone knew that the people who had perpetrated these regrettable incidents were all dead now. The playwright's task, then, in these dramas, was to find a way of shocking the audience into attention. Sylvanus's solution was an adaption of the Pirandellian method.

Pirandello's intention was either to involve the audience in the action and make it believe it was a part of it (e.g., *Each in His Own Way*) or to convince the spectators that their lives were themselves plays no more real than those depicted onstage (e.g., *Six Characters in Search of an Author, Right You Are, If You Think You Are*). Sylvanus realized that not even this was enough to arouse the audience any more. A new, more elaborate and sophisticated device was needed to arouse the jaded and apathetic consciences of the spectators. He hit upon the device of having them watch a group of ordinary people like themselves—the actors—become involved in the communal guilt of the mass murders. Instead of showing them a story and hoping that they would be affected by it, Sylvanus shows his spectators a group of actors becoming affected by the story as they rehearse it. These actors have the same background as the audience—they too had willingly functioned as cogs in the Nazi machine and they too had shifted the blame to cleanse themselves in the soothing waters of hypocrisy. As the audience watches these people who, with their professional actors' cynicism become caught up in their parts, it should become caught up too. Sylvanus felt that the Germans are so fortified with a sense of their own blamelessness that they could be affected only through a vicarious assumption of guilt. The nature of the theatrical experience is such that the audience's emotions are insidiously caught up by the activities and feelings of the characters; it is only when the audience's involvement is a *fait accompli* that it realizes that the "characters" are not characters at all but real people exactly like themselves. Sylvanus's play is one of the most brilliant demonstrations of the practical effectiveness of the Pirandellian method.

It is interesting to note that the extraordinarily bitter idea of *Dr. Korczak and the Children,* which appeared in 1957, took twelve years to percolate. There are two reasons for this. First, unless it is a spontaneous reaction to a sharp emotional stimulus, drama does not immediately reflect a social condition. The artist usually requires a period of five to ten years for thought and observation before he can reproduce his reaction. Second, *Dr. Korczak and the Children* was not written in direct reaction to the horrors of the war, as *The Outsider* was, but in direct reaction to something which, to such writers as Sylvanus, Hochhuth and Weiss, seemed perhaps even more morally appalling: the fantastic ease and rapidity with which the horrors had been forgotten. Plays such as *Dr. Korczak and the Children,* Hochhuth's *The Deputy,* and Weiss' *The Investigation* were written in order to rake up the horrors of the war again. They are savagely evocative

threnodies, full of moral indignation at the crimes perpetrated by
the Germans during the war, but even more at the way in which
those crimes have already been relegated to oblivion. These
writers have had as their stimulus the incredibly insouciant assumption of guiltlessness by their fellow countrymen, and their
dramas are attempts to erect expiatory wailing walls. The attempts
have been frequently brilliant, always laudable, and inevitably in
vain.

Playwrights who have tried to depict the refined bestiality
which might be said to have been the chief characteristic of
World War II have not always chosen to confront it directly, as
Borchert and Sylvanus did. Some, like Wolfgang Hildesheimer,
have felt it necessary to approach it obliquely. Like the post-
World War I surrealists, who felt that life was too false to be depicted directly and therefore distorted it in order to mock it and
rise above it, Hildesheimer removes his story to a vaguely symbolic
plane. The actions of the two characters in his *Nightpiece* have
verisimilitude, but none of the logic of everyday reality: they are
pregnant with meaning rather than meaningful.

During the war Hildesheimer, who had fled Nazism, was a
British Army liaison officer in Palestine. He is now an expatriate
again, living in southern Switzerland. The *Weltanschauung* dis-
played in his play *Nightpiece* is interestingly close to that of his
adopted fellow countryman, Friedrich Dürrenmatt. Like Dürrenmatt, Hildesheimer keeps his play free of specific applications to
reality but shows a detached, sardonic attitude shot through with
a despairing bitterness attributable to a single cause—the same
that provoked the anger of Borchert and Sylvanus.

Nightpiece is a study in madness—in which madness is shown
to be correct. The main character suffers from a compulsion neu-
rosis. His two great fears are that a burglar will some night succeed in entering his bedroom and that he will not be able to
sleep. For years, therefore, he has been unable to go to bed without performing a complex rigmarole of ritualistic precautionary
measures. The room has to be hermetically sealed by a series
of predetermined steps which are compulsively followed and
frequently repeated over and over again, since the play's victim (a
more accurate designation than protagonist in this case) con-

stantly forgets what he has already done. Inside the room stands
a huge wardrobe filled with bottles, jars, and boxes full of
sleeping pills of varying strengths, each narcotic level representing a stage in the victim's nervous disintegration. Three of these
stages are recounted in considerable detail: an eerie choirboys'
concert, a procession of cardinals in Rome, and a parade of el-
derly, shriveled women carrying laurel wreaths along the Champs
Elysées behind a military band. As the victim recounts them,
Hildesheimer's symbolic play becomes clearer. The victim seems
to be the tragically impotent humanist in the modern world.
Hemmed in by the powers of darkness—the forces of religious
superstition and social totemism—he is so appalled by what he
sees that he seeks refuge in the deeper darkness of self-induced
anesthesia. The humanist, the intellectual, is no longer able to
function. He does not understand what is going on around him;
he cannot comprehend what has happened to his ideal world;
the barriers he tries to throw up against it and its mysterious in-
trusions (represented by the enigmatic phone calls) are useless.
Although he has sealed his room—his refuge, his ivory tower—he
has forgotten to lock the front door. Although he has looked
under the bed, he has not seen the intruder there. The house
around his room has been ransacked. The elaborate precautions
he has planned in case a burglar does get in are useless: the burglar has no difficulty extricating himself from the complex, carefully designed system of knots with which the victim ties him.
And by the time the burglar is free, the victim has destroyed
himself with his narcotics. The burglar, of course, understands
the mysterious, senseless, encroaching, businesslike phone calls
perfectly well, for they are the code of the forces of organized
idiocy that have taken over the world. It is both instructive and
illuminating to note in this connection that Hildesheimer's
characterization of the burglar makes him seem blood-brother
to Willie the Arsonist in Max Frisch's *The Firebugs*.

Hildesheimer's mind typically works in a hermetic manner. In
Nightpiece, and even more in his symbolically titled *Plays in
which Darkness Falls* (*Spiele in denen es dunkel wird*), he has
clearly been profoundly influenced by the technique of French
surrealism. It is as if he were looking at the world from a slightly

distorted angle—obliquely from a parallel track, as it were.
Hildesheimer's parallel world is somewhat nearer to the world of
reality than the completely surrealistic world is, and here and there
it seems to be joined to it by connecting ties. Its spirit seems to
be less dissociated and ridiculing, more involved and therefore
more despairing than the world of pure surrealism. But, like the
neo-Dadaist Laszlo, he is clearly out of the traditional main-
stream of German drama. It is Borchert, with his self-centered
protesting hallucinations, who continues the tradition of German
drama begun in World War I by Sorge, Hasenclever, Goering,
Bronnen, Kornfeld, and others, a tradition carried on by Kaiser
and Sternheim between the wars. Hildesheimer, Laszlo, and the
French surrealists stand apart. They have preferred to resign
from a world they consider hopeless and not worth saving. To the
despairing and self-lacerating inverted ecstasy of the expressionistic *schrei*, they oppose the raised eyebrow and the twisted
smile. Their quiescent urbanity and cynicism provide a contrast
to the frantic outrage and masochistic abandon of the German
tradition. In the event it has taken on the appearance of a healthy
contrast, for frantic outrage remains undirected for just so long
and masochistic abandon soon passes over into its opposite. Even
Borchert's play, originally an outburst against the Nazis insofar
as it was an outburst against anything specific today takes on
a different meaning when self-pity and self-justification have
combined in the German mind to redirect Borchert's accusations
outside Germany's borders.

A different attitude of detachment just as extreme as that of
the surrealists marks the work of Friedrich Dürrenmatt. Dürrenmatt's urbanity and cynicism are intensified to such a degree
that his work can only be characterized as sardonic. He practices
an almost inhuman detachment and adopts the position of a
puppeteer-God toward his characters. It would be tempting to
attribute his objective attitude to his Swiss nationality were it
not for Max Frisch. Frisch has the same reasons or excuses as
Dürrenmatt for detachment, but plays like *The Chinese Wall*
and *The Firebugs* amply demonstrate his involvement. Dürrenmatt's *Weltanschauung* must therefore be attributed to personal
temperament. Neither specifically surrealistic or expressionistic

in technique, Dürrenmatt's technical eclecticism nevertheless places him in the forefront of contemporary theatrical experimenters. In *Incident at Twilight*, a play originally written in 1959 for radio performance, he employs the circular construction he had previously used in his full-length play, *The Marriage of Mr. Mississippi* (1950). In the latter play the beginning of the last scene was shown at the opening of the play, like a preview of coming attractions. In *Incident at Twilight* the play ends with its opening, so that Dürrenmatt gives the idea of continuous and endless repetition of the play's grotesque horror.

Like all of Dürrenmatt's plays, *Incident at Twilight* has a first-class suspense plot. The tremendously effective denouement comes when Korbes reveals that his crimes are not only well-known but actually condoned and abetted by society. We are again, in other words, in a condition of society where lawlessness is the accepted norm. Nobel Prize winner Korbes is a more sophisticated version of Willie the Arsonist and Hildesheimer's Burglar. Famous people are proud to be his friends; the Archbishop of Czernowitz himself is fully cognizant of his crimes. Only Feargod Hofer, the insignificant little bookkeeper, is unaware of the conspiracy of silence around him, just as Hildesheimer's victim is unaware of the meaning of the phone calls. Dürrenmatt, however, is typically more cynical about his presentation of Hofer: Hildesheimer's victim is simply helpless; Dürrenmatt's is tainted with self-interest. Hofer wants to become a part of the evil he has uncovered, to travel with the great man and be his confidant, to participate in Korbes's thrill-murders by proxy. His punishment is the discovery that Korbes himself commits his thrill-murders by proxy, so to speak: that as a murderer Korbes acts only as a surrogate for the sublimated wishes of the whole world. Korbes and Hofer are both puppet figures in what Dürrenmatt, arguing against the suitability of traditional concepts of tragedy in the modern world, so aptly calls "the Punch and Judy show of our century":

> Tragedy emphasizes guilt, despair, moderation, an all-encompassing vision, and a sense of responsibility. In the Punch and Judy show of our century there are no longer people who are

guilty or people who have responsibility. It wasn't anybody's fault, and nobody wanted it. Everything really did happen without anyone's actually doing anything about it. Everyone was swept along and caught somewhere. We are collectively guilty, collectively enmeshed in the sins of our fathers and of our fathers' fathers. We are simply the children of other children. That is not our guilt: it is our misfortune. Guilt exists only as a result of personal effort, as a religious deed. Comedy alone is suitable for us.[4]

Max Frisch, Dürrenmatt's compatriot and rival as the most consistently interesting and significant dramatist writing today, is hardly a "moralist without a moral," as one critic has called him. Quite the contrary. In such plays as *The Chinese Wall, The Firebugs,* and *Andorra* Frisch proves that he is probably the most indefatigably moralistic playwright active today. In *The Great Fury of Philip Hotz,* a light farce about that most terrible of all personal situations, the inability of a man to escape his fate, Frisch confines his moralizing to a more personal level. As in his early plays, *Santa Cruz* and *Count Öderland,* he sets up a Paradise-on-Earth, an illusory freedom which beckons the entrapped hero and promises him a release from his hidebound existence. In *Santa Cruz* the paradise is Hawaii; in *Count Öderland* it is the Isle of Santorin in the Aegean Sea. The Captain never makes it to Hawaii, and Count Öderland sees his dream turn to ashes when he attains it. Hotz, a far more comic character than either of his predecessors, wants to join the French Foreign Legion, but he too discovers that he can escape only in imagination.

The identification of imagination with freedom is also the theme of Tankred Dorst's *Freedom for Clemens,* in which a man is taught that life in a prison cell is just as free as life outside. At the end the door of his cell is open, but Clemens remains inside, preferring to communicate with his Clementine not by human speech, but by the tapping code of the prison. When Clemens first enters his cell all he can think about is his release from it. He hopes his appeal will go through, and he counts the days until his sentence will be over. Neither Clemens nor the

[4] Friedrich Dürrenmatt, *Theaterprobleme* (Zürich: Verlag der Arche, 1955), pp. 47–48.

prison Warden has any idea why he has been imprisoned. Dorst, like many of us, is aware that he is living in a world which Kafka has defined. As the play progresses, Clemens slowly realizes that he has no real reason for wanting to be released. The kind of life he has led in freedom he can live just as adequately within the prison walls. When the door is finally opened for him, he no longer feels any urge to go out.

This little allegory of freedom existing only in the imagination is, appropriately enough, composed in a very imaginative, highly theatrical way. Gesture and motion—which even at some points approach slapstick—are primary. In a note which precedes the play, Dorst specifies that "the movements of the characters should be pointed, rapid, stylized, almost dancelike . . . the actors . . . must be jugglers and acrobats capable of using dialogue the way a tightrope-walker would use a pole to enable him to keep balance on a swaying rope."

In Carl Laszlo's two playlets, *Let's Eat Hair!* and *The Chinese Icebox*, and in Günter Grass's *Rocking Back and Forth*, the concern with theatrical style is virtually total. Grass's skit about a group of hardboiled showbusiness people discussing a clown with callous insensitivity to his presence is, as near as we can give a definite interpretation to its deliberate vagueness, a comment on materialism encroaching on the life of the artist. Conelli the clown continues to ride his rocking horse and remains in his fantasy world while the materialists unfeelingly discuss his "possibilities." Laszlo's plays are even more experimental in technique. An Hungarian refugee living in Switzerland, Laszlo is the founder of Panderma, which is best described as a neo-Dada movement. Laszlo himself, however, would object to this description, as he would to any other, since the principal tenet of Panderma is that it has no connection with anything else and is a totally new and totally isolated artistic phenomenon. Laszlo has a reason for this statement since one of the purposes of Dada was to destroy itself, an aim in which it clearly succeeded despite the sporadic attempts of such aged and nostalgic Dadaists as Huelsenbeck to revive it. In its contemptuous and nihilistic attitude toward the world, however, Panderma approximates the philosophy of Dada, and it is best described as a re-creation of that movement. Both of Laszlo's plays in this anthology express a Dada-like disgust with tradition of any sort. *The Chinese Icebox* presents us with a cast of characters (an Overcoat, a Bat, the Queen of Aragon, etc.) bemoaning the fact that "We've been forgotten!" This threnody rises until finally it is uttered by the entire cast in urgent unison— and while yawning. *Let's Eat Hair!* is a play about language itself. Here high and low phrases—old-fashioned poetic phrases such as "The eagle flies low, with the night in its claws" and commercial phrases such as "Let's eat toothpaste—DENTO-GRIND"—are placed in curious and interesting juxtaposition. Laszlo's point about the impermanence and inadequacy of language is made in the final lines:

> DANIELE: Language is tranquilly disintegrating . . .
> JEAN-CLAUDE: The syllables . . .
> DANIELE: We're disappearing . . .
> JEAN-CLAUDE: Into the soft waves of the alphabet sea . . .

Though Dorst's and Laszlo's plays state the problem with lightness and even charm, the manner in which language is used—and misused—is a concern of many postwar German writers. The editor of one of the most important literary periodicals of the postwar period, *Akzente* (founded in 1945), the poet and essayist Walter Höllerer, has gone so far as to place indifference to language as among the chief characteristics of Nazi thought. For Höllerer, as for many observers both inside and outside Germany, the deadening of language is not only esthetically bad, but an immoral act tending ultimately to an abusive politics:

> Almost worse than the coarsening of the language of politics in Hitler Germany was the misuse of language in the literature sponsored by the regime. Apart from war books, this literature was neither vigorous in tone nor aggressive in attitude. There was nothing revolutionary about it. Instead, it was pseudo-idealistic, emotionally soothing, glorifying the tritest of virtues. . . . Things went along as though there had never been a technological world. This uncritical literature made things easy for the wielders of power. While literature prattled of landscape and love, reality could commit the most monstrous crimes, to a great degree unnoticed.[5]

[5] *Evergreen Review*, Vol. 5, No. 21, November–December, 1961, p. 120.

Like Dada, Panderma is interested in the breakdown of artistic form and conventional ideas of semantic precision as a protest against an irremediably meaningless world. The seeming insanity of Laszlo's two little plays is a calculated attempt to ridicule the everyday world and everything it represents. So extreme is this ridicule, indeed, that it is actually a resignation from the world.

Peter Weiss is a German-born dramatist who has lived in Sweden since before the war. Although, like Grass and Hildesheimer, he has done serious work as a graphic artist and has made many experimental films, his most successful work—as evidenced by the worldwide acclaim it has already received—is in dramatic form. The subject of Weiss's first play, *The Tower*, appears again in the two startling plays which followed it, *The Persecution and Assassination of Marat as Performed by the Inmates of the Asylum of Charenton under the Direction of the Marquis de Sade* and *The Investigation*. All three plays attempt to examine representatives of basic human types under the theatrical microscope. The cross-section of society in *The Investigation* and the opposition of Marat and Sade, representing the views of the political and the animal-sexual man, are matched in *The Tower* by a kind of psychological allegory. Pablo, the significantly gifted "escape artist," is the man who longs for freedom from all constricting bonds. The tower and its inhabitants represent all those barriers to liberty which man must overcome to be truly free: the past, one's family, habits, loves, and occupations, as well as all tradition. Throughout his shifting grid of implications Weiss carefully keeps the "realistic" metaphorical surface of circus life intact. As is true of *Marat-Sade* and *The Investigation*, the play—though its theme is abstract—is shot through by the intensely animating light of its clinical, prison-like setting. *The Tower*, in its realism, is doubtless the least horrifying of Weiss's plays. It is full of bizarre imagery, animated by hints of magic tricks, freaks, and acrobatic feats. The play unfolds as a kind of dream which overwhelms its chief character, Pablo. He imagines himself in a vague, circus-like atmosphere, a disembodied phantasmagoria of the painful and afflicting memories which assail him. It is only at the end of the play that the circus metaphor is definitively broken. Pablo has what one might call a successful return engagement at the tower—but, as he bursts his bonds one last time, Weiss has a disembodied voice make an astonishing analogy: "The rope dangles down from him now like an umbilical cord." The tower is not only the past, not only all tradition, but the world of the womb from which every human freedom that exists is basically a departure.

Both in the special examples which we have selected for inclusion here and in its general development, the tendency of the postwar German theater is clearly toward a radical rejection of the past. As we have noted, a strong distrust of simple messages, not to mention easy panaceas, characterizes much of the very best of recent German drama.[6] This disillusioned scepticism, combined with an interest in formal experimentation, is what chiefly characterizes the new German drama. Postwar German drama has come from the serious, idealistic, singleminded reformism of Brecht and the expressionistic protest of Borchert to a merging of this moral current with the surrealistic stream emanating from post World War I French drama. In Hildesheimer, Dorst, and Grass among the native Germans, and in Dürrenmatt, Frisch, and Laszlo among the "foreign" Germans, we can see German drama becoming more open, more experimental, and more international. The singleminded moralizing, the schoolmasterish didacticism, the self-righteous missionary quality and its corollary feeling of intolerance, and the sense of barely controlled hysteria which are so typical, in whole or in part, of German drama from expressionism on, are all absent in these "new German dramatists." And, undeniably brilliant though many of the typically German dramatists were, there can be little argument about the ultimate healthiness of this absence. In building from the ground up, the new German dramatists have not only wrecked the old ruins,

---

[6] Considerations of space aside, it is for this reason that we have not included any examples of East German theater. In a sense, even the most talented and interesting playwrights of East Germany continue an earlier tradition of simple solutions. Although there are undeniably gifted dramatists in East Germany—men such as Peter Hacks, Joachim Knauth, and Harald Hauser —they are committed to a particular point of view, one that involves the writer's deliberate intellectual subjugation to the service of a doctrinaire ideal. As a result, the East German plays, in which aesthetics equals doctrine, are interesting only from a sociological viewpoint, seldom from an artistic one.

but they have created structures which can stand on their own among the creations of the contemporary theater. The new German theater is liberal, humanistic, and no longer characteristically national. It is a European, rather than a German theater.

* * *

For convenience's sake, the editors of this anthology agreed that one of them should assume responsibility for the Introduction. I must, however, acknowledge my gratitude to Michael Benedikt for his ideas concerning Laszlo, Weiss, Dorst, Grass and the paragraph concerning Höllerer and the misuse of language which will be found on page xxiv.

GEORGE E. WELLWARTH

THE RAFT OF
THE MEDUSA

by GEORG KAISER

TRANSLATED BY GEORGE E. WELLWARTH

In September, 1940, a ship carrying children from the bombed cities of England to Canada was torpedoed on the high seas. Only a very few of the children were able to escape in the lifeboats. The following scenes describe what happened in one of these lifeboats during the seven days it drifted: how eleven of the thirteen in the boat were eventually saved and how the rescue plane came too late for the other two.

Characters

ALLAN

ANN

SECOND BOY

THIRD BOY

FOURTH BOY

FIFTH BOY

SIXTH BOY

SECOND GIRL

THIRD GIRL

FOURTH GIRL

FIFTH GIRL

SIXTH GIRL

LITTLE FOX

PILOT

PROLOGUE

Since it is night, only sounds and flashes of fiery light mark the work of destruction. Out of the initial darkness and the almost noiseless rocking of the waves burst the first blinding light of the explosion and the crash made by the breaking plates of the iron ship.

The roar of the flames drowns out human voices—and human forms are too diminutive to be seen against the overwhelming flood of flame and smoke.

Nothing but sounds and light.

Forked-lightning flames flash up, followed by thunderclaps from exploding boilers.

Flaming bits of wood shoot into the air and shower dancing sparks down from far overhead.

Yet these are still isolated fires, kindling sudden but separate bursts of flame.

The ship is as yet only partly in the grip of fire. The fury of the flames even seems to subside for a moment.

The scene becomes quieter and darker.

During this interval the lifeboats are lowered with a rattling of chains. The rattling sound knifes through the crackling of the lurking fire.

One of the boats hits the water with a violent, explosive splash. Several other boats follow

Then the intense heat ignites the ship's fuel. A hail of glowing pieces of steel sails upward into night and emptiness: the oil has burst out of its tanks and pipes.

The fire flows liquid-like over the deck; the ship's flaming outline is now unbroken.

The stark design of the sacrifice is complete—now it can become reality.

The iron hull breaks in two. The water rushes in and drags both sections down into the depths. The bow and the stern stand up on end like harpooned whales, and, capped by a cloud of steam and smoke, sink further and further until even the faintest glimmer of fiery light has faded away. The ship and all its cargo has now been wiped out utterly by the waters.

NIGHT

The blackness thickens over the sea,
whose aimless thudding flood roars dully back and forth.
Sometimes waves break, as if lamenting hands
were to be clapped together.
   Thus the sea mourns.
Then the wind raises its lamenting voice.
At first a sighing wail—swelling up; dying away.
Returning with stronger cries—joining with
other sounds from far away. Uniting with them—
   and the wailing forms a word:
     MEDUSA
     MEDUSA
     MEDUSA
     MEDUSA
The sounds disperse, and only a muffled sighing
echoes for a moment—
     then it, too, dies away.

THE FIRST DAY

The lifeboat emerges from the dawn mist. It is swept from sight again by other, thicker mists. Once again it appears—then disappears once more into the fog.

The fog dissolves at last, and nothing remains to hide the boat. Twelve children—six boys and six girls—crouch on its benches, huddled in sleep. They are ten—eleven—twelve years old.

They are an indistinguishable mass in their colorless raincoats. Their heads are bare.

One boy—Allan—wears a white wool muffler.

One girl—Ann—clasps an object to her breast.

The boat lies motionless on the leaden surface of the sea.

The early morning light becomes brighter.

Ann is the first to blink her eyes and awake. She peers cautiously out of half-opened eyes, taking in only what is directly before her: the middle of the boat—and nothing but the middle of the boat. She cannot prevent herself from opening her eyes a little wider now: the water beyond the edge of the boat is real—it is unalterable reality. Now her eyes sweep to the left and take in her shipmates in that half of the boat; now to the right, where the others crouch.

This exhausts the possibilities of discovery.

Now she becomes aware of the object she is hugging to her breast. She loosens her grasp: the object is a Thermos bottle. She unscrews the cap, which also serves as cup, and pours out some liquid, which she drinks.

Allan wakes up. He too slowly surveys the boat and his shipmates —until he notices Ann.

ANN (*showing him the cup*): Want some?

ALLAN: (*Looks at her and smiles.*)

ANN (*shaking her head*): Sure?

ALLAN: All right.

ANN: (*Pours.*)

ALLAN: What is it?

ANN: Milk.

ALLAN (*repeating*): Milk.

ANN: Or don't big boys drink milk?

ALLAN: How old do you suppose I am?

ANN (*calculating*): Twelve.

ALLAN: (*Nods.*)

ANN: I'm twelve too.

ALLAN: That isn't the same thing, though.

ANN: What isn't the same thing?

ALLAN: Twelve-year-old girls are older than twelve-year-old boys.

ANN: Is that better or worse for the boys?

ALLAN: That's why they can't marry.

ANN (*amused*): Who—us?

ALLAN: I mean people who are the same age don't marry.

ANN (*laughing*): But I was fibbing—I'm really only eleven.

ALLAN: That makes a big difference.

ANN: Can you marry me now?

ALLAN: That's something you'll have to think about.

ANN: And how about you?

ALLAN: I don't need to think about it.

ANN (*offering the cup*): Here, take some.

ALLAN (*taking the cup with his outstretched hand, amazed*):
    Warm milk!

ANN: Drink some.

ALLAN (*drinking*): It's really hot.

ANN: It's from the Thermos bottle.

ALLAN: You managed to rescue it?

ANN: And you?

ALLAN (*after he has finished drinking*): My muffler. (*Unwinding
    it.*) Here, it's yours if you want it.

ANN: No.

ALLAN: You gave *me* a drink from your Thermos bottle.

ANN: That was just a swallow.

ALLAN: I'm warm now.

ANN: I'm not cold.

ALLAN: But you will be—and you've got to promise me you'll take the muffler then.

ANN: I promise.

ALLAN *(after a pause)*: What's your name?

ANN: Ann.

ALLAN *(repeating)*: Ann.

ANN: And you?

ALLAN: Allan.

ANN: Really?

ALLAN: Sounds nice, doesn't it: Allan and Ann?

ANN: You say that as if we were—

ALLAN: As if we were all alone in the world: Allan and Ann.

There is a short pause during which both children look away from each other, out over the water. The stiff forms of the boat's other occupants slowly come to life.

SECOND BOY *(rubbing his eyes and getting up)*: Where's the ship?

THIRD BOY: What ship?

SECOND BOY: Our ship.

FOURTH BOY: It got torpedoed, silly!

FIFTH BOY: It couldn't stay afloat if it got torpedoed, now, could it?

SIXTH BOY: It went up in flames right after it got torpedoed!

FIFTH BOY: The oil caught fire.

FOURTH BOY: If there hadn't been any wind to blow the smoke away—

THIRD BOY: —We'd have suffocated in the smoke.

SECOND BOY: Now we don't have any ship anymore. *(He sits down and buries his face in his hands.)*

The children are silent for a short time.

ALLAN (*giving Ann the cup back*): The milk will get cold if you don't put the top back on.

ANN (*takes the cup and looks around the boat*): Anyone thirsty?

SECOND GIRL (*raising her hand*): I am.

ANN: No one else?

THIRD GIRL: You don't have enough there for all of us.

ANN: Yes, I do—if I divide it up.

ALLAN: I've had some already.

ANN: Me too. How many are there?

FOURTH GIRL (*counting heads*): Five boys.

SECOND BOY (*also counting*): And five girls.

ANN: All right, ten. Ten half-cups. Sit still or I'll spill some. (*She pours.*) Who's first?

SECOND GIRL: I'm first. (*She takes the cup and hands it back after she has drunk.*)

ANN (*pouring again*): Who's second?

THIRD GIRL: I'm second. (*She drinks and hands the cup back.*)

ANN (*pouring*): Who's third?

FOURTH GIRL: I'm third. (*She drinks and hands the cup back.*)

ANN (*pouring*): Who's fourth?

FIFTH GIRL: I'm fourth. (*She drinks and hands the cup back.*)

ANN (*pouring*): Who's fifth?

SIXTH GIRL: I'm fifth. (*She drinks and hands the cup back.*)

ANN (*pouring*): Who's sixth?

SECOND BOY: I'm sixth. (*He drinks and hands the cup back.*)

ANN (*pouring*): Who's seventh?

THIRD BOY: I'm seventh. (*He drinks and hands the cup back.*)

ANN (*pouring*): Who's eighth?

FOURTH BOY: I'm eighth. (*He drinks and hands the cup back.*)

ANN (*pouring*): Who's ninth?

FIFTH BOY: I'm ninth. (*He drinks and hands the cup back.*)

ANN (*pouring*): Who's tenth?

SIXTH BOY: I'm tenth. (*He drinks and hands the cup back.*)

ANN (*shaking the Thermos bottle*): Twelve of us have drunk now, and the bottle still isn't empty. The rest is for the first one to feel faint.

SECOND GIRL (*anxiously*): Why are we supposed to feel faint?

SECOND BOY: In case it takes a long time.

THIRD GIRL: In case what takes a long time?

THIRD BOY: Till we sight land.

FOURTH GIRL: Are we that far from land?

FOURTH BOY: There's nothing but sea all around us.

FIFTH GIRL: Are we right in the middle of the sea?

FIFTH BOY: We put out to sea three days ago, so there can't be any land anywhere near us.

SIXTH GIRL: What did we ever leave for?

SIXTH BOY: They said children shouldn't live in cities that were getting bombed.

SECOND GIRL (*after a pause*): That's right—we're only children! Our whole ship was full of children, that's all. We play games, we sing songs, and we don't do anyone any harm. And if we did, anyone could come along and punish us. Why should they want to drop bombs on us anyway? We're not bad, are we? We're not grownups yet, are we? We only want to run away from the terrible things grownups do. They're just wicked—but we're children and we never do any of those horrible things they do. If they could only see us now, they'd never be so cruel again. If they could only see how one of us gives up the little milk she's saved even though she needs it just as much herself! (*Losing control.*) They should put it in all the papers of the world—how children act when they're together and left alone just to be themselves! Why don't the grownups care what harm they do?! (*She bursts into tears, hiding her face in her arms.*)

Pause.

ALLAN (*loud*): Let's search the boat! Every lifeboat has emergency rations which are supposed to last the grownup crew for a long time. We're only children and need less food. Sometimes I get full-up with just a few bites, myself. Anyone who wants half my share can have it.

SECOND BOY: I wouldn't take it for anything. Not me!

THIRD GIRL: Anyone who'd take it, wouldn't be behaving right.

THIRD BOY: That's right—he'd simply be doing wrong.

FOURTH GIRL: He couldn't expect any girl in this boat to take any notice of him.

FOURTH BOY: The girls should get more to eat than us.

GIRLS (*jumping up*): No—less!

BOYS (*jumping up*): No—more!

ALLAN: The boat's rocking—don't capsize it!

Everyone becomes silent at once and sits down.

ALLAN: Let's get the oars out now. The food's stowed away under them. Everyone give a hand.

Working all together, the children pull the four long oars out from under the benches and stow them lengthwise along the inside of the boat. Then they rest, breathing heavily.

ALLAN (*pulling out another pole*): The boathook. That's for keeping the boat fast to something else. We can't do without that. Take care of it. (*He hands it to several of the others. Then he stoops down in the bow of the boat.*) Here's something! (*He lifts up a sailcloth and calls out:*) Bags—boxes! Biscuits—sugar—ham! And lots of cans of water! They haven't forgotten a thing. We'll have plenty of provisions if we're careful. We won't start till midday and then we'll try and do without another meal as long as we can. (*He folds the sail-*

cloth down again, turns round and looks over the boat.) What's back there?

SECOND BOY *(in the stern)*: Here?

ALLAN: What's that stuff covered up back there?

SECOND BOY *(helped by some of the others, he removes the crumpled sailcloth)*: Here's someone else!

All the children look at the find.

THIRD GIRL: Is he dead?

FOURTH GIRL: His eyes are open.

THIRD BOY: He's alive.

FOURTH BOY: Don't you want to get up?

THIRD GIRL: Can't you get up?

SECOND BOY: Are you hurt?

FOURTH GIRL: He'd be crying if he was.

SECOND BOY: Let's sit him on the bench and ask him how he got into the boat.

As he is lifted up on to the bench, we see that the newcomer is a nine-year-old boy with red hair and freckles, dressed in a rust-red sweater. He has a flashlight attached to a string hanging on his chest.

FIFTH GIRL *(as she sees him)*: Red as a little fox!

The children laugh.

SECOND BOY: Okay—you're a little fox. We've dragged you out of your hole. You might have suffocated in there. Why didn't you crawl out by yourself?

The Little Fox remains silent and stares at the children.

SECOND BOY: Can't you talk?

The Little Fox remains silent and stares.

SECOND BOY: You still upset because we were torpedoed and everything was burnt?

The Little Fox remains silent and stares.

B*

SECOND BOY: That's all over now: the noise—the explosion—the fire. I bet you still see sparks before your eyes, right?

The Little Fox remains silent and stares.

SECOND BOY: You must have run off and jumped into the boat right away. You don't even have a coat—just a flashlight. Does it work? (*He switches it on.*) It works—so what are you so sad about? No reason at all. Believe me, *I'd* be pretty happy if I had a flashlight with fresh batteries. (*He switches it off and turns to the others.*) Hey—anybody here who wouldn't like to have a flashlight just like the little fox's here?

THIRD GIRL (*after a pause*): We should give him something to drink.

FOURTH GIRL: There was still some warm milk left.

THIRD GIRL (*to Ann*): Give us the Thermos bottle.

ANN: Do you know how to open it?

THIRD GIRL: Why don't you open it?

ANN: You go ahead.

THIRD GIRL (*takes the bottle, unscrews the cap and fills it*): There—now drink, Little Fox.

The Little Fox seizes the cup convulsively and empties it.

THIRD GIRL: Now everyone has had his share of the milk—and now the bottle is empty! (*To Ann*) There's your empty bottle.

ALLAN (*clapping his hands*): Come on now—let's all row!

SECOND BOY: Where to?

ALLAN: Toward land.

THIRD BOY: But we're in the middle of the ocean!

ALLAN: How do you know? Ships always sail a zigzag course in wartime—it lessens the danger. Maybe we're not far from land at all—we might even reach it today. Put the oars into the oarlocks.

SECOND BOY: The oars are too big and heavy for children.

ALLAN: If we work three to an oar, we'll manage.

SECOND GIRL: We challenge the boys to see who can last longer.

The girls take over one bench and the boys another. With considerable effort the oars are put into position.

ALLAN: We have to stay in a one-two rhythm. Oars into the water at one—out at two. Everyone count: one—

ALL (*in chorus*): One—two—one—two—one—two—

The oar-strokes start the boat moving. The Little Fox sits on the bench in the stern of the boat as if paralyzed. The boat disappears, and the children's chorus fades away.

The Second Day

The clouds of mist sweep aside. The boat with its cargo of sleeping children becomes visible. The oars have been shipped and lie lengthwise along the inner edge of the boat. A sound like whimpering and baying—somewhat like the yelping of a small dog—is heard in the boat. It awakes the children, who straighten up from their crouching positions.

SECOND GIRL: Did a puppy get in our boat or something?

THIRD GIRL: During the night?

FOURTH GIRL: From the ship?

FIFTH GIRL: It's barking again.

All of them sit still and listen.

FOURTH BOY: Dogs can't keep swimming for a whole day and night.

FIFTH BOY: And anyway, they couldn't climb up over the edge of the boat after that.

SIXTH BOY: Maybe it's a seal.

SECOND BOY (*lifting up the sailcloth in the stern*): It's Little Fox. He's crept under the sailcloth again. Wake up, Little Fox.

The dogs aren't after you. No one's biting you. (*He shakes him.*) There. Now you're wide awake again. Come on, get up. It's morning.

FIFTH GIRL: He never gets up by himself.

SECOND BOY: Come on—we'll lift you up on the bench. (*Together with the Fifth Boy, he lifts the Little Fox on to the stern bench.*) You must have been having a nightmare. Who was chasing you anyway? Big, snarling dogs, all ready to tear you to pieces with their jaws? Well, where are they now? Gone! Now you see us. We're not wild dogs chasing you and tearing you to pieces, are we? You're not scared of people's faces, are you? Of children's faces—we're not even people yet really? You're not scared of us, are you?

THIRD GIRL: He's got to recover a bit yet.

FOURTH BOY: Well, let's leave him alone till he does.

They turn away from him.

ALLAN (*in the bow*): We'll start the day with a bag of biscuits. (*He brings out the bag.*) This is some knot! I can't get it undone. Who's got better fingers for this?

ANN (*taking the bag*): I have.

ALLAN (*watching her*): You're really good at it! I've never seen fingers like that. They're like ivory.

ANN: That's because I'm an elf.

ALLAN: How come you're an elf?

ANN: Because I—(*Opening the bag.*) Because I've undone the knot. (*She hands the bag back.*)

ALLAN (*still looking at her*): No—you are one anyway. I wouldn't even be surprised if you could fly.

ANN: If I could, I'd fly away and come back with a big airplane to rescue us.

ALLAN: Yes—I bet you'd do that.

ANN: I will, too—if I get some biscuit right now.

ALLAN: If everyone just takes two, there'll be enough.

The bag passes from child to child, each one taking two biscuits. The Fifth Girl offers the bag to the Little Fox.

SECOND BOY: You'll have to give him his—he'll never take it by himself.

FIFTH GIRL: Here, Little Fox—take one in each of your little fox paws. Now eat. Eat with us. Just like everyone else. Now we're all eating together.

The Little Fox follows the example of the others, who are all busily eating their biscuits.

ANN (*stopping suddenly*): Thirteen!

Several children direct their attention at her.

ANN: We're thirteen!

The other children take no notice.

ANN: Are you all deaf? Stop eating! We're thirteen!

SIXTH BOY: There's plenty of room here for thirteen.

ANN: There's room for more than thirteen. For fourteen—fifteen—sixteen. But we can't have thirteen.

FOURTH BOY: Says who?

THIRD GIRL (*bursts out laughing*): Says who!

FOURTH BOY: Well, I'm a city boy, you know—I don't know anything about rules of the sea.

SECOND GIRL: It's got nothing to do with rules of the sea!

FOURTH BOY: Well, with what?

ANN: With Christianity!

THIRD GIRL: Aren't you a Christian?

FOURTH BOY: Sure I am.

ANN: Who isn't a Christian here?

SECOND BOY: We're all Christians here, of course!

ANN: Well, there you are. We're thirteen Christians—and so we're all lost!

Pause.

THIRD BOY: That's not always certain.

THIRD GIRL: What do you mean, not certain?

THIRD BOY: That thirteen Christians always—

SECOND GIRL: Thirteen Christians—not thirteen heathens!

FOURTH GIRL: It doesn't apply to heathens anyway!

THIRD GIRL: The heathens aren't like us. They're just heathens!

THIRD BOY: I'm not talking about heathens—I'm talking about Christians! I don't even *know* any heathens.

FOURTH GIRL: And what do you know about Christians?

THIRD BOY: You can have thirteen Christians in a bus, can't you? And the bus doesn't just go and tip over then, does it?

ANN: That's when you're traveling—the bus doesn't have to tip over in that case.

THIRD BOY: Well, there you are!

ANN: They're not eating. You don't sit at table and eat in a bus. But we are eating here in this boat. That's the big difference.

THIRD BOY: No, it isn't—there's no table here.

ANN: Well, we're actually drinking from the same bottle and eating out of the same bag—isn't that much worse? Jesus didn't do anything like that—and he was crucified anyway!

THIRD GIRL (*after a pause*): Yes, that's right—it all comes from Jesus.

ANN: It comes from the Last Supper—and there isn't anything more sacred than that. Or maybe you think it doesn't apply to us because we're better than Jesus and his disciples?

THIRD BOY (*timidly*): I never said I was better.

SECOND GIRL: Well, maybe it just sounded that way.

THIRD BOY: I don't always say what I mean.

FOURTH GIRL: You won't be able to do that when you're before God in Heaven.

THIRD BOY: But I believe in the same things you believe in.

SECOND GIRL: Now you're just being a coward.

THIRD BOY: Me—a coward? (*To the other boys.*) If anyone here blasphemes against Jesus or makes fun of the Last Supper, I'll—(*He shakes his fists.*)

ANN: Well, it looks like you've learned your lesson finally. They certainly don't seem to have taught you very much where you went to school. Jesus leads everyone into temptation, so that they will believe in him. That's why we're in this boat. The ship would never have been torpedoed if you'd felt more respect for Jesus and his twelve apostles—who make thirteen altogether. We've got you to thank that we're out here in the middle of the ocean now, all ready to sink if a storm comes up. And with thirteen here it will come up!

Silence reigns in the boat.

ALLAN (*reassuringly*): There won't be any storm.

ANN (*pointing at him*): *That* is a heathen!

ALLAN: My baptism was just as Christian as any other in our country.

FOURTH GIRL: Then you have to believe.

ALLAN: But not in the storm.

ANN: But the storm is the result of true belief.

ALLAN: Is it true belief?

THIRD GIRL: What else could true belief be but true belief?

ALLAN: Superstition.

THIRD GIRL: All right, then. I'll tell you a story about how my parents behaved. And they're grownups—big grownups. You should see my father—he's not afraid of anybody. And my mother—she's just as fearless as my father. But once we had company to dinner and I was already in bed. Suddenly my mother dashed into my room, shook me until I woke up, and cried: "You've got to get up right away—one of the guests isn't coming—we're thirteen now." Nobody would have sat down—and all that lovely food would have been spoiled.

The guests looked pale as corpses and their hands shook when they used their knives and forks—and all because they would have been thirteen if my parents hadn't counted carefully. The guests kept thanking my parents the whole evening—and the next day one of my aunts came and brought my mother a present because she'd been so alert. That's how seriously eating thirteen at table is taken.

SECOND GIRL (*sighing*): Yes—it's terribly serious.

FOURTH BOY (*after a pause*): I know of a case too.

SEVERAL GIRLS: What kind of case?

FOURTH BOY: Well, this is something I overhead. I've got big parents who aren't afraid of anything either. I was sick once and couldn't get up or they'd have come and taken me in with them, too. My room was right next to the hall, and I could hear the guests arriving. The door kept opening and shutting and pretty soon just about everyone was there. Then I heard my parents coming into the hall and opening the door themselves when it rang again. My parents took turns talking: "My dear doctor, you must go away again." "Heaven knows how it happened, but we miscalculated, and now we're thirteen." Then I heard the doctor, very startled, call out: "Don't tell the others about the mistake—it could have unpleasant consequences." "God forbid," whispered my mother, "we'll say we haven't seen you for days." Then I heard the sound of the party going on half the night. They didn't even dare *tell* that the thirteenth had *almost* appeared. And, believe me, I kept my mouth shut as if it had been sealed up.

THIRD BOY (*his head in his hands*): It could have turned out terribly if you hadn't!

ALLAN: You can't tell how it would have ended.

SECOND GIRL: Of course nobody can tell since they went and took the proper precautions.

ALLAN: What I'm just wondering is if it really has to end so terribly. All I'm saying is there's no proof.

ANN: You don't think all that was proof? All right then, I'll give you a proof. My uncle has a big estate—it's like a world without end! I used to go there during the holidays and I

could ride and swim there—anything I wanted to do I could.
My uncle was a great hunter. He'd even hunted dangerous
animals in other parts of the world! I think he's even killed
snakes! That's the most daring thing of all. He never boasted
about what he'd done, though. Sometimes he used to talk
about his gardener, who had eleven children. But my uncle
didn't think that was too many. He used to say, "If only he
had twelve, then they wouldn't always be sitting thirteen at
table. As long as they're thirteen, they'll never get away from
their misery." Then one of the children died, and my uncle
was really happy for the sake of his gardener's family. "At
last," he said, "the curse is lifted—the dead child has freed
the living." And from then on there was nothing but peace
and happiness in the gardener's house. But only after the
thirteenth died.

SIXTH GIRL (*after a pause*): Did your uncle really hunt lions and
snakes?

ANN: Yes—and that's the proof of the whole thing, because a man
like that knows what's dangerous and what isn't. Snakes and
lions are less dangerous than thirteen who eat and drink together.

*The children now sit despondently and hesitate to take any
more bites out of the biscuits in their hands. The Little Fox
does not eat either, since the others have stopped.*

ALLAN (*jumping up*): Let's keep rowing. Somewhere there's land
—some island which maybe we can reach with just a few
strokes. Then we'll laze around under the palm trees and let
the natives feed us. Everyone will have his own hut and he'll
eat and drink alone as much as he likes. Come on—let's row!
(*He steps over the benches in order to take a seat near the
Little Fox.*) You count cadence, Little Fox. Can you count
like this: one—two?

ANN: Little Fox can't do anything. We have to do everything
ourselves.

*The long oars are put back into rowing position. The children
—boys and girls all mixed up together this time—swing the
oars out and, counting cadence, move the boat forward.*

ALL (*echoing*): One—two—one—two—one—two—

The Third Day

The morning mists melt away.

The children are crouched asleep in the boat.

Only the Second Girl sits upright, awake. Carefully holding her right hand out away from her, she pulls her handkerchief awkwardly out of her right-hand coat pocket with her left hand. Once she has the handkerchief, she moves to the edge of the boat. She leans out over it and soaks the cloth in the water. Slowly she pulls it out again and straightens up. Working awkwardly with her left hand, she wraps the wet cloth around her right hand. As soon as she has done this, a shrill scream breaks from her. The scream becomes wild sobbing as the girl writhes in pain.

The other children wake up and turn their heads in the direction of the noise.

SECOND GIRL (*waving her right hand*): Tear it off!—Tear it off!— I'm burning!

THIRD BOY: What do you mean, you're burning?

SECOND GIRL: You don't care if I burn up—how mean you are!

FOURTH BOY: You want that handkerchief off?

SECOND GIRL: Tear it off before my hand burns up!

THIRD GIRL (*taking it off*): What happened?

SECOND GIRL (*whimpering*): What—what—it was salt water, of course. I forgot that sea water is salty. And salt on an open wound—it's like touching fire!

SIXTH BOY: How can you even stand the pain?

SECOND GIRL: I can't stand it. I couldn't even stand it before. It wouldn't let me get to sleep. I've been awake the whole night, but I was afraid that I'd fall out of the boat if I leaned over the water in the darkness. Then when it finally got to be morning and a little brighter, I used my left hand—'cause it wasn't so bad as the other one—to get my hanky out of my other coat pocket and dipped it in the water and wrapped it around my bad hand. Now it's bleeding. There, you can all see the blood running out! (*She lifts her right hand.*)

FOURTH BOY: If it bleeds, it'll get better faster.

SIXTH BOY: That way the salt'll run out.

FIFTH BOY: You just let it bleed.

THIRD GIRL (*covering her eyes*): I can't bear the sight of blood!

SIXTH GIRL (*same action*): It's terrible—human blood!

THIRD BOY: It's dripping into your sleeve.

FOURTH BOY: Boy, you've got it all over you.

SECOND GIRL: Where?

FIFTH GIRL: It's all over your face because you wiped your eyes.

SECOND GIRL: I wiped my tears. Can't I cry since it hurts so much?

ALLAN (*after a pause*): Does it still hurt a lot?

SECOND GIRL (*sobbing*): Tears are salty too—like the sea.

ALLAN (*taking an empty biscuit bag*): I'll make you a bandage out of this bag. Both hands?

SECOND GIRL: This one isn't bleeding yet, but it might start any moment if I hit it on something.

ALLAN: All right, two bandages. First I'll dampen it—with some better water than you used. (*He brings out a canister.*)

SEVERAL CHILDREN: Drinking water!

ALLAN: Can't I use my share any way I want?

FIFTH BOY: You want to die of thirst?

ALLAN: Die of thirst? I don't get thirsty so fast if I don't want to. (*He soaks the strips of linen in the canister. To the Second Girl:*) Here, give me your hands—I'll bandage them. Does that cool it off? (*She nods.*) That's the way. If you'll hold the bandaged hands up in the wind, it'll feel like ice. Dampness feels colder in wind. Remember that.

SECOND GIRL (*smiling*): I'll remember.

ALLAN: You can learn all sorts of things on an adventurous sea journey. (*He goes back to his seat in the bow.*)

SECOND GIRL (*looking around*): Do I look terrible?

THIRD GIRL: Wipe the blood off your face.

SECOND GIRL (*lifting her bandaged hands*): I don't have any fingers.

THIRD BOY: Oh, leave it. A little blood won't hurt you.

FOURTH BOY: We're not very hoity-toity here anymore.

SIXTH BOY: You said it! We can't even wash anymore.

FIFTH BOY: Little Fox is the only one who never gets dirty. You can still see those freckles of his. (*He bends and helps Little Fox on to the stern bench.*) It's morning again, Little Fox. Show your little spotted face. How many have you got? Didn't you ever count your freckles? You want us to guess? Whoever guesses right wins—the flashlight. It still works. That's what I call a brilliant prize! I'd give anything in the world for that flashlight.

THIRD GIRL: You can't count that many freckles.

FOURTH BOY: We could if Little Fox just kept still.

FIFTH BOY: I'll try. (*He kneels and, surrounded by the other children, silently starts counting Little Fox's freckles.*)

Allan and Ann are alone in the bow of the boat.

ALLAN (*taking one of Ann's hands and opening it*): Are your hands all right?

ANN: I don't hurt so easily.

ALLAN: Really? Is ivory as tough as all that?

ANN: I've done a lot of rowing in my life.

ALLAN: Where?

ANN: On my uncle's estate. It's got its own lake.

ALLAN: With swans?

ANN: Black, Australian ones.

ALLAN: Black—Australian—

ANN: Don't you believe that there are black swans?

ALLAN: I'm just imagining—how beautiful it must be—you rowing among the black swans—

ANN: In a white dress, naturally.

ALLAN: I never imagined it any other way.

ANN: Riding makes the hands tough too. Or don't you believe that?

ALLAN: I believe anything you say.

ANN: The reins do it. Naturally you wear gloves, but that only half protects you. The leather straps press through them anyway. That's what makes the hands tough after a while.

ALLAN (*looking at the palms of her hands*): I've never seen hands like yours.

ANN (*withdrawing them*): I could go on rowing for another twenty days. The others couldn't.

ALLAN: What others?

ANN: The other children. They've all got blisters on their hands already, and tomorrow they'll be bleeding. (*Calling out.*) Who hasn't got blisters?

The children turn away from Little Fox.

THIRD BOY (*holding his hands up*): I can't row anymore.

THIRD GIRL: I only pretended to row yesterday. Today I couldn't even pick up anything.

FOURTH GIRL: Row until *my* hands start bleeding? No thanks— no more rowing for me!

SEVERAL TOGETHER: No more rowing!

ALLAN (*jumping up*): But then we won't be able to move from this spot. We can't just play around here in the boat until our food gives out. We don't have that much to eat stored in the lifeboat. There's thirteen people here who want to eat, after all!

ANN (*after a pause—quietly*): One of them must eat no more.

ALLAN: What—what do you mean?

ANN: I say: one of us must eat no more.

ALLAN: Where did you get that idea?

ANN: It's the penance for our sin.

ALLAN: What sin?

ANN: We were thirteen who ate and drank together. That was what we realized yesterday. And today it'll be much worse if we do it again since we *know* now that we're thirteen.

ALLAN (*turning to the others*): Anybody here agree to any of this?

ANN: Anybody here agree that tomorrow his hands will bleed too, and that he'll whimper the way she's whimpering now?

ALLAN (*to the Second Girl*): Is it burning again?

SECOND GIRL (*squirming*): Like fire!

ALLAN: Then we'll have to put it out again.

SECOND GIRL (*shaking her head*): No more water—it's for drinking.

BOYS AND GIRLS (*grumbling*): That's drinking water!

ALLAN: I have no right to order you to do anything. All I can do is give up my own share.

THIRD BOY: But you've already done that.

FOURTH BOY: That's right—you've given up your whole share for today already.

ALLAN: I don't need any.

THIRD GIRL (*after a pause*): Well, who's the one here who's supposed to give up eating?

ANN: Who'll volunteer? Who will save us in our need and swear a holy oath that he will eat no bite nor drink no drop until our rescue, even if he should die—without complaint, like our holy Jesus for the salvation of mankind, which shall find eternal life through his crucifixion?

A deep silence falls over the boat.

ANN: I can't do it either. I don't blame anyone for not volunteering. We're still just children and can't carry out anything so colossal that it'll be set down in books after we're gone. We're only children, and if we have to fulfill Christ's commandment, then let it be decided by lot.

SECOND BOY (*after a pause*): He doesn't really have to die of starvation, does he?

ANN (*shrugging her shoulders*): No—not if we sight land first.

FIFTH GIRL: Can he eat right away again when we reach land?

ANN: Once we're on land again, it's all over.

FOURTH GIRL: Some people can't fast as well as others.

THIRD BOY: And we're all weak already.

FOURTH BOY: Not a single bite?

ANN: Not one!

Silence.

SECOND BOY: Here, you can use my notebook. I know how to cast lots. I'll draw a circle on twelve pieces of paper and a cross on the thirteenth. If you draw a circle, you're in luck. If you draw the cross—

ANN: —You're lost!

The Second Boy tears thirteen pages out of his notebook and draws the signs on them. Then he rolls them up.

SECOND BOY (*to Allan*): Have you got another empty bag over there?

ALLAN (*handing him one*): I wouldn't want to spoil the game.

ANN: It's no game—it's a matter of life and death!

The lots are put into the bag, which is shaken vigorously.

SECOND BOY: Who's first?

THIRD BOY: The one who started this.

ANN: Me. (*She takes the bag.*)

SECOND BOY: Don't look at it until everyone's drawn his.

ANN: All right, I'll wait.

The bag goes round. Finally it is offered to Little Fox, who does not move.

SECOND BOY: Here, Little Fox—grab the last one.

Little Fox stares and does not move.

SECOND BOY: Shall I draw for him?

ANN (*clapping her hands*): No! Everyone has to draw his own lot! (*As she says this, her own lot rolls off her lap.*)

ALLAN: (*Picks up Ann's lot, opens it, and starts.*)

THIRD BOY: But he doesn't even know what he's supposed to do.

ALLAN (*loudly*): He's not supposed to do anything!

ANN (*startled*): Where's my lot?

ALLAN: Chucked into the water. Together with mine. (*He goes through the boat, tearing their lots away from the children.*) Over the side with them, all of them! (*He throws the bag overboard too.*) We're not going to be saved just because one of us doesn't eat or drink anymore. Since our hands can't hold the oars anymore, we'll have to run up a pennant so they can find us. Without a pennant no one will be able to see us. I'm going to put up a mast now and fix a pennant to it! (*He goes forward again and ties the boathook upright to a bench. Then he unwinds his white muffler and fixes it to the hook.*)

ANN (*crying out*): It's getting foggy. No one's going to see that pennant in the fog. We'll be completely lost with you and your pennant!

A fogbank approaches and covers the boat and the children.

THE FOURTH DAY

The fog sweeps over the scene.

The time of day is uncertain.

Nothing is visible.

Suddenly a reverberating sound is heard, somewhat like the sound of a muffled drum played in an irregular rhythm.

The fog swirls apart, revealing the boat.

The children are sitting on the benches, wide awake.

The Little Fox sits rigidly on the stern bench.

The Sixth Boy continues to beat with an iron oarlock on an empty tin can which is set up on a bench.

SECOND BOY (*loudly*): We're out of the fog now!

SIXTH BOY: (*Continues drumming.*)

SECOND GIRL (*holding back his arm*): You can stop drumming now.

SIXTH BOY (*stopping*): Why?

THIRD BOY: The fog's gone.

SIXTH BOY: I couldn't have gone on any longer anyway. (*He throws the oarlock away.*) Just a lot of nonsense anyway.

ALLAN: It wasn't nonsense. If there had been a ship in the vicinity it couldn't have seen us in the fog, but it could have heard us from far away. Fog carries sound.

SIXTH BOY: Fog as thick as that?

THIRD BOY: Yes. It's all in accordance with precise physical laws.

SIXTH BOY: Do they hold good everywhere?

THIRD BOY: Where do you suppose they wouldn't?

SIXTH BOY: Right here—where *we're* drumming away and waiting for help.

THIRD BOY: That doesn't make any difference.

SIXTH BOY: In that case it's a good thing there are such laws.

Silence.

THIRD GIRL: The pennant!

All the children look up at the boathook. The pennant is gone.

FOURTH GIRL: The pennant's gone!

FIFTH GIRL: It's been blown away by the wind.

SIXTH GIRL: How are they ever going to find us in this big ocean without a pennant?

THIRD GIRL: The pennant would have saved us.

ALLAN (*after a pause*): I'll make a new pennant.

ANN: Have you got another muffler?

ALLAN: I'll tie two shirt sleeves together. That'll make an even longer pennant than my muffler. I can always figure something out.

ANN (*shaking her head*): You can't figure something out for us now.

ALLAN: Why not?

ANN: You could tie shirt sleeves a mile long on that hook and it still wouldn't help us.

ALLAN: Naturally it would help all of us if someone saw my pennant. They wouldn't just rescue me; they'd rescue the whole boat.

ANN: The boat isn't going to be rescued.

ALLAN: Pretty soon someone's sure to see us or to hear our drumming. In fact, if there's any more fog, we'll drum on *two* cans.

ANN: The drumming doesn't do any good and the pennant doesn't do any good and the rowing just gives us sore hands. There's a deep reason behind all this. That's why the pennant flew away, too. There wasn't any wind—but the pennant flew away. If that isn't a sign, then I don't know what a sign looks like.

ALLAN: I didn't tie it on properly.

ANN: That's just an excuse. The real reason is obvious.

FIFTH BOY (*after a pause*): Well—tell us: why aren't we going to be rescued?

ANN: Count—and see how many we are.

The children look around at each other.

SECOND BOY: We haven't got less.

SECOND GIRL: Or more.

ANN: We can't become more—only less.

Silence.

THIRD GIRL: Do we have to wait—until one of us dies?

ANN: We'll all die if we remain thirteen.

Silence.

ANN: We weren't allowed to cast lots. One of us tore the lots out of our hands and threw them into the sea. Maybe he had some special reason for doing it.

ALLAN (*smiling*): Maybe.

ANN: Maybe he drew the cross himself and took a peek at his lot before we others unrolled ours.

ALLAN: Who—me?

ANN: If the shoe fits, wear it.

ALLAN: I swear I didn't open my lot.

ANN: Then why did you stop us from looking at ours?

ALLAN: Because you don't play for lives. Life is a serious matter.

ANN: Now you're saying it yourself. And twelve lives are twelve times as serious as one life. (*To the other children.*) It's easy as pie, figuring that out. (*Exultingly.*) And when it's a matter of thirteen lives, one of them isn't important enough not to be sacrificed for the other twelve. (*Quietly.*) Since we weren't allowed to draw lots . . . we'll have to use force.

Silence.

THIRD BOY (*hesitatingly*): Force?

FOURTH GIRL (*to Ann*): What do you mean—force?

ANN: One of us has to leave the boat. One of us must no longer eat and drink and sleep with us. One of us is our Judas—like the Judas who betrayed his Savior.

Silence.

ALLAN: There's no Judas here.

ANN: Judas returns again in every thirteenth person, and if he doesn't die right away—the boat is going to sink right away. We've stayed too long in one boat with him already. We can no longer remain thirteen—that would be tempting God. And God doesn't permit that—particularly by children. Even grownups are afraid of making up the Judas-number. Think of the real-life examples we talked about before. If you asked everyone, those examples would be multiplied a thousandfold and more. A hundred-thousandfold! Assuming that the people you ask are Christians—like us, of course.

THIRD GIRL: I was dragged out of bed so that there'd be fourteen.

FOURTH BOY: I listened while someone was sent away so there'd only be twelve.

ANN: The gardener's family had good luck only after one child died. Before that they were thirteen.

Silence.

FIFTH GIRL: Are we tempting God now?

ANN: He is still giving us warning out of the goodness of his heart.

SIXTH GIRL: How is he giving us warning?

ANN: The pennant flew away without any wind and the fog came. That was the last warning—after that the storm breaks.

SECOND BOY: A storm will sink the boat.

ANN: That is inevitable.

Silence.

ALLAN (*opening his coat and shouting*): Now I'm going to make the pennant!

ANN (*as loud as Allan*): We'll do it now!

ALLAN: Do what?

ANN: Do it by force—since we couldn't cast lots!

ALLAN: You want to kill one of us here in this boat?

ANN: The thirteenth!

ALLAN: And who's going to let you do that to him?

ANN: Little Fox! He can't do anything: he can't row, he can't count cadence when *we* row, he can't drum. He can't do anything—not a thing—not one single thing! He was just lying there in the boat and would have died long ago anyway if we hadn't found him. He can't blame us for picking him. He won't feel a thing when we throw him into the water. I bet he'll quit breathing with his first swallow. He's just in the way here—and that's why it has to be him!

The children turn and look at Little Fox.

ANN: One push and he'll be gone—let's do it now!

ALLAN: Anyone who touches Little Fox—anyone who just tries to touch him—!

ANN (*flaring up*): Heathen!

ALLAN: All right then, I'm a heathen.

ANN: And with a heathen one should . . . (*Her voice fades.*)

ALLAN: A heathen who knows the Christian commandments. Better than you do. One of them is, "Thou shalt not kill."

Silence.

ALLAN: You can't say anything against that, can you? It's all cut and dried. A deaf man can read it and a blind man can feel it through his fingers. So why can't someone with all his five senses about him understand it? This is our religion, the religion we try to convert the heathens with, isn't it? And aren't those the proudest words our lips can say: "Thou shalt not kill!"?

Silence.

ALLAN: Those are God's words, just as they are preached, just as they are written. And I'll repeat it once again: not even the blind and deaf can escape from this knowledge. There's no way you can avoid it and even if you twist yourself like a snake around the truth that everyone who calls himself a Christian knows, you still cannot escape it: "Thou shalt not kill!"

Silence.

ALLAN: Or maybe there's someone here who's really worse off than the deaf and blind?

Silence.

ALLAN: Then obey this commandment and act like Christians: do not kill!

ANN (*after a pause*): You don't have to be deaf and blind to understand that it only applies to the church. In life it's all quite different.

ALLAN: Isn't the church our life?

ANN: If it was, we wouldn't need any church. We wouldn't need any church for God's word to be preached in. What would the sermons be about if everything happened in life just the way we hear about it in church? Who'd want to go to church again if he only learned there what was already happening in real life? The preacher wouldn't have anything to say anymore; he might just as well disappear altogether. The whole church and everything that depends on it wouldn't have to exist anymore. There's a whole world of preachers who wouldn't be here at all if all the commandments were obeyed. Particularly the commandment, "Thou shalt not kill." In fact, didn't you ever see priests actually blessing weapons—the ones they use to kill more and more people with all the time? Maybe even the bombs that drove us out and the torpedo that sank our ship were blessed—that is, if those people *let* the priests bless them. They're ready to do it, all right. It's the same in all countries where Christians live. That's the reason they're Christians—because they only kill with weapons that have been blessed. But they have to kill; if they didn't, there wouldn't be anything else to say in our churches. That's the whole difference—that's what you have to understand: commandments are for the Sunday sermon and sound great in church. But outside it's quite different: out here the greatest evil is thirteen!

ALLAN: That's a difference that you've thought up for yourself.

ANN: The difference between church and life?

ALLAN: Some day the commandments will be obeyed.

ANN: And all churches will be superfluous then, I suppose?

ALLAN: Jesus will live again.

ANN: Jesus lives in Heaven.

ALLAN: I mean he'll return to earth and will be crucified no more.

ANN: He'll return on Judgment Day. Then he'll hold court. And woe to him who has sinned, whether his sin was big or small.

ALLAN: Killing is the greatest sin!

ANN: Who's asking *you* to do it? (*She turns away from him.*)

ALLAN (*jumps from his bench and makes his way to the stern. He picks up Little Fox and carries him back to the bow*): Now I'm going to build a tent for us, Little Fox. We'll live in there the way we want to; and we won't let anyone else come in. That's the way it's going to be—and I pledge myself for your safety. (*With a few skillful, quick movements he builds a tent by fastening a sailcloth to the boathook. He hides Little Fox in it.*)

A new fogbank rolls onto the scene.

ALLAN (*barely visible at the entrance of the tent*): We'll have to start drumming again. We're not going to be saved if we don't make any effort. Our rescue is up to us—don't kid yourselves. Drum—drum—drum!

The fog hides the boat. Only the sound of the drumming testifies to its existence. But the drumming sounds like Negro drums in the primeval jungle.

THE FIFTH DAY

Fog; calm sea.

The only sound is the drumming—rhythmic and tinny.

Then the mist thins—disappears.

The boat is there, with the tent in the bow hiding Allan and Little Fox.

The Third Girl puts the oarlock down and, tired out like the other children, slumps down on a bench.

ALLAN (*ducking out of the tent*): It's my turn to do the drumming. Why don't you call me when it's my turn? Oh, I see—the fog's gone. (*He sits down opposite Ann, who is wiping the water off her face with her hands.*) Why don't you go into the tent? It's drier in there, and there's room for three.

ANN: I don't sleep in a tent with boys.

ALLAN (*after a pause*): You were in the tent anyway.

ANN: I haven't moved from my bench.

ALLAN: I'm not saying you have. Still, there are ways of meeting one another without actually moving around.

ANN: In dreams.

ALLAN (*nods*): I dreamt of you. Shall I tell you the dream?

ANN: But people always forget their dreams when they wake up.

ALLAN (*forcefully*): Not this one, Ann. Ann, I really believe that things happen which can change a person's whole life—and that they happen just as suddenly as the way things happen in dreams. If we couldn't dream, our lives wouldn't mean anything anymore. If I hadn't had this dream, I wouldn't be alive anymore.

ANN: Oh, did you dream of a golden castle?

ALLAN: I dreamt of you.

ANN: If you dreamt of me the way I look now, you didn't dream of anything very wonderful.

ALLAN: The dream didn't take place here.

ANN: Oh, where then?

ALLAN: On your uncle's estate. Do you remember the story you told about your stay there?

ANN (*reluctantly, drawing her words out*): Yes—I remember.

ALLAN: The lake—the black Australian swans.

ANN: I shouldn't have said all that—there wasn't any point.

ALLAN (*eagerly*): Yes—swans that circle around under the willows —that swim through water lilies.

ANN: Have you been there yourself?

ALLAN: Why?

ANN: Because it's all exactly the way you describe it.

ALLAN: There!—you see how powerful dreams are! They're much more powerful than any reality. I'll show you that right away. How old are you now?

ANN: I told you that once already.

ALLAN: Eleven or twelve?

ANN: That's my secret.

ALLAN: In my dream you were grownup—it didn't matter whether you were eleven or twelve. That's what I meant by my question.

ANN: I'm twelve.

ALLAN: That doesn't spoil the vision I had of you. Not anymore. I don't think I'll ever see you any other way. Eighteen.

ANN (*amused*): Me, eighteen?—Then you must have been nineteen.

ALLAN: (*Shakes his head.*)

ANN: Twenty?

ALLAN: (*Shakes his head.*)

ANN: Well, how old were you?

ALLAN (*seriously*): Twenty-one.

ANN: And I'm supposed to believe that?

ALLAN: You will believe it when I tell you how I went to your uncle's estate in order to ask him—(*he hesitates*).

ANN: You wanted to ask my uncle something?

ALLAN: I wanted to ask him if I could kiss you.

ANN: And—did my uncle get mad at you?

ALLAN (*dreamily*): It was wonderful. The room was very bright. Usually rooms with lots of books round the walls are dark. This one had bookcases going up to the ceiling. They gave

C

out so much power—and so much silence—that everything became timeless. It was as if eternal silence had swallowed up all sound and changed all knowledge into a mystery. You could feel there was a completely different way of valuing the things we do in there—that the things we do now were completely forbidden there. It was wonderful to be outside oneself like that and yet to see much deeper into oneself.

ANN: Actually my uncle *does* have a lot of books.

ALLAN (*happily*): It's all true?

ANN: And what did you talk about?

ALLAN: We talked about you. Your uncle spoke: I didn't have to explain anything to him. He said, "After you kiss my niece, you will never forget your stay in this room. For through this room lies the path—there is no other—that makes a man worthy and immortal." (*After a pause, looking up.*) He must have meant love when he said immortality, mustn't he? And you become worthy when you—(*He sighs.*) That's the most difficult thing of all—becoming worthy—

(*He falls silent and pensively rests his head on his hand.*)

ANN: And—did we kiss?

ALLAN (*looking at her*): Just like grownups kiss—that's how we kissed.

ANN: We held each other really close?

ALLAN: As if we would never be parted.

ANN (*after a pause*): What a thing to dream!

ALLAN: Yes—that was my dream. Are you angry with me?

ANN: Why should I be angry with you?

ALLAN: Because I kissed you.

ANN: But my uncle allowed it.

ALLAN (*hesitatingly*): And would you kiss me—

ANN (*looking around the boat*): If the others allowed it. (*She laughs. Suddenly she stops and then claps her hands.*) We want to get engaged!

The other children, suddenly wide awake, all turn toward Allan and Ann.

ANN (*to Allan*): Or wasn't that a proposal?

ALLAN: I've already said that this dream is even realer for me than life.

ANN: There—did you all hear? His dream ordered him to kiss me. And when you kiss, you become bride and groom.

ALLAN: Yes, that's true.

ANN: Well then, kiss me.

ALLAN (*hesitating*): In front of the others?

ANN: Where else?

ALLAN: In the tent.

ANN: With Little Fox there?

ALLAN: (*Takes her silently into his arms and kisses her.*)

SECOND GIRL (*waving her bandaged hands*): We've got a pair of lovers in the boat!

SECOND BOY: Kiss again!

Allan and Ann kiss again.

THIRD BOY: Let's all take a bride!

THIRD GIRL: Everyone take a groom!

ANN (*loudly*): No! Just me and him!

FOURTH GIRL: Why do you want only you two kissing?

ANN: Because we're going to marry too. We're going to get married tomorrow. You can only have a wedding for one couple at a time. I'll explain that to you later. There isn't even enough room in the boat for so many couples.

SIXTH BOY: There was plenty of room up to now.

ANN: But not for marriage. Marriage is different. Wait a bit and I'll explain it to you.

ALLAN (*amazed*): Ann—are you absolutely serious?

ANN: As truly as I kissed you, so too will I marry you. Just as if I was eighteen.

ALLAN (*impulsively*): This is even more wonderful than my dream! We've got to show that this isn't a dream anymore— I've got to—(*He thinks for a moment, then bends down and gets the Thermos bottle.*) Everyone has to sign to show that this isn't a dream anymore. We'll send a message to the world so that it'll know the reality. The world needs messages like this in its troubles. (*To the Second Boy.*) Have you got any more notepaper?

SECOND BOY (*pulling his notebook out of his pocket*): Yes.

ALLAN (*unscrewing the bottle—to Ann*): You gave me a cup of milk and I looked at you. I fell in love with you at first sight. It was all meant to be the way it is now. Now we'll marry— and this will testify to it. I'll write it. (*He tears a page out of the notebook, writes, and hands it to Ann.*) Now sign it.

Ann reads, signs, and passes it on. All the children sign.

ALLAN (*getting the paper back*): And Little Fox.

ANN (*blurting it out*): Him too?

ALLAN: He mustn't be left out.

ANN: But he can't even write!

ALLAN: Then I'll write for him: "and Little Fox." (*When he has written this, he folds up the paper and inserts it into the bottle, which he then closes tight. He throws the bottle into the water with a wide swing of his arm.*) Bottle-post with unknown destination. Whoever finds it shall proclaim that Allan and Ann are one in life and one in death!!

The children stare at the disappearing bottle.

FOURTH BOY: Bet that'll never sink.

FOURTH GIRL: Red's easy to see, too.

FIFTH BOY: Do you think someone really *will* see it?

ANN (*loudly*): We've got to prepare for the wedding now. It's got to be a real celebration.

ALLAN: What are you cooking up there?

ANN: Something you're not allowed to know about. (*To the other children.*) No, Allan mustn't know anything about it in advance. You go on into the tent, Allan, while we make plans. Come on, help me to get him to go to his little fox!

SIXTH BOY: Go on, go to your little fox!

SIXTH GIRL: To your little fox!

SEVERAL CHILDREN: To your little fox!

ALL THE CHILDREN (*with their fists instinctively raised*): To your little fox!

ALLAN: (*Smiles uncomprehendingly and ducks into the tent.*)

The children continue to stare at the entrance of the tent.

FIFTH BOY (*to Ann*): You were going to explain to us—

SECOND GIRL: What were you going to explain to us?

THIRD BOY (*turning round*): Look at the fog!

ANN: Come around me here so I can whisper—and then I'll explain what this marriage . . .

As the children gather round Ann, the fog closes in on them. Ann's voice can no longer be heard from the fog. But there is one sound which can be heard ever louder and louder: it is the word "Yes" repeated excitedly and finally chanted in perfect unison. Then the drum is heard again—triumphant and wild.

THE SIXTH DAY

Silence over the calm sea.

A thick, languid fog.

The silence is shattered by a vaguely bell-like sound.

The fog parts; the boat becomes visible.

Allan and Ann are sitting on the bench in the bow.

The other children are in the stern, gathered around a water canister, on which one of the boys is beating. The children ac-

company his regular strokes with the ding-donging of voices as
they imitate bells.

This goes on until Ann raises her hand.

Silence.

ANN (*to Allan*): Now we've reached the church.

ALLAN: How lovely the journey through the streets was with all
the bells ringing.

ANN: And the sun shining brightly.

ALLAN: Did you see the crowd in front of the church door?

ANN: Of course I did—what else did you expect to see?

ALLAN: When Allan and Ann marry . . .

ANN: Quiet. We mustn't talk anymore. Now they're going to sing.

(*She gives another sign to the others.*)

THE CHILDREN (*singing with their pure young voices*):
Praise the Lord, the mighty king of love!
Praise him, O soul, at one with the heavenly dove!
Come for his sake,
Psalter and harp awake!
Raise the song of praise above!

Praise the Lord, who has blessed thee from on high,
Whose rays of love stream down from out of the sky.
Meditate and view
What the Almighty can do—
His love is always nigh!

Praise the Lord, and praise his name!
Raise up your voice and sing his fame!
He is your light!
He drives away all night!
Praise him forever! Amen.

ANN (*softly, to Allan*): After the hymn the priest comes out. You
have to imagine everything. You've been at a wedding before,
haven't you?

ALLAN: I didn't really pay close attention.

ANN: Then just do as I do. (*Staring before her.*) There he is. Look at him the same as I do. He's addressing us. Naturally he doesn't talk as long as he does to grownups. After all— we're still children.

ALLAN: He talks as seriously as if he were talking to grownups, though.

ANN: That's just habit with him.

ALLAN: It's making me feel hot and cold all over.

ANN: Quiet! Now he's marrying us. Give him the rings. Now he's exchanging them. Now he's putting them on our fingers. He's still got to give the blessing. (*She bows her head.*)

Allan bows his head too. He has obeyed Ann's whispered directions and imitated her in corresponding gestures throughout the last speech. Ann straightens up suddenly.

ALLAN (*imitating her*): Are we—?

ANN: We're still in the church. Another hymn! (*She gives the sign.*)

THE CHILDREN (*in their pure, clear young voices*):
    The Heavens praise the glory of the Lord.
    Their sound spreads forth the splendor of his name.
    The earth and sea bow down in mute accord.
    Accept, O men, the signs of his fame!

    Who bears the Heavens' countless stars?
    Who leads the sun out of his tent?
    He comes and laughs and lights us from afar,
    And like a hero runs his course.

ANN (*turning round*): Time for the wedding feast. Here are our guests now!

THE CHILDREN (*offering their hands to Ann and Allan*): Congratulations!—Congratulations!

SECOND GIRL: What a wonderful wedding dress!

THIRD GIRL: Is it silk?

ANN: Brocade. It got awfully crumpled in the car. Oh well, that doesn't matter though—you only wear it once.

FOURTH GIRL: What a lovely lace veil!

ANN: It's old lace.

FIFTH GIRL: It looks like new!

ANN: Old lace is worth more than new.

FOURTH GIRL: That's the way it is with lace.

FIFTH GIRL: How am I supposed to know that?

ALLAN: We mustn't let our guests get hungry!

ANN: Everything's ready!

SIXTH BOY: What's to eat?

ANN: Oh—it's a pretty long menu. We'll have to hurry if we're going to eat it all. (*To Allan.*) Give me one of the bags.

ALLAN (*bends down and brings out a bag of biscuits*): Rare imported oriental delicacies, right?

ANN: Even better than that! Something that no one has ever eaten before: fruits of the imagination.

THE CHILDREN: Ahh—that must taste good!

ANN: (*Opens the bag, takes out two biscuits, and passes the bag to Allan.*)

ALLAN: Two for everybody, right?

ANN: You mean you want more than me?

ALLAN: Do *you* want mine?

ANN: Everyone gets his share.

The bag is passed round and comes back to Ann. It is not quite empty.

ALLAN (*taking it*): Give it to me. (*He takes the last two biscuits out and puts them into his coat pocket.*)

ANN: You *are* taking more for yourself.

ALLAN: They're not for me.

Instantly a visible change passes over the children: they lower their heads and nibble their biscuits, casting nervous glances at each other.

ANN (*jumping up*): That's the end of the wedding dinner. What do we do now, Allan?

ALLAN: Now?

ANN: Don't you know?

ALLAN: Don't I know what?

ANN: What people do when they're married.

ALLAN: I want to do everything you're supposed to do.

ANN: They have to sleep in one room!

ALLAN: You mean you'd sleep with me in one room?

ANN: I have to.

ALLAN: We can't just imagine a room.

ANN: A tent can be a room.

ALLAN: And we do have a tent here.

ANN: Then let's go into the tent. (*She opens the tent flap and then backs out again.*) We're not alone.

ALLAN: Little Fox is in there.

ANN: I'm not asking you about Little Fox: I'm just saying we have to be alone.

ALLAN: But it's only Little Fox.

ANN: I can't follow you into that tent if we won't be alone. If that's the way you wanted it, I could have saved myself the trouble of the wedding dress and the veil and all the rest. The bells were rung and they sang two hymns—everything was serious and you said yourself how it made you go hot and cold all over. Now you're telling me all that was just a lie. Show me yourself—teach me a lesson I can remember my whole life—show me how much I can count on your love.

ALLAN: Crying makes you even prettier.

ANN: Is that why you want me to cry?

ALLAN: Now you're acting as if you were eighteen.

ANN: Why can't I be alone with you then?

c*

ALLAN: We are alone.

ANN: And what about Little Fox?

ALLAN: He won't be in the tent. (*He looks at her ardently.*)

ANNS (*Offers her lips.*)

ALLAN: (*Kisses her.*)

ANN: (*to the other children*): Now get Little Fox!

> *The Second and Fifth Boys clamber through the boat, enter the tent, and come back out carrying Little Fox.*

ALLAN: Wait a minute! Let him have his biscuits! (*He takes the biscuits out of his pocket and offers them to Little Fox.*)

SECOND BOY: Go on, take them—they're yours.

FIFTH BOY (*taking the biscuits*): He doesn't want to eat them now.

SIXTH BOY: Couldn't we use his flashlight?

FIFTH BOY: We could make signals with it at night.

ALLAN (*forcefully*): Don't do that! All ships are blacked-out now. A little ray of light could give a whole ship away. They might even take this boat for a freighter and shoot at the light. Then we'd be killed for sure. (*Reaching for the flashlight.*) Give it to me. I want to be sure that none of you puts it on and gives the enemy a target! (*He pockets the light.*)

ANN: Look at that fog!

ALLAN: It's never been this black!

FIFTH BOY: We'll drum—you go on and stay in the tent!

ANN (*pulling Allan with her*): Come into the tent!

> *The wall of black fog covers the boat. A wild drumming ensues, drowning out all other sounds.*

THE SEVENTH DAY

The fog hangs heavily over the sea, smothering daylight. Gradually the mist thins and the boat becomes visible. The children are crouched between the benches, relaxed and silent. Now a droning sound is heard from the sky.

SIXTH BOY (*wakes up and listens; suddenly he flings up his arms*): Airplanes!

Gradually the other children wake up and look up into the sky.

SECOND GIRL: I don't see it.

THIRD BOY: You can't see him yet.

FOURTH BOY: The fog's lifting.

SECOND BOY: He's above the fog.

FIFTH BOY: The fog has to get out of the way first.

SIXTH GIRL: Then he'll see us.

FOURTH GIRL: Then the plane will rescue us!

THE CHILDREN (*breaking out in wild joy*): The plane—the plane!

Allan ducks out of the tent.

SECOND GIRL (*to Allan*): A plane's coming to rescue us.

FIFTH BOY: I heard him first.

ALLAN (*worried*): I hope he doesn't fly past us.

FOURTH GIRL: Our plane?

THE CHILDREN (*joyously*): It is our plane—it is too our plane!!

Ann ducks out of the tent.

ALLAN: Ann, there's a plane up there somewhere. It might come to our rescue.

ANN: It will come to our rescue.

ALLAN: Are you sure?

ANN: I'm sure. (*To the other children.*) Or do I have any reason not to be sure?

The children bow their heads and make no answer.

ANN: The others are sure too. There's no doubt that it's come to rescue us.

THIRD BOY (*after a pause*): There's the plane!

FOURTH BOY: It's a flying-boat!

SECOND BOY: It's circling over us!

FIFTH BOY: There—the pilot's spotted us!

THE GIRLS (*clapping their hands*): The pilot's spotted us!

ALLAN: —He's coming down in wide circles.—That's a sure sign he wants to rescue us.—There's plenty of room for everyone in there—in that big fuselage. (*To the others.*) Who's going to get in first?—I know! Little Fox—he's the smallest!—Where's Little Fox? (*The children fall silent again.*) Is he back under that sailcloth again, sleeping through the rescue?—Wake him up! (*The children remain silent and motionless. Allan shoves part of the sailcloth aside. They remain as before.*) Why don't you do as I say?

FIFTH BOY (*defiantly*): He isn't under the sailcloth.

ALLAN: Then where is he?

Deep silence.

ALLAN (*suddenly comprehending*): What have you done to Little Fox? (*Hesitatingly.*) Did you—have you—(*Turns to Ann.*) They've thrown Little Fox out of the boat—(*His voice fails.*)

ANN (*firmly*): Yes—and now we're saved.

ALLAN: (*Stares at her.*)

ANN: That's how I knew we'd be rescued.

ALLAN (*painfully*): Is that why you didn't want me to keep Little Fox in the tent—?

ANN: Yes, that was why. Anyway, that was one of the reasons.

ALLAN: Ann—it isn't true. Say it isn't true, Ann. You didn't plan this—you couldn't treat me like this—you couldn't—I believed everything you said—I still believe you, Ann. You just have to say it, just say you didn't stay in the tent with me just to get Little Fox out of it. You loved me, Ann, didn't you?

ANN: I loved you.

ALLAN: And now you don't love me anymore?

ANN: I wouldn't say that . . .

ALLAN: Never mind—if only Little Fox hadn't died that way!

ANN: What way?

ALLAN: By being murdered.

ANN: *I* haven't murdered anyone.

ALLAN: The others did, and with your help. (*To the others.*) Are you murderers or aren't you?

FIFTH BOY: You mean you'd betray us?

ANN: Traitors are contemptible.

ALLAN: Do you want to deny that Little Fox was here in the boat with us?

SECOND GIRL: Who's going to know we were thirteen?

THIRD GIRL: Who counted us?

ALLAN: You counted yourselves. The message is there in the Thermos bottle—and I wrote "Little Fox" at the bottom!

ANN (*flaring up*): You deserve to be spat on for that!

SIXTH BOY (*shouting*): The flying-boat's landed!

The droning of the motors has stopped. An enormous wing and one of the floats of the plane appear. The pilot remains unseen, but his voice can be clearly heard.

PILOT: Hello down there—have you got the boathook ready? The boathook—got it? You've got to keep the boat fast to the float with it. Who's your strongest boy? Have him hold on as hard as he can—otherwise we won't be able to get you out of your boat. (*Allan rapidly takes down the sailcloth and unfastens the boathook: from now on he will hold the boat fast to the plane with it.*) We're going to let down a rope ladder. See that it swings clear! And remember—safety first! (*Sounds of activity from the plane.*) Lady Luck's been good to you kids. A patrol boat picked up your red Thermos bottle. That was one cracking good message you wrote! The newspapers have got hold of it already—you're all practically celebrities now. Particularly the country's youngest married couple. That's what's bowled everyone over most. You two have become a

national model of how to behave in time of danger. Never
mind danger and let yourself go! Every day's a wedding day!
And the others who signed the message: every one of you's a
little hero! (*More sounds of activity from the plane.*) And
where's Little Fox? Where's the little dog you listed? That
was a real cute idea—letting a dog join human society. Isn't
he in the boat anymore? What's the matter, did he starve?
Couldn't take it, eh? Just fell overboard while you were
playing with him probably. Never mind—don't take it to
heart: a dog's just a dog, after all. You're safe: that's more
important than your Little Fox, when you come right down
to it! (*The rope ladder is let down.*) Come on up now, one
after the other. Keep the line moving—don't wait for one to
get up before the next one starts. That ladder's strong, and
you're not heavy. Seven days on the open sea sure have done
their work: you look like a bunch of little devils! If I didn't
feel sorry for you, I'd be scared of you!

The children crowd around the ladder.

SIXTH BOY: Girls first!

PILOT: Attaboy!

Ann and the five girls disappear into the plane.

SECOND BOY: We'll climb faster than that!

The five boys disappear as well. Allan keeps on holding the boat.

PILOT: You can let go now—you've got lots of time to climb up
here with us before the boat drifts away.

ALLAN (*suddenly hysterical*): I won't climb up there with you!

PILOT: What's that?

ALLAN: I don't want to—don't want—don't want to live without
Little Fox!

PILOT: Did he belong to you or something?

ALLAN (*beside himself*): No, he didn't belong to me—he belonged
to the whole world. The whole world is guilty of his death!

PILOT: Don't forget that men die too.

ALLAN: Yes, they kill—kill—kill. They're dead set on doing wrong, no matter where or why!

PILOT: People will be better some day—they'll be just like children again.

ALLAN: No, children will be like grownups—because they're like them already!

PILOT: Do children kill?

ANN (*invisible above*): Allan—save yourself!

ALLAN: Is that you, Ann?

ANN: I meant it about the marriage!

ALLAN: And I meant it when I saved you, Ann. You drew the cross in the lottery. I took a look at it secretly and threw it into the sea with the others.

ANN: You're telling me that too late!

ALLAN (*tears streaming down his face*): Because it's the last thing I wanted to tell you. Now I've got nothing more to say! (*He frees the boathook and throws it into the water.*)

PILOT (*shouting*): We've just got word we're being pursued. We can't stick around here any longer. Come on now, you're a bright lad—grab that ladder! We're going to pull it up—grab it!

The ladder disappears. Allan remains in the boat.

The motors start. The flying-boat glides away. The sound of its motors fades away.

The scene becomes darker.

From the opposite direction another plane can be heard in the darkness.

Allan—clearly visible in silhouette—stands on one of the benches and takes the flashlight out of his coat pocket.

When the enemy plane is almost overhead, Allan swings the light to and fro.

The plane soon discovers the target.

Allan is hit by a burst of machine-gun fire.

The noise of the plane fades away.

It becomes darker.

EPILOGUE

The sun rises blood-red above the sea
    And the waves seem to change to blood.
And on this sea of blood the boat drifts on,
Half sunk, because its sides are full of bullet-holes.
Allan lies with arms outstretched upon the center bench:
            As if crucified
The water rushes in and laps at Allan's body.
        The boat sinks deeper.
A sudden wave rushes over it,
And when the wave recedes, the boat has disappeared.
And once more the crime is consummated.

THE OUTSIDER

by WOLFGANG BORCHERT

TRANSLATED BY MICHAEL BENEDIKT

For Hans Quest
A play which no theater will produce
and no audience will care to see

Characters

BECKMANN, one of the many

his WIFE, who forgot him

her BOYFRIEND, who loves her

a GIRL, whose husband came home on one leg

her HUSBAND, who dreamt of her a thousand nights

a COLONEL, who is very jovial

his WIFE, who gets the chills in her own living room

the DAUGHTER, right in the middle of supper

her smart HUSBAND

a CABARET PRODUCER, who would like to be decent,—but then decides against it

MRS. KRAMER, who is simply Mrs. Kramer, which is just what's so awful

the OLD MAN, in whom no one believes anymore

the UNDERTAKER with the hiccoughs

a STREET CLEANER, who isn't really one at all

the OTHER ONE, whom everyone knows

the ELBE

A man comes home to Germany.

He's been away for a long time, this man. A very long time. Perhaps too long. And he returns looking a lot different from the way he did before. Outwardly he is a near relation of those figures which stand around in the fields to scare birds (and sometimes, at least at night, scaring people too). Inwardly—he's the same. He has waited outside a thousand days in the cold. And as the price of admission he's had to forfeit his kneecap. And after he's waited outside in the cold a thousand nights, he really finally comes home.

A man comes home to Germany.

And there he sits through rather an astonishing piece of film. He has to pinch his arm continually during the performance, because he doesn't know whether he's waking or sleeping. But then he notices to the right and the left of him other people all living through the same experience. So he thinks that all this must really be the truth. Yes: at the very end when he's standing in the street again with an empty stomach and cold feet, he realizes that it was really a perfectly ordinary, everyday film. About a man who comes to Germany, one of many. One of the many who come home, but then don't come home, because there's no home for them any more. And their home starts being outside the door somewhere. Their Germany is outside the door somewhere, in the rain at night in the street.

That is their Germany.

Prologue

The wind moans. The Elbe laps against pilings. It is evening. The undertaker. Against the evening sky a man's silhouette.

UNDERTAKER (*punctuating his words with belches*): Urp! Urp! Just like—Urp! Just like flies! Yes, just like flies! Aha! There's one now, there on that dock over there. Looks as though he's wearing a uniform. Yes, that's an old army overcoat. He's got no cap—and his hair's short as the bristles of a brush. He's standing rather near the water. Almost too near the water, actually. That's suspicious. People who stand near the

53

water in the darkness are either lovers or poets. Or else he's one of that great gray number who've simply had it—who throw in their hand and won't play anymore. Yes, he looks as if he were one of those, that one over there does. Standing dangerously near the water. And pretty much alone there. Not a lover, he'd have someone with him there, then. Nor a poet—poets have long hair. And this one here has hair like the bristles of a brush. Interesting case, this one, very interesting.

(A *loud, abrupt splash. The silhouette has vanished.*)

Urp! There! He's gone. Jumped in. Standing too close to the water. Got him down, no doubt. And now he's gone. Urp! A man dies. So what? So nothing. The wind goes on blowing. The Elbe goes on gurgling. Streetcar bells still ring. Whores still lie, soft and white, there in their windows. Mr. Kramer rolls over on his other side and goes on snoring. And not a single clock falters in its onward course! Urp! A man is dead. So what? So nothing. Only a few circles in the water prove that he was ever there. And even they quickly disappear. And when they're gone, he's forgotten, without a trace, as if he'd never even existed. And that's all. Aha! I hear someone crying. Interesting. An old man just standing there and crying. Good evening!

OLD MAN (*not complainingly, but more or less totally crushed*): Children! Children! My children!

UNDERTAKER: What are you crying about, old man?

OLD MAN: Because there is nothing I can do, oh my, because there is nothing I can do.

UNDERTAKER: Urp! Pardon me! That's certainly awful, yes indeed —but you've certainly no reason for breaking down that way like an abandoned bride or something. Urp! Pardon me!

OLD MAN: Oh, my children! They're all my children, don't you see?

UNDERTAKER: Aha! (*Pause.*) Who are you, anyway?

OLD MAN: The God in whom no one believes any more.

UNDERTAKER: And you're crying because—? Urp! Pardon me!

OLD MAN: Because I can do nothing about it. They shoot themselves. They hang themselves. They drown themselves. They go on murdering themselves, today a hundred, tomorrow a hundred thousand. And I, I can do nothing about it.

UNDERTAKER: Rough, rough, old man. Very rough. But nobody believes in you any more, that's the way it goes.

GOD: Bad, bad, very bad. I am God—the God in whom no one believes any more. Very bad indeed. And I can do nothing about it, my children, I can do nothing about it. Bad, bad very bad.

UNDERTAKER: Urp! Pardon me! Like flies! Urp! Dammit!

GOD: Why do you keep belching so disgustingly. It's absolutely dreadful!

UNDERTAKER: Yes, yes, it's terrible. Just terrible. Occupational disease. I'm an undertaker.

GOD: What— Death? Oh, you're in good shape. You're the new God. They believe in you. They love you. They fear you. You can't be deposed. You can't be denied. No one can blaspheme against you. Yes, you're in good shape, all right. You're the new God. No one can slip through your fingers. You're the new God, Death, but you've grown fat. I remember you as quite different. Much thinner, drier, bonier, but you've grown round and fat and good-tempered. Before, Death used to look so starved.

DEATH: Why, yes, I have put on a wee bit of weight this century. Business has been good. One war after another. Like flies! The dead hang on the walls of this century just like flies. Like flies they lie stiff and dry on the window sill of the era.

GOD: But this belching? Why all this hideous belching?

DEATH: Overeating. Plain overeating. That's all. You just can't keep from belching nowadays. Urp! Pardon me!

GOD: Children! Children! And I can do nothing about it. Children, my children! (*Exit.*)

DEATH: Ah me, good night then, old man. Go to sleep. And watch out you don't fall in the water too; we lost one just a moment ago. Take very good care, old man. It's dark now, very dark. Urp! Go home, old man. There's nothing you can do about it anymore. Don't cry over the one who just splashed in over there. The one with the bristly hair, in the old army overcoat. You'll cry yourself to pieces! All these people who stand by the water at night—they're no longer lovers or poets. The boy who was here before—he's just one of those who simply can't go on, and who won't go on. And those who simply can't go on, at night, somewhere or other, step quietly into the water. Plop. Done with. Forget him, old man, don't weep. You'll just weep yourself to pieces. He was only one of those who can't go on, one of that great gray company —only *one*.

THE DREAM

In the Elbe. Monotonous lapping of little waves.

BECKMANN: Where am I? My God, where am I?

ELBE: With me.

BECKMANN: With you? And—who are you?

ELBE: Who do you think I am, my little chickadee, when you throw yourself into the water from the landing stage at St. Pauli?

BECKMANN: The Elbe?

ELBE: Yes, that's who. The Elbe.

BECKMANN (*astounded*): The Elbe? You?

ELBE: Well, that's opened your baby blue eyes for you a little, anyway, right? I bet you thought I was a romantic young maiden with a pale green complexion—the Ophelia type, with water lilies amid her flowing hair, right? You thought that when the End came you could spend eternity in my sweet-scented lily-white arms, right? That was a mistake, my boy, quite a mistake. I'm neither romantic nor sweet-scented. A decent river stinks. Yes indeed—of oil and fish. Now, what do you want in here?

BECKMANN: Sleep. I can't take it anymore up there. I'm through. I want to sleep and be dead. Be dead for life. And sleep. Sleep in peace at last. Sleep for ten thousand nights.

ELBE: You mean, what you want to do, you little baby you, is cut out! Is that right? You think you can't stick it out up there, right? You like to kid yourself that you've been through enough, right? How old are you? you faint-hearted little tenderfoot you.

BECKMANN: Twenty-five. And now I want to sleep.

ELBE: Just think of that, twenty-five! And he wants to sleep away the rest of it. Twenty-five, and in the fog and darkness he steps into the water, because he can't take it anymore. Just what can't you take, you poor sad old thing?

BECKMANN: Everything. I can't bear anything up there anymore. I can't bear starving anymore. I can't bear limping around up there anymore and standing by my own bed; and then limping out of the house again because the bed's been taken. My leg, my bed, even my bread—I can't stick it out anymore, don't you understand?

ELBE: No. You snotty-nosed little suicide. No, do *you* understand? Do you really suppose that just because your wife won't go beddy-by with you anymore, because you've a limp and your stomach rumbles, you're entitled to creep in here under my skirts? To go jumping into the water—just like that? Listen, if everyone who's hungry decided to drown himself, our good old earth would be as bare as an old man's dome, just as bare and as bright and shiny. No, my boy, we can't allow that to happen. You won't get around me with that sort of excuse. You're not going to get taken on around here. You're asking for a smack on your bottom, my little one. Yes indeed—even if you were a soldier for six years. Everyone was. And they're all limping around somewhere. If your bed isn't vacant, find yourself another. I don't want your miserable little slice of life. You're small fry to me, baby. Listen to an old woman's advice: live a little first. Let them kick you around a bit—and then kick back! And when you're fed up, thoroughly fed up, fed up right to here, when you're trampled out flat and when your heart comes around crawling on all fours, then maybe we can take up your case once again. But no nonsense just yet, is that clear? And now, my pretty one, get out of my sight. Your little handful of life is *too* damned little for my purposes. Keep it. I just don't want it, babykins. And now, keep your mouth shut a moment for a change: I'm going to tell you something, very quietly, for your ear alone. Come here. Now: I shit on your suicide! You suckling. Just watch what I'm going to do with you. (*Loudly.*) Hey, boys! Throw this baby out on the sand here at Blankenese. He's going to have another go at it—he's just promised me. But be gentle, he says he's got a bad leg, the little rascal, the quitter, the little damp-behind-the-ears beginner!

Scene 1

Evening at Blankenese. The sound of wind and water. Beckmann. The Other One.

BECKMANN: Who goes there? In the middle of the night! Here by the water. Hello—who's there?

THE OTHER ONE: I am.

BECKMANN: Thanks a lot. And who's I?

THE OTHER: I am the other one.

BECKMANN: The other one? What other one?

THE OTHER: The one from yesterday. The one from long ago. The one from always. The one who says Yes. The one who answers.

BECKMANN: The one from long ago?—and from always? You're the other one from the school bench, from the iceskating rink? The one from the stairwell?

THE OTHER: The one from the snowstorm near Smolensk. And the one from the bunker at Gorodok.

BECKMANN: And the one—the one from Stalingrad, that one, are you that one too?

THE OTHER: That one too. And also the one from last night. And the one from tomorrow morning.

BECKMANN: Tomorrow. There is no tomorrow. Tomorrow has no you in it, in any case. Beat it. You've no face.

THE OTHER: You won't get rid of me. I am the other one, the one who is always here. Tomorrow. In the afternoons. In bed. During the night.

BECKMANN: Beat it. I have no bed. I'm lying here in the dirt.

THE OTHER: I am also the one from the dirt. I am always there. Escape from me is impossible.

BECKMANN: You have no face. Go away.

THE OTHER: You cannot escape me. I have a thousand faces. I am the voice that everyone understands. I am the other one, the one who is always here. The other Self, the answerer. Who laughs while you weep. Who drives you on when you're tired, the slave driver; I am the secret, disturbing one. I am the optimist who sees good in evil itself and light in the deepest darkness. I am the one who believes, who laughs, who loves! I am the one who marches on, lame or not. And the one who says yes, when you say no, the yea-sayer. And the . . .

BECKMANN: Say yes as much as you like. Go away. I don't want you. I say No. No. No. Go away. I say No. Do you hear me?

THE OTHER: I hear you. That's why I'm staying. Who are you, you nay-sayer, you pessimist?

BECKMANN: My name's Beckmann.

THE OTHER: Have you no Christian name, pessimist?

BECKMANN: No. Not since yesterday. Since yesterday my only name has been Beckmann. Just Beckmann. The way a table is called a table.

THE OTHER: Who calls you table?

BECKMANN: My wife. No, the woman who was my wife. You see, I was away for three years. In Russia. And yesterday I came home again. And that's where I went wrong. Three years is quite a while, you know. And my wife called me Beckmann.

Beckmann—plain and simple. Three years—and Beckmann is what she called me, as one calls a table, Table. Beckmann. A piece of furniture. Put it away, that Beckmann over there. So you see, that's why I don't have a Christian name anymore. Do you understand?

THE OTHER: And why are you lying here on the sand? In the middle of the night? Here by the water?

BECKMANN: Because I can't get up. You see, I happen to have brought back a game leg with me. As a kind of souvenir. Souvenirs aren't a bad idea, you know; otherwise wars are forgotten so, so quickly . . . and I didn't want that to happen at any price. It was all just too, too beautiful. Oh my oh my was it beautiful!

THE OTHER: And that's why you're lying here in the middle of the night, beside the water?

BECKMANN: I fell.

THE OTHER: Oh! You fell. You mean you fell into the water?

BECKMANN: No, no! No—listen closely now: I decided to *let* myself fall in. Deliberately! Couldn't take it any more all this lameness and all this sameness. And then that little matter of the woman who used to be my wife—just called me Beckmann, as you call a table, Table. And the other fellow, the one who was with her then—he just grinned. And then all these ruins. This rubbish heap at home. Here in Hamburg. And somewhere underneath lies my boy. A bit of mud and mortar and debris. Human mud, bone mortar. He was just one year old, and I'd never seen him. And now I see him every single night. Under ten thousand stones. Debris, nothing but a bit of debris. I couldn't bear it, I thought. And so I decided to let myself fall in. It would be very easy, I thought: Off the end of the dock—plop! Done for. Finished.

THE OTHER: Plop? Done for? Finished? You've been dreaming. You're lying right here in the sand.

BECKMANN: Dreaming? Yes. Dreaming out of hunger—out of longing. I dreamt that she spat me out again, the Elbe, that old . . . she didn't even want me. I ought to have another crack at things, she said. I had no right to what I wanted.

I was too green, she said. I shit on your lousy little life, that's what she said. She whispered it in my ear: "I shit on your suicide." Shit, she said, that damned old bag—and she screeched like a fishwife. Life is so grand, she said, and here I am lying around in my wet rags on the shore at Blankenese, ice cold. I'm always ice cold. I had enough cold in Russia. I'm sick of this everlasting freezing. And that damned old Elbe, that miserable old *bag*— Oh yes, I've been dreaming out of hunger. (*Pause.*) What's that?

THE OTHER: Someone's coming. A girl or something. There now! There she is!

GIRL: Is anyone there? Just now someone was talking I'm sure— Hello! Is there anyone there?

BECKMANN: Yes, lying here. Here. Down here by the water.

GIRL: What do you think you're doing there? Why don't you get up?

BECKMANN: As you can see, I'm lying here—half on land and half in the water.

GIRL: And whatever for? Stand up—I thought at first it was a dead man when I saw that dark heap by the water.

BECKMANN: Yes indeed, dark heap is right all right.

GIRL: You've a funny way of talking, you know? Well, actually there are often dead bodies lying down here in the evening by the water. Sometimes they're all swollen and slippery. And as white as ghosts. That's why I was so frightened. But you're still alive, thank God. You must be wet through and through, though.

BECKMANN: Right you are. Wet and cold like a genuine corpse.

GIRL: Well then, stand up now. Or have you hurt yourself?

BECKMANN: Yes I have. They stole my kneecap from me. In Russia. And now I have to go limping through life with a stiff leg. And it always seems to be going backward instead of forward on me. So there's no question of my ever getting up again.

GIRL: Come along, come along. I'll help you. Otherwise you might slowly start turning into a fish.

BECKMANN: If you think I won't start flopping off backward again, we might give it another try. Ah. Thank you.

GIRL: You see, you've even gone *upwards* now! But you're ice cold and wet to the skin. If I hadn't come by, you really would have turned into a fish soon. And you *are* just about speechless. May I make a little suggestion? I live right around here. And I have some dry things back at the house. Will you come with me? Yes? Or are you too proud to let me change those damp clothes of yours for you. You semi-fish, you! You dumb, soggy fish, you!

BECKMANN: You'll take me with you?

GIRL: Yes, if you like. But only because you're so wet. I hope you're very ugly and unbothersome so I'll never have any cause to regret any of this. I'm only taking you with me because you're so wet and cold, is that clear? And since—

BECKMANN: Since? Since what? No—only since I'm so wet and cold. There's no other "since."

GIRL: But there is. There is indeed. Since your voice is so hopelessly sad. So colorless and disconsolate—oh, that's all nonsense, isn't it? Come on now, you, my dumb, soggy old fish.

BECKMANN: Hey—stop! You're running away from me. My leg can't keep up with me. Slowly!

GIRL: Oh yes, that's right—so then: slowly. Like two prehistoric, age-old, ice-cold, soggy fishes.

THE OTHER: They're gone now. That's how they are, these strange bipeds, these two-legged creatures. Really bizarre people live here in this world! First they let themselves drop into the water, dead set on dying. Then quite by accident along comes through the darkness, this one with a skirt, with a bosom and long hair. And then life is suddenly sweet and splendid again. Then nobody wants to die anymore. They want *never* to be dead, then. And just because of a few locks of hair, a white skin and the scent of a woman. Then they leap up from their deathbeds as good as new, like ten thousand sprightly stags in the springtime. Then even half-drowned bodies come to life again. All those people who really and truly couldn't stand it any more on this wretched, miserable, damned old globe. Drowned people start wriggling again—and all because

of a pair of eyes, all because of a little softness and warmth
and sympathy, all because of two little hands and a slender
neck. Even the drowned! Those bipeds! Those bizarre people
here on this earth—

SCENE 2

(A *room. Evening. A door creaks and slams shut. Beckmann. The
Girl.*)

GIRL: There! Now we'll see just what sort of a fish we've caught.
Lights on! Well— (*She laughs.*) Well, in heaven's name,
what are those supposed to be?

BECKMANN: These? These are my glasses. Yes—just go on and
laugh. These are my glasses. Unfortunately.

GIRL: You call those glasses? I do believe you're trying to be
funny.

BECKMANN: Yes, my glasses. You're right: perhaps they do look
a little funny, with these gray tin strips going around the
lenses. And then these gray bands that you have to fix
around your ears. And this other gray band right across the
nose! You get a kind of gray, standardized face. A sort of
tin robot's face. A sort of gas-mask face. But then they're
gas-mask glasses.

GIRL: Gas-mask glasses?

BECKMANN: Gas-mask glasses—for soldiers who wore glasses. So a
soldier could see with a gas mask on.

GIRL: But what do you still go around in them for? Don't you
have another pair somewhere?

BECKMANN: No. I did have a pair, but they were shot to pieces.
No, they're not exactly pretty, but I'm glad I've at least got
these. They're extraordinarily ugly—I know that. And it does
make me sort of nervous when people laugh at me. But it
can't be helped. I can't do without them—without them I'm
hopelessly lost. Really, absolutely helpless without them.

GIRL: Oh? You're absolutely helpless without them? (*Gaily, not
at all unkindly.*) Then give me those disgraceful things at

once! There—now what do you say? No, you're not getting them back again until you have to go. In any case, it's more reassuring to me to know that you're absolutely helpless. Much more reassuring. And you know—without glasses you immediately look like a changed man to me. I really believe you make such a melancholy impression because you have to go around looking through these appalling gas-mask glasses.

BECKMANN: Everything's just a blur to me now. Come on—hand them over. I can't see a thing. Even you seem to be far away. Absolutely blurry.

GIRL: Wonderful! That suits me perfectly. And it suits you much better too. With those glasses you look like a ghost.

BECKMANN: Perhaps I am a ghost. One from yesterday, whom nobody wants to see today. A ghost from the war, temporarily repaired for peace.

GIRL (*sympathetically and warmly*): And what a grouchy, gray old ghost you are! I really think that you wear a pair of these gas-mask glasses inside you, too, you self-appointed fish. Leave the glasses with me. It's not at all a bad idea for you to see things a little blurrily for one evening. Do those trousers fit you at least? (*Looks.*) Well now—I guess they'll do. Here, take the jacket.

BECKMANN: Look at this, will you! You pull me out of the water and then you inundate me again. This jacket was made for an Olympic weight lifter. You must go around robbing giants.

GIRL: The giant is my husband—was my husband.

BECKMANN: Your husband?

GIRL: Yes. Did you think I ran a haberdashery here?

BECKMANN: Where is he? Your husband?

GIRL (*quietly, bitterly*): Starved, frozen, killed—how should I know? He's been missing since Stalingrad. It's been three years.

BECKMANN (*stunned*): Stalingrad? In Stalingrad, yes. Yes, many were killed in Stalingrad. But some come back again. And they put on the clothes of those who don't. The man who was your husband, the giant, who owns these clothes, he was left lying there. And I, I come back now and put them on. That's wonderful, isn't it? Isn't that wonderful? And his jacket's so big I practically drown in it. (*Hurriedly*.) I must take it off. Right. I must put on my own wet one. This jacket's killing me. It's choking me, this jacket. I'm a joke in this jacket. A dirty, vulgar joke, made by the war. No—I won't wear this jacket.

GIRL (*warmly, desperately*): Be quiet, Fish. Keep it on, please. I like you this way, Fish. In spite of your funny haircut. You brought that from Russia with you too, didn't you? With the glasses and the leg. See—I thought so. You musn't think I'm laughing at you, Fish. No, Fish, I'm really not. You look so wonderfully sad, you poor gray ghost: in that floppy jacket, with your hair and your stiff leg. Relax, Fish, relax—I don't think it's so funny. No, Fish, you look wonderfully sad. I could cry when you look at me with those unconsolable eyes. And you're so quiet. Say something, Fish, please. Say anything. It doesn't have to make sense, just anything at all. Say something, Fish, the world's so terribly quiet. Say something, then it won't seem so lonely here. Open your mouth, please, Fish Man. Don't stand there all night. Come. Sit down. Here, beside me. Not so far away, Fish. No harm in coming closer, you can only see me blurrily anyway. Come on; you can even close your eyes as far as I'm concerned. Come and say something, so there's something here. Don't you feel how horribly quiet it is?

BECKMANN (*confused*): I like looking at you. Yes—you. But I'm afraid that any step I take is going to be backward. Very afraid.

GIRL: There you go again. Forward, backward. Upward, downward. Tomorrow we may all be lying in the water, white and fat, quiet and cold. But today we're still warm. Still warm, Fish—come on and say something, Fish. You're not going to swim away this evening. And don't talk so much: I don't believe a word. And now I think I'd better lock the door.

BECKMANN: Don't do that. I'm no fish, and you've no need to lock the door. No—God knows I'm no fish.

GIRL (*affectionately*): Fish! Oh Fish! You gray, wet, patched-up ghost.

BECKMANN (*suddenly far off*): Something's smothering me. I'm sinking. I'm strangling—it's because I can't see properly. It's all completely blurred to me now—and it's strangling me.

GIRL (*fearfully*): What's the matter? What's the matter with you? What's happening?

BECKMANN (*with increasing horror*): Now I'm slowly but surely going crazy. Give me my glasses. Quickly. It's happening because everything's so misty now. There! I have the feeling that a man is standing behind your back. He's been there from the start. A big man. Like a sort of athlete. Like a giant, you know. But that's only because I haven't got my glasses —and the giant has only one leg. He's coming nearer, the giant's coming nearer with one leg and two crutches. Do you hear them—tick, tock. Tick tock. That's the sound of the crutches. Now he's standing right in back of you. Don't you feel his breath on your neck? Give me my glasses, I don't want to see him anymore! He's standing there now, right behind you!

(*The Girl screams and rushes out. A door creaks and slams shut. Then, very loudly, the "tick-tock" of crutches is heard.*)

BECKMANN (*whispering*): The giant!

ONE LEG (*in a flat, toneless voice*): What are you doing here? You. In my clothes? In my place? With my wife?

BECKMANN (*weakly*): Your clothes? Your place? Your wife?

ONE LEG (*tonelessly and apathetically*): I'm asking you: what are you doing here?

BECKMANN (*almost mumbling, and stumbling for words*): That's what I asked the man who was with *my* wife last night. In my shirt. In my bed. What are you doing here? I asked. And he shrugged his shoulders and let them fall again and said: "Yes, what am I doing here?" That's what he answered. Then I shut the bedroom door again—no, first I put out the light again. And then I was outside.

ONE LEG: Let me see your face in the light. Come closer. (*In a hollow voice.*) Beckmann!

BECKMANN: Yes. That's me. Beckmann. I didn't think you'd recognize me again.

ONE LEG (*quietly, but with immense reproach*): Beckmann . . . Beckmann . . . Beckmann!!!

BECKMANN (*in agony*): Shut up, you. Don't use that name to me! I won't have that name! Shut up!

ONE LEG (*tauntingly*): Beckmann. Beckmann.

BECKMANN (*screaming*): I'm not. I'm not that anymore. I won't be Beckmann any more!

(*He runs out. A door creaks and slams shut. Then the wind is heard, and a man running through the silent streets.*)

THE OTHER: Stop! Beckmann!

BECKMANN: Who's there?

THE OTHER: I. The other one.

BECKMANN: Are you here again?

THE OTHER: Still here, Beckmann. Always here.

BECKMANN: What do you want? Let me past.

THE OTHER: No, Beckmann. That path leads to the Elbe. Come, the road's up here.

BECKMANN: Let me by. I want the Elbe.

THE OTHER: No, Beckmann. Come. You want this road.

BECKMANN: Take this road? You mean I'm supposed to live? You mean I'm supposed to carry on? Supposed to eat, sleep, all the rest?

THE OTHER: Come, Beckmann.

BECKMANN (*more apathetic than actually angry*): Don't say that name. I won't be Beckmann anymore. I have no name anymore. So I'm to go ahead and live, when there's somebody —somebody with only one leg, somebody who's got only one leg thanks to me? Who's got only one leg because there was once a Sergeant Beckmann who said: "Corporal Bauer, you'll hold your ground to the very last." I'm supposed to go on living, when there's this one-legged man who keeps repeating the name, Beckmann? Always, always—Beckmann! Spoken as if he were pronouncing the word Grave, or the

D

word Dog, or the word Murder. Who speaks my name the way you might say the word Doom! Desperately, threateningly and hopelessly. And you say I ought to go on living? I'm outside, outside again. Last night I was outside. Today I've been outside. I'm outside forever. The doors are permanently shut. And yet I'm a man with legs that are tired and heavy. With a stomach that yells with hunger. With blood that's freezing out here in the night. And the one-legged man keeps saying my name. And at night I can't even sleep any more. So where am I supposed to go, you? Where? Let me by!

THE OTHER: Come, Beckmann. We'll take the road. We'll pay a certain somebody a visit. And you'll give it back to him.

BECKMANN: Give what back?

THE OTHER: The responsibility.

BECKMANN: We'll pay somebody a visit? Yes, let's do that. And I'll give the responsibility back to him. Yes, we'll do that. I want a night's sleep without cripples. I'll give it back to him. Yes! I'll take the responsibility right back to him. I'll bring his own dead right back to him. To him! Yes, come, we'll pay somebody a visit, a certain somebody who lives in a nice warm house. In this town, in every town. We'll pay a man a visit, we want to give him a present—a dear, sweet, brave man, who his whole life long has only done his duty, always his duty! But it was a cruel duty! It was a frightful duty! A cursed—cursed—cursed duty! Come on now! Come on!

SCENE 3

(A room. Evening. A door creaks and slams shut. The Colonel and his family. Beckmann.)

BECKMANN: *Bon appetit*, Colonel.

COLONEL (*chewing*): Pardon?

BECKMANN: *Bon appetit*, Colonel.

COLONEL: You're interrupting supper. Is your business here that important?

BECKMANN: No. I only wanted to decide whether to drown myself tonight, or go on living. And if I am to go on living, just how to go about doing it. Days I'd like a little something to eat now and then, perhaps. Nights, I'd like to sleep. That's all.

COLONEL: Come, come, come! Don't talk such unmanly nonsense. After all you were a soldier, weren't you?

BECKMANN: No, sir.

SON-IN-LAW: What do you mean, no? You're wearing a uniform, aren't you?

BECKMANN (*in a flat voice*): Yes, that's right. For the last six years. But I always thought that even if I went around wearing a postman's uniform for ten years, I'd still be far from being a postman.

DAUGHTER: Daddy, do ask him what he really wants. He keeps on staring at my plate.

BECKMANN (*not unkindly*): Your windows look so warm from outside there. I just wanted to remember again what it's like to look through windows like that. But from inside, from inside. Do you know what it's like to see such bright, glowing windows in the evening, and to be standing out there?

MOTHER (*without malice, but full of horror*): Father, tell him to take off those glasses. It makes me shiver all over just looking at them.

COLONEL: Those are so-called special gas-mask glasses, my dear. Introduced into the armed forces in 1934 for personnel with bad eyesight, designed to be worn beneath one's gas mask. Why don't you throw those things away? The war's over.

BECKMANN: Yes, yes; it's over. That's what they all say. But I still need the glasses. I'm nearsighted; everything looks completely blurry without them. But with them on, I don't miss a thing. From here for example I can see quite clearly what you've got on that table . . .

COLONEL (*interrupting*): Tell me now, just how did you get that remarkable haircut? You've been in jail, right? Been in a bit of a jam, right? Come on now, confess, you broke in someplace, right? And they caught you, right?

BECKMANN: Quite right, sir. Helped break in somewhere. Into Stalingrad, Sir. But the job got bungled, and they nabbed us. We were sent up for three years, the whole hundred thousand of us. And our head man put on civvies and ate caviar. Three years of caviar! And the others lay under the snow with the sands of the steppes in their mouths. And we just went on spooning hot water from our soup bowls. But our head man had to eat caviar. For three years! And they shaved our heads. Either right down to the throat, or else just the hair, there was no definite ruling on that particular point. The ones with the amputated heads were the luckiest. At least they didn't have to go around eating caviar all the time.

SON-IN-LAW (*very annoyed*): What do you think of that, Father! Did you hear? Well? What do you think of that?

COLONEL: My dear young friend, you're completely distorting the whole business, you know. We're all Germans—after all! Let's stick to good old German truth, my dear fellow. He who believes in the truth fights best—that's what General Clausewitz says.

BECKMANN: Right, sir. That's just fine, sir. I'm willing to play this game of truth. We eat until we're full, sir, really full. We put on a new shirt and a new suit with none of its buttons missing, and with no holes in it. And then we light the stove, sir, for indeed we do have a stove, sir. And we put on the tea kettle so as to make some nice hot rum. And then we lower the blinds and drop into an armchair, for we have an armchair too, after all. We can smell our wife's fine perfume— but not blood, isn't that right sir, no blood—and we think about the clean white bed we have, just we two, sir, the bed that's waiting for us upstairs in the bedroom, so soft, so white, so warm. And then we believe in the truth, sir, our good, old German truth.

DAUGHTER: He's mad.

SON-IN-LAW: Nonsense, he's just drunk.

MOTHER: Please put a stop to it, Father. This person's giving me the chills.

COLONEL (*still mildly*): You know I definitely get the impression that you're one of these people whose sense of things has been somewhat confused by that little touch of warfare. Why didn't you become an officer? You'd have traveled in different circles then—had a decent wife and a decent house by now, too. You'd have been quite a different person. Yes —why didn't you become an officer?

BECKMANN: My voice was too quiet, sir. My voice was just too quiet.

COLONEL: There you are: you're too quiet. Tell the truth: you're one of those kind of tired, run-down types, right?

BECKMANN: That's right, sir. That's it. Kind of quiet. Kind of run-down. And tired, sir, tired, so tired! You know I can't sleep, sir, same thing every night. And that's why I'm here, why I've come to see you, sir. I know you can help me. I want to be able to sleep again at last! That's all I want. Just sleep. Deep, deep sleep.

MOTHER: Father, protect us! I'm afraid. He gives me the chills.

DAUGHTER: Nonsense, Mother. He's just one of those people who haven't got all their marbles anymore—you know. Perfectly harmless.

SON-IN-LAW: I think the "gentleman's" quite uppity, myself.

COLONEL (*in a superior sort of way*): Just leave everything to me, children, I've met this type before among the troops.

MOTHER: My God, he's half asleep on his feet.

COLONEL (*almost paternally*): They have to be dealt with a little sharply, that's all. I'll settle this, just leave it to me.

BECKMANN (*far away*): Sir?

COLONEL: Well, what is it you want?

BECKMANN (*far away*): Sir?

COLONEL: I'm listening, I'm listening.

BECKMANN (*drunk with sleep, dreamily*): You're listening, sir?
That's fine then, if you're able to listen, sir. I'd like to tell
you about my dream. The dream I dream every night. Then
I wake up, because somebody's screaming so horribly. And do
you know who's screaming? It's me, sir, I am. Funny, isn't it,
sir? And then I can't fall asleep again. Every night, sir, just
think of it, lying awake every night. That's why I'm tired,
sir, so horribly tired.

MOTHER: Protect us, Father. I feel cold.

COLONEL (*interested*): And your dream wakes you up, you say?

BECKMANN: No, it's when I scream. It's not the dream but the
scream.

COLONEL (*interested*): But the dream is the cause of the scream,
right?

BECKMANN: There you are—you've got it. Dream causes scream.
And it's a most unusual dream, I ought to tell you, too. I'll
just describe it a little to you. You're listening, sir, aren't you?
A man stands there playing the xylophone. He plays the most
wild, abandoned rhythm. And he sweats, this man, because
he's extraordinarily fat. And he's playing on a gigantic xylophone. And because he's so fat he has to lunge about wildly
to reach all the notes. And he sweats, because he's really very
fat. But it's not sweat that he sweats, that's the odd thing.
He sweats blood, steaming, dark blood. And the blood runs
down his trousers in two broad red stripes, so that from far
away he looks like a general. Like a general! A fat, bloodstained general. He must be quite a seasoned old campaigner
of a general, too, for he's lost both arms. Yes, he plays with
long artificial arms that look like mechanical grenade launch-
ers, wooden, with two metal rings. He must be quite an odd
old musician too, this general, because the keys of his xylophone aren't made of wood. No, believe me, sir, believe me,
they're made of bones. Believe me, sir, bones!

COLONEL (*quietly*): Yes, I believe you. They're made of bones.

BECKMANN (*still in a trance, in a haunted voice*): Yes, not wood,
bones. Wonderful white bones. He's got skull bones, shoulder
blades, pelvises. And for the high notes, arms and leg bones.
And then ribs—thousands of ribs. And finally, right at the end

of the xylophone, where the very highest notes are, he's got little finger-bones, toes, teeth. Yes, right at the end come the teeth. And that's the xylophone played by the fat man with the general's stripes. Isn't he a joke of a musician, this general?

COLONEL (*uncertainly*): Yes, that's right, a joke. A great big joke!

BECKMANN: Yes, and now it really gets going. Now the dream really begins. Now: the general stands in front of his gigantic xylophone of human bones, and with his artificial arms beats out a march. "Glory be to Prussia" or "The Badenweiler." But mostly he plays "The Entry of the Gladiators" and "The Old Comrades." Mostly he plays those. You know that one, sir, don't you, "The Old Comrades"? (*Hums.*)

COLONEL: Yes, yes. Of course. (*Also hums.*)

BECKMANN: And then they come. Then they advance, the Gladiators, the Old Comrades. Then they rise up from their mass military graves, and their bloody moaning and groaning stinks to the high white moon. And that's what makes the nights the way they are. As piercing as cat pee. As red, as red as raspberry juice on a white shirt. That's when the nights become so close that we can't even breathe. That's when we smother if we have no mouth to kiss and no liquor to drink. That bloody moaning and groaning stinks to the moon, sir, to the high white moon, when the dead come, the lemonade-spotted dead.

DAUGHTER: I told you—he's crazy! He says the moon is supposed to be white! White!—The moon!

COLONEL (*soberly*): Nonsense. The moon is quite obviously yellow, and always has been yellow. Like honey bread. Like an omelette. The moon's always been yellow.

BECKMANN: Oh no, sir, Oh no! These nights when the dead go walking around she's white and sick. Like the belly of a pregnant girl drowned in a stream. So white, so sick, so round! No, sir, the moon is white on these nights when the dead go walking around and the bloody moaning and groaning stinks to the moon, as cutting as cat pee against the white sick moon. Blood. Blood. Then they rise up from their mass graves with rotting bandages and bloodstained uniforms. They materialize from forests, from streets and ruins, they desubmerge from the oceans, from the steppes and the marshes, frozen black, green, moldering. They come up out of the steppes, one-eyed, one-armed, toothless, legless, with their insides torn to shreds, without skulls, without hands, shot through, stinking, blind. They come together in a fearful flood, immeasurable in numbers, immeasurable in agony! The fearful immeasurable flood of the dead overflows the banks of its graves and rolls thick, pulpy, diseased and bloody over the earth. And then the general with his stripes of blood says to me: "Sergeant Beckmann, assume command—it's your responsibility. Count off!" And then I stand there, before the millions of grinning skeletons, before all those bits and pieces of bone, stand there with my responsibility, and order them to count off. But the company won't count off. Their jaws twitch horribly—but they won't count off for me. The General orders fifty deep knee bends for punishment. The rotting bones rattle, lungs hiss and wheeze, but they won't count off. Is that not mutiny, sir? Outright mutiny?

COLONEL (*whispers*): Yes, outright mutiny.

BECKMANN: They'll all be damned if they'll count off. But then these ghosts do line up, get into formation—and form choruses. Thundering, droning, hollow-voiced choruses. And do you know what they roar, Colonel?

COLONEL (*whispers*): No.

BECKMANN: Beckmann, they roar. Sergeant Beckmann. Always Sergeant Beckmann. And the roaring grows. The roaring rises, brutal as the cry of some God, strange, cold, gigantic. And the roaring grows and rolls, grows and rolls!—It grows so huge, so smothering and huge that I can't breathe anymore. And then I scream, then I scream out in the night. Then I have to scream, scream so terribly, so terribly. And it always wakes me up. Every night. Every night the concert on the bone xylophone, every night the choruses, and every night the terrible screaming. And then I can't go back to sleep again, because I had assumed command, because I had assumed the responsibility. Yes, the responsibility was mine. And that's why I've come to you, sir, because I want at last to be able to sleep again. I want to sleep once more, and that's why I've come: just to be able to sleep, just sleep.

COLONEL: What do you want of me?

BECKMANN: I'm bringing it back to you.

COLONEL: What?

BECKMANN (*in a naïve voice*): Why, the responsibility. I'm bringing you back the responsibility. Have you completely forgotten, sir? The fourteenth of February? At Gorodok. It was forty-two below zero. You came to our post, sir, and said: "Sergeant Beckmann." "Here," I shouted. Then you said, and your breath hung like ice on your fur collar—I remember that quite distinctly because you had a very beautiful fur collar—then you said: "Sergeant Beckmann, I'm giving you responsibility for these twenty men. You'll patrol the forest to the east of Gorodok and if possible take a few prisoners, is that clear?" "Very good, sir," I answered you. And then we set off and patrolled. And I—I had the responsibility. We were on patrol all night, and there was some shooting, and when we got back to our post, eleven men were missing. And I had the responsibility. And that's all, sir. But now the war's over, now I want to sleep, now I'm giving you back the responsibility, sir, I don't want it any more, I'm giving it back to you, Colonel.

COLONEL: But, my dear Beckmann, you're exciting yourself unnecessarily. It wasn't meant like that at all.

BECKMANN (*without excitement, but earnestly indeed*): It was. It was, Colonel. It must have been meant like that. Responsibility is not simply a word, a chemical formula for transforming warm human flesh into dark cold earth. You just can't let men die for the sake of an empty word. Somewhere along the line we've got to take our responsibility. The dead don't answer. God doesn't answer. But the living go on asking. They go on asking every night, sir. While I lie there awake, they come and they ask. Women, sir, sad, lamenting women. Old women with gray hair and hard, cracked hands—young women with lonely, longing eyes; children, sir, children, a *very* great number of little children. And out of the darkness they whisper: Sergeant Beckmann, where is my father, Sergeant Beckmann? Sergeant Beckmann, what did you do with my husband? Sergeant Beckmann, where is my son, where is my brother, Sergeant Beckmann, where is my fiancé, Sergeant Beckmann? Sergeant Beckmann, where? Where? Where?

D*

And so they whisper, until it gets light. There are only eleven women, sir, only eleven women who come to me. How many come to you, sir? A thousand? Two thousand? Do you sleep well, sir? Then I suppose it won't make any difference to you if I add to your two thousand the responsibility for my eleven. Can you sleep, sir? With two thousand ghosts every night? Can you even live, sir, can you live a single minute without screaming? Sir, sir, do you sleep well at night? If you can, this won't bother you, and I'll be able to sleep again at last—if you'll only be so kind as to take it back from me, this responsibility. Then finally my soul will be able to sleep in peace. Peace in my soul, yes, that's what I want—just a little peace in my soul, sir!

And then: sleep! Oh my God, sleep!

COLONEL (*He finally seems a bit affected by all this. But then he laughs aloud, not disagreeably—with rough joviality, quite good-naturedly; then he says, rather uncertainly*): Young man, young man! I just don't know about you—I really just don't know. You aren't deep down one of these pacifists, are you? Just a soupçon of the nihilist in you, perhaps? But—(*He begins to laugh quietly to himself; then, his hearty old Prussianism taking over, he bellows at the top of his lungs:*) My dear boy, my dear boy! I'd almost suspect you of being a bit of a wag, you know that? Am I right? Well? You're a joker, isn't that it? (*He laughs.*) Delicious, you're absolutely delicious! You're a regular pro at it! That good old basic humor! You know (*he is again overcome with laughter*), you know, with that material, with those gags, you should really be on the stage! (*The Colonel actually doesn't wish to offend Beckmann, but he is so hearty, so naïve and so much the old soldier that he can only grasp Beckmann's dream as a joke, a prank.*) Those absurd glasses, that silly mess of a haircut! You should be set to music. (*Laughs.*) My God, that priceless dream of yours! The deep knee bends, those deep knee bends to that xylophone music! My dear boy, you'd be a smash hit on the stage with all that! The whole world will laugh itself half to death over it! Oh my God! (*Laughs wheezingly, with tears in his eyes.*) I honestly didn't realize at first that it was all a comic routine. I figured you didn't have all your marbles or something. I never would have taken you for such a comedian at first. Now, my dear young man, you've given us a delightful evening, and that's worth something in return.

You know what! Go down to see my chauffeur, get some hot water, wash yourself, get rid of that stubble on your chin. Make yourself human. And then have my chauffeur give you one of my old suits. Yes, I'm absolutely serious! Throw those rags of yours away and put on one of my old suits. Go on, you can accept in all good conscience, my boy! And then you'll feel yourself becoming human again at least!

BECKMANN (*coming to; also coming out of his apathy for the first time*): Human? Become? I'm supposed to become human again at least? (*Yells.*) I'm supposed to become human at least you say? What are you supposed to be then? Human? Well? Human? Are you supposed to be human? Are you?

MOTHER (*screams shrilly and jumps up; something is knocked over*): Oh no! He'll kill us all! Oh no, no!

(*Great tumult; the voices of the family are heard shrieking at one another:*)

SON-IN-LAW: Somebody grab the lamp!

DAUGHTER: Help! The light's out! Mother upset the lamp!

COLONEL: Quiet, children, quiet!

MOTHER: Put the light on!

SON-IN-LAW: Where did the lamp go?

COLONEL: Look—it's right over there.

MOTHER: Thank God we've got our light back.

SON-IN-LAW: And that character's gone. I suspected right off there was something the matter with that guy.

DAUGHTER: One, two, three—four. No, everything's still here. But the serving dish is broken.

COLONEL: Damn it, it is. What on earth could he have been after?

SON-IN-LAW: Perhaps he really was just plain crazy.

DAUGHTER: No—look! Our bottle of rum's missing!

MOTHER: Oh my, Father, all your lovely rum.

DAUGHTER: And that half-loaf of bread—it's gone too!

COLONEL: What's that? Our bread?

MOTHER: He ran off with that loaf of bread? Whatever would he want with half a loaf of bread?

SON-IN-LAW: Perhaps he wants to eat it. Or sell it someplace. Those people stop at nothing!

DAUGHTER: Yes, that's right, perhaps he wants to eat it.

MOTHER: Yes, maybe—but just plain dry bread—?

(A door creaks and slams shut.)

BECKMANN (out in the street again. A bottle gurgles): Those people are right. (Gradually getting drunker and drunker:) Down the hatch! That warms you up, all right. No, those people are right. Are we all supposed to sit around and think about Death, when he's right on our heels? Down the hatch! Those people are right. The dead are piling up over our heads. Ten million yesterday. Today—thirty million. Tomorrow somebody's going to come along and blow up an entire continent. By next week they'll be able to manage the murder of everyone on earth with ten grams of poison, all in about seven seconds. And we're supposed to just sit around and mourn? Down the hatch! I've got a deep dark suspicion that pretty soon we should start looking around for another planet for ourselves. Down the hatch! Those people are right. I'm off to the circus. They're right all right. The Colonel laughed himself silly. He says I should go on the stage. Limping, with this coat, with my face and with these glasses on it, with my brush-bristle hairdo on my head—the Colonel's right, humanity's going to laugh itself to death. Down the hatch! Long live the Colonel! He's saved my life. Hail, hail, the Colonel. Down the hatch! Long live bloodshed! Long live laughter at the expense of the dead! Yes, I'll go to the circus, people will laugh themselves silly when it gets really gruesome, with blood and bodies lying all over the place. Come on, let's toast it all again! This booze has saved my life, my brains are submerged, I'm soused. Down the hatch! (Grandiosely and drunkenly:) Whoever has booze or a bed or a broad, let him dream his last! Tomorrow may be too late! Let him build a Noah's Ark of his dream and sail sousing and singing over all the horror and into eternal darkness. Let the others drown in dread and despair! Whoever has booze shall be saved! Down the hatch! Long live the bloodstained Colonel! Long live responsibility! All hail, all hail! I'm off to the circus. Long live the circus! The whole damned circus!

SCENE 4

(A *room. A cabaret producer. Beckmann, still slightly tipsy.*)

PRODUCER (*with great conviction*): So you see, it's precisely here in the field of Art that we really need Youth most again, a Youth which will take a fresh, active stand on all our problems today. A courageous, sober—

BECKMANN (*to himself*): Yes, it absolutely must be sober.

PRODUCER: —and revolutionary Youth. We need the spirit of a Schiller, who wrote his play "The Robbers" at the age of twenty. We need a Grabbe, a Heinrich Heine! That's the kind of aggressive genius we need today! An unromantic, realistic, sturdy Youth which looks the dark side of life straight in the eye, unsentimentally, objectively, with detachment. We need a *true* Youth, a generation that understands the world as it is, and loves it the way it is. Which prizes truth, which has plans, projects. They needn't be the most profound truths in the world, of course—for heaven's sake, we want nothing finished, mature, serene. It should all be like a cry, a cry from the heart. Questions, hopes, longings, hungers!

BECKMANN (*to himself*): Hunger, ah, yes, that we have.

PRODUCER: But this Youth must be young, passionate, courageous. Particularly in Art! Now look at me: when I was seventeen years old I stood there on the cabaret stage and showed all those petty bourgeoisie in the audience my teeth—I spoiled the taste of their cigars, believe me. What we lack is an avant-garde, the kind perpetually poised to present the living gray suffering face of our times!

BECKMANN (*to himself*): Yes, yes: "present," and then "present" again. They "present" faces. They "present" arms. They "present" ghosts. They've always got to "present" something.

PRODUCER: Did you say face? That reminds me: why do you run around in those grotesque glasses? Where did you ever find such weird things, anyway? Just looking at you gives me the hiccups. That's really quite a bizarre piece of mechanism you've got sitting on your nose there.

BECKMANN (*automatically*): These are my gas-mask glasses. We got them in the army—at least those of us who needed them did—so that even in gas masks we could recognize the enemy and strike him down.

PRODUCER: But the war has been over for months now! We've been lolling around in the lap of civilian luxury for ages! How can you possibly still show up in that military regalia?

BECKMANN: You mustn't hold it against me—I just arrived from Siberia the day before yesterday. (*Half to himself:*) The day before yesterday? Yes, the day before yesterday.

PRODUCER: Siberia? Dreadful—just dreadful! Oh, that terrible war! But those glasses—don't you have another pair?

BECKMANN: I'm lucky to have these at least. They've been my salvation. It's the only salvation there is—the only pair of glasses I have, I mean.

PRODUCER: My dear fellow, why didn't you just put aside a spare pair somewhere?

BECKMANN: Where? In Siberia?

PRODUCER: Oh. Of course. That silly Siberia! Look here—observe how I've covered myself on this matter of glasses. (*He digs in his pocket.*) Yes, my boy! I am the proud possessor of three pairs of first-class hornrimmed glasses. (*He holds up three pair.*) Genuine horn, my friend! A yellow pair for work. An unobtrusive pair for going out. And in the evening—for stage purposes, you understand—a heavy black pair. And the result, my friend: class!

BECKMANN: And I don't even have anything I could give you in exchange for one. I know I look all thrown together and patched up. (*Pointing at glasses.*) I know how preposterous these things seem, but what can I do? Couldn't you perhaps—

PRODUCER: My dear man, whatever are you thinking of? I can't spare a single one. All my inspirations, my moods, my whole *effect* depend on them.

BECKMANN: That's the problem: all mine do too. And it's hard to get a drink every day these days, too. And when that's gone, life is like lead: rough, gray, and worthless. But just think— on stage these fantastically hideous glasses would probably be quiet effective.

PRODUCER: What? How do you mean?

BECKMANN: I mean: they'd seem humorous. People laugh them- selves sick when they see me in these glasses, right? And then there's the haircut and the coat. And my face, just think, my face! It's all terribly funny, don't you think?

PRODUCER (*gradually contracting a slight case of the creeps*): Funny? Funny? The laughter will probably stick in their throats, my dear man. Just looking at you will send cold horror creeping up their necks: naked fear in the face of a ghost from the underworld. You know, really, people want to use art for pleasure, to be elevated, edified by—they can do without looking at visions of icecold ghosts. No, we can't just let you loose on them like that. The approach has to be more genial, more self-assured—cheerier. Positive! Yes, my dear man, positive! Consider Goethe! Think of Mozart! The Maid of Orleans! Richard Wagner! Max Schmeling! Shirley Temple!

BECKMANN: Well, I can't really compete with names like that, I'll admit. I'm just Beckmann. Begins with B—ends with eckmann.

PRODUCER: Beckmann? Beckmann? At the moment it doesn't ring a bell with me in cabaret. Have you been working under a stage name?

BECKMANN: No, I'm sort of new. I'm a beginner, in fact.

PRODUCER (*complete about-face*): A beginner? Now look—things in this life aren't quite that easy. Not quite that easy in the least! You can't just walk into a career just like that! You underestimate the promoter's responsibility! Presenting a be- ginner can mean absolute ruin. The public wants names!

BECKMANN: Goethe, Schmeling, Shirley Temple and so on, eh?

PRODUCER: Precisely. Not beginners, newcomers, complete un- knowns! How old are you?

BECKMANN: Twenty-five.

PRODUCER: There, you see. Let the wind blow past your nose a little, young man. Inhale the fragrance of life. What sort of thing have you been doing up till now?

BECKMANN: Not much. War. Been starved, frozen; used a rifle: war. That's all.

PRODUCER: Is that all? Well what's that supposed to amount to? Let yourself mature on the battlefield of life, my dear boy. Work! Make a name for yourself, then we'll make you a star. Learn to know the world, then come back again. Become somebody!

BECKMANN (*who has thus far been subdued, now gradually becomes more and more excited*): And where shall I start? Where? A man has to be given a chance someplace. Somewhere or other a beginner must begin. The wind didn't go blowing past our noses too much in Russia, did it; but then metal did, a great deal of metal. Hot, hard, heartless metal. Where are we to begin then, anyway? Tell me, exactly where? Yes, we want to get the show on the road, damn it!

PRODUCER: Take it easy, take it easy. After all, I didn't send anybody off to Siberia—that had nothing to do with me.

BECKMANN: That's right: nobody sent us to Siberia. We went on our own. All of us, on our own. And some decided to stay out there, all on their own. Under the snow, under the sand. The ones who stayed out there had a chance, the dead ones. But as for us—we can't get a start anywhere. Nowhere.

PRODUCER (*resigned*): All right, all right. Start, then. Please. Just stand there and start. But don't take too long. Time is money. Please, now: be so kind as to proceed. Begin. I'm giving you your big chance, a real opportunity. You're a very lucky man: I'm lending you my ear now. You should appreciate that, young man, you should appreciate that—believe me! So in God's name, start. Please. Ah. Here we go now—

(*Soft xylophone music. The tune of "Tapferen kleinen Soldatenfrau" may be recognized.*)

BECKMANN (*Sings, almost speaking, softly, apathetically and monotonously*):

Brave little soldier's wife
That old song haunts my life
Oh that sweet, that charming song
But really: everything went wrong.

Refrain:
I hear the whole world's laughter
At the things I suffer.
And the mists of a long, long evening
Cloud over everything.
Only a grinning moon
May be seen
Through one of the holes in my curtain.

Coming home just now I saw
My bed was far from empty.
If I cared about anything anymore
I'd find some way to end this misery.

Refrain:
I hear the whole world's laughter
At the things I suffer.
And the mists of a long, long evening
Cloud over everything.
Only a grinning moon
May be seen
Through one of the holes in my curtain.

By the time that midnight came
I'd had myself another woman.
About Germany we made very little fuss,
And Germany didn't bother us.
The night was short, morning came,
I saw him standing there in the door:
Mr. One-leg, her husband,
And that was in the morning—around four.

Refrain:
I hear the whole world's laughter
At the things I suffer.
And the mists of a long, long evening
Cloud over everything.
Only a grinning moon
May be seen
Through one of the holes in my curtain.

Now I run around outside again
Remembering, remembering the old refrain:
The song of the fast—
The song of the fast—
The song of the fastidious little soldier's wife.
(*The xylophone dies away.*)

PRODUCER (*cowed*): Well—that wasn't so bad at all, no, not so
bad. A good try—and for a beginner, very good. But of course,
my dear boy, the whole thing could use a little more spirit!
It doesn't sparkle enough. It lacks a certain polish. And of
course it's not really a true lyric yet. It lacks the delicate tone,
the discreet, piquant erotic quality which the infidelity theme
demands. The public wants to be tickled, not *pinched* like
that. But still, it's a very good try, considering your youth.
The moral, the sense of a deeper wisdom, are lacking, but
still, as I say, not at all bad for a beginner. It is, though, a
bit too explicit, too obvious—

BECKMANN (*to himself*): Too obvious . . .

PRODUCER: —Yes, too loud. Too direct, if you follow me. Of
course, with your youth you lack that genial—

BECKMANN (*slowly, to himself*): Genial . . .

PRODUCER: —sense of serenity, of assurance. Think of that great
old master, Goethe. Goethe! who accompanied his Duke to
the battlefield, and there, around the old campfire, wrote an
operetta.

BECKMANN (*softly, to himself*): An operetta . . .

PRODUCER: That's genius for you! That's what makes all the difference!

BECKMANN: Yes, one must admit, there's quite a difference there.

PRODUCER: My friend, tell you what—let's wait a couple of years,
all right?

BECKMANN: Wait? I'm hungry! I've got to work!

PRODUCER: Yes, but your art needs time to mature. So far your
delivery lacks elegance, lacks experience. It's too bleak, too
naked. You'll upset my public! No, we can't force black bread
on people when—

BECKMANN (*softly, to himself*): Black bread . . .

PRODUCER: —When what they want is cake. Have a little patience. Work on yourself, become slicker, smoother—mature! Yes; nice try, as I say, a very nice try; but still—it's not art.

BECKMANN: Art! Art! But it's the truth!

PRODUCER: Truth! Truth has nothing to do with art!

BECKMANN (*softly, to himself*): No . . .

PRODUCER: Truth won't get you anyplace!

BECKMANN (*softly, to himself*): No . . .

PRODUCER: No—it'll only make you unpopular! Where would we all be if everybody suddenly started telling the truth? Who wants to know anything about things like truth these days? Well? Who? Never let yourself forget that fact.

BECKMANN (*bitterly*): Yes, yes. I understand now. And I thank you. Slowly I'm beginning to understand. It's a fact you can't forget. (*His voice gets harsher and harsher; by the time he opens the door he is almost shouting.*) You musn't ever forget: truth won't get you anywhere. Truth will only make you unpopular. And who wants to hear anything about truth these days? (*Very loud now:*) Yes, slowly I'm beginning to understand, these are the facts—

(*Beckmann goes out without any leave-taking. A door creaks and slams shut.*)

PRODUCER: Hey—hey, young man! Why did you suddenly get so touchy!?

BECKMANN (*outside; despairingly*):
              The booze was finished
              The world turned hard
              As the skin of some savage beast—
              Armored.
And this road heads straight down to the Elbe.

THE OTHER: Stay here, Beckmann. This is the road! Here! Up here!

BECKMANN: That road smells of blood. They massacred truth there. My road goes to the Elbe. And that's the one down here.

THE OTHER: Come, Beckmann. Don't give in! Truth lives!

BECKMANN: Truth is like the town whore. Everybody knows her, but nonetheless, it's embarrassing to meet her in the street. Therefore one must try it out at night, and in secret. In the daylight they're gray, raw and ugly—both the whore and the truth. And some never stomach either of them as long as they live.

THE OTHER: Come, Beckmann. There's always a door open somewhere.

BECKMANN: Yes, for Goethe. For Shirley Temple or Schmeling. But I'm just Beckmann. Beckmann with the funny glasses and the funny haircut. Beckmann with the game leg and the old Santa Claus suit. I'm just a bad joke made by the war, a ghost of yesterday. And because I'm just Beckmann and not Mozart, every door is shut tight. Bang. That's why I stand outside. Bang. And again: Bang. Always, always: Bang. Here I am outside again: Bang. And because I'm a beginner I can't begin anywhere. And because I'm too quiet I wasn't commissioned. And because I'm too loud I frighten the public. And because I've a heart that cries at night for the dead I'm told that I have to become "a little human again." And in the Colonel's old suit!

> The booze is finished
> The world turns hard
> As the skin of some savage beast—
> Armored.

That road stinks of blood, because they massacred truth there, and every door is shut. I want to go home, but all the streets are dark. Only the path to the Elbe is light. Oh, how light!

THE OTHER: Stay here, Beckmann. This is your road up here. This is the way home. You must go home, Beckmann. Your father is sitting in the living room and waiting. And already your mother's standing at the door. She recognized your footsteps.

BECKMANN: My God! Home! Yes, I'll go back home. I'll go to my mother. I'll go at last to my mother!!! To my—

THE OTHER: Come. This is your way, straight home. It's true: the place one should go first is always the last one thinks of.

BECKMANN: Home, where my mother is, my mother—

Scene 5

(A *house*. A *door*. *Beckmann*.)

BECKMANN: Our house is still standing! And it has a door—and
that door is open just for me. My mother is there and my
mother will open the door and I'll enter. To think that our
house is still standing! And listen—the steps still creak, too.
And there—our door. My father comes out of it every day at
eight in the morning. And every evening at six he enters it
again. Except for Sundays. He fumbles with his bunch of
keys and mumbles a little to himself. Every single day. A
whole lifetime. And there my mother goes in and out—three,
seven, perhaps ten times a day. Every single day. Her whole
life long. That, *that* is our door. Behind it the kitchen door
squeaks, behind it the clock with its deep, deep tones ticks
away the irrecoverable hours. Behind it I used to sit on a chair
turned around backwards and pretend it was the seat of a
racing car. And behind it my father coughs. Behind it the
running faucets gurgle and the kitchen tiles click as my
mother fusses about. That's our door. Behind it a life is un-
wound from an inexhaustible reel. A life which has gone on,
unchanged, for thirty years. And which will always go on.
War has passed this door by. It hasn't broken it down, it
hasn't ripped it off its hinges. It has left our door standing, purely by chance; an oversight. And now the door's
there for me. It will open for me; it will close behind
me, and I won't be outside anymore. Then I'll be home
—*home*. That's our old door with the paint peeling off
and the dented letterbox. With the wobbly white bell-push
and the shining brass plate, which my mother polishes every
morning and which bears our name: Beckmann—

No! the brass plate's missing! Why isn't the brass plate there?
Who's taken our name away. What's this dirty card on the
door? With this strange name? Nobody named Kramer lives
here! Why isn't our name still on the door? It's been there
for thirty years. It can't simply be removed and another just
stuck in its place! Where's our brass plate? The other names

in the house are still on their doors. As always. Why isn't Beckmann there too? You can't simply nail on a new name when Beckmann's been there for thirty years! Who's this Kramer, anyway?

(*He rings. The door opens.*)

MRS. KRAMER (*with an indifferent, chilling, cheery amiability, more terrible than any outright rudeness or outright brutality*): What can I do for you?

BECKMANN: Oh, good morning, I was just—

MRS. KRAMER: Yes?

BECKMANN: Do you know where our brass plate's gone?

MRS. KRAMER: What do you mean, "our brass plate"?

BECKMANN: The nameplate that's always been here—thirty years!

MRS. KRAMER: How should I know?

BECKMANN: Then you don't know where my parents are?

MRS. KRAMER: Who are they? And who are you?

BECKMANN: My name's Beckmann. I was born here. This is our apartment.

MRS. KRAMER (*still chatty and mildly snotty, rather than deliberately nasty*): No, you're wrong there, it's our apartment. For all I care, you *were* born here, but this isn't your apartment. It's ours.

BECKMANN: Yes, yes, I see—but what's happened to my parents then? They must be living somewhere.

MRS. KRAMER: You're the son of those people, the Beckmanns, is that it? Your name is Beckmann?

BECKMANN: Yes, of course, Beckmann. I was born here in this very house.

MRS. KRAMER: That's fine—I really couldn't care less one way or the other, though. You see, the apartment's *ours* now.

BECKMANN: But my parents! Where are my parents staying? Can't you tell me where I can find them?

MRS. KRAMER: You mean you actually don't know? Well, you're a fine son, you are. You actually don't know?

BECKMANN: For God's sake where could those old people have gone!? They've lived here thirty years, and now they're simply not here any more? Tell me—they must be someplace!

MRS. KRAMER: They are. As far as I know: Plot Five.

BECKMANN: Plot Five. What's Plot Five mean?

MRS. KRAMER (*resigned to the effort of explanation; still casual, rather than simply brutal*): Plot Five at Ohlsdorf. Do you know what Ohlsdorf is? It's a cemetery. Do you know where Ohlsdorf is? It's near Fuhlsbüttel. Three city train lines have last stops out there. In Fuhlsbüttel the prison, in Alsterdorf the insane asylum. And in Ohlsdorf the cemetery. Do you see —that's where they stay now, those old people of yours. That's where they live now. Moved away, left, departed. And you really didn't know?

BECKMANN (*dazed; half to himself, half to Mrs. Kramer*): What are they doing out there? Can they really be dead? But they were alive just now. How could I know anything about this? I've been in Siberia three years—more than a thousand days. They're dead? But they were here just now. Why did they have to die before I could get home? There wasn't anything wrong with them. My father had a cough—but he'd always had it. And my mother used to say that the tiles on the kitchen floor gave her cold feet all the time. You don't die of things like that. They had no reason to die. They can't just have suddenly, mysteriously died like that.

MRS. KRAMER (*vulgar, familiar; and with a sudden touch of coarse sentimentality*): You're really too much—just too much, you silly son you! Oh well, all right, skip it. A thousand days in Siberia is certainly no joke at that—I guess it really can knock your feet out from under you. Well, what happened was that the old Beckmanns just couldn't take it anymore. You know. They went just a wee bit overboard during the Third Reich —if you follow. Why should an old man like him want to go around wearing a uniform, anyway? And he was a bit nutty about the Jews, as his son you know that, don't you? Your old man couldn't stand them—in fact, they gave him fits. He was always announcing that he'd like to chase them all back to Palestine, single-handed. In the air raid shelter, you know, every single time a bomb went off he'd let loose about the Jews. He was a bit too active, your old man. He gave a bit too much of himself to the Nazis. Then, when the Brownshirts disappeared, he found himself high and dry, your father did. And all just over the Jews. He really did overdo it. Why couldn't he keep his mouth shut, anyway? He was just too involved, old Beckmann was. And when it was over with those brown-shirted boys, the authorities came around and touched him on his sore spot. Yes, and a very sensitive sore spot it was, too, believe me, very sensitive by that time. And— you know, I have to tell you: you're really killing me with those ridiculous things you've got on your nose for glasses. You're an absolute holy terror in them. You can't tell me those are sensible glasses. Haven't you got a regular pair, young man?

BECKMANN (*automatically*): No. These are the gas-mask glasses which soldiers were issued who—

MRS. KRAMER: I know that all right—but you wouldn't catch me going around with those things on. I'd stay at home first. You know what my dear better half would say to you if he saw you? He'd say: *achtung*, young man, off with that bridgework!

BECKMANN: Yes—go on: what happened to my father? You're confusing me—go on, Mrs. Kramer, go on!

MRS. KRAMER: Well, there's really nothing else to say. They gave your dad the sack, without benefit of pension, of course. And then they had to get out of the house, too—and all they could keep were the shirts on their backs. It was a sad, sad situation, of course. I guess that pretty much finished them off. The old people just couldn't cope with it all. They didn't even want to, I guess. So—they denazified themselves once and for all. That was very consistent of your old man, I'll say that about him.

BECKMANN: What was that? You say they—

MRS. KRAMER (*chattily; still not consciously being mean*): Denazi-fied themselves. Just an expression, you know. Sort of a little private joke with us. Yes, those parents of yours had had it. They were found one morning stretched out stiff and blue in the kitchen. Pretty stupid, my better half said; with all that gas we could have done a month's cooking!

BECKMANN (*softly, but with enormous menace*): I think it would be a very good idea if you shut that door now, and shut it fast. Fast! And you'd better lock it! I'm warning you to shut that door!

(*Mrs. Kramer screams; the door slams shut.*)

BECKMANN (*softly*): I can't stand it! I can't stand it! I can't stand it!

THE OTHER: Yes, Beckmann, yes. One can stand it.

BECKMANN: No! I can't—I can't anymore! Go away! You soft-headed optimistic idiot! Go away!

THE OTHER: No, Beckmann. Your road's up here. Keep going, Beckmann, keep going—you've still a long way to go. Come!

BECKMANN: You filthy swine! Oh, sure, "one can stand it," oh, sure. You can stand it, *you* can stand going on this way. Sometimes it takes your breath away—other times you want to kill someone. But you go on breathing anyway and the murder doesn't happen. And you don't scream anymore and you don't sob anymore. You stand it. You stick it out. Two corpses! Who bothers these days about two little corpses.

THE OTHER: Quiet, Beckmann. Come!

BECKMANN: Naturally it's rather vexing when they happen to be your parents, these two little corpses. But then, two corpses, two old people? Too bad about the gas, though! We might have done a month's cooking with it!

THE OTHER: Never mind, Beckmann. Come. The road's waiting for you.

BECKMANN: Yes, never mind. When one has a heart that's screaming, a heart that'd commit murder in a minute. A poor idiot of a heart that would murder these mourners who regret only the passing away of—gas! A heart that wants to sleep, deep in the Elbe—do you understand me! A heart that has screamed itself hoarse; and no one has even heard it. No one below. No one above. Two old people have wandered off to Ohlsdorf cemetery. Yesterday it was perhaps two thousand, the day before yesterday perhaps seventy thousand. Tomorrow it'll be four hundred thousand or six million—all just wandered off into the world's mass graves. Who cares? No one. Not a soul below—not a God above. God sleeps, and we just go on living.

THE OTHER: Beckmann! Beckmann! Don't think about it, Beckmann. You see everything through your gas-mask glasses. You see everything distortedly, Beckmann. Pay no attention. There was *once* a time, Beckmann, when people reading the evening newspapers under the greenish lights of Capetown would sigh, sigh deeply for two little girls frozen to death in the ice of Alaska. There was *once* a time when they couldn't sleep in Hamburg because a child had been kidnaped in Boston. There was *once* a time when it could happen that they mourned in San Francisco if a balloonist crashed in Paris.

BECKMANN: There was once a time, once, once! When was it? Ten thousand years ago? It takes casualty lists running to seven digits to get any kind of reaction now. And people don't even sigh in the lamplight any more, they sleep deeply and peacefully—at least when they still have a bed to sleep in. People stare right past each other, stunned by so much agony: hollow-cheeked, hard, bitter, warped, and lonely. They're fed with numbers, numbers that are so long they can hardly pronounce them. And what the numbers stand for—

THE OTHER: Don't think about it, don't think about it.

BECKMANN: No, *do* think about it, think about it until you go to pieces! The numbers are so long you can hardly pronounce them. And what the numbers stand for are—

THE OTHER: Don't think about it!

BECKMANN: Yes, think about it! They stand for the dead, the half-dead, men killed by grenades, by shrapnel, starvation, bombs, freezing, drowning, despair, the lost, the bewildered, the lifeless. And those numbers have more digits than we have fingers!

THE OTHER: Never mind, never mind—the road is waiting for you, Beckmann, come!

BECKMANN: Tell me, tell me for the love of God, where does it lead? Where are we now? Are we still here? Is this still the

old earth? Haven't we grown fur yet? Or tails? Or fangs? Or
claws? Do we really still go around on two legs? Man! Man!
What kind of road are you? Where do you lead? Answer
me that, you other one, you great optimist! You eternal
Answerer—answer me that!

THE OTHER: You're losing the way, Beckmann; come, stay up
here, your road is here! Don't think, don't. The road goes
both up and down. Don't cry out when it goes down, and
everything falls into darkness—the road goes on, and everywhere there are lamps and lights: the sun, stars, women,
windows, lightbulbs and opened doors. Don't cry out if you
have to stand alone at night for half an hour in the fog.
You'll come across others eventually. Come on, boy, don't
get tired! Don't listen to that sweet xylophone player's senti-
mental tripe, don't listen.

BECKMANN: Don't listen? And that's your answer? Millions of the
dead, half-dead, unaccounted for—and that just doesn't matter? And you tell me: just don't listen! I've lost my way, you
say? Yes, this road's gray, terrible, abysmal. But we're out
here on it just the same—limping, weeping and starving;
poor, cold and tired! And the Elbe threw me up again like
rotten meat. The Elbe won't let me sleep. I'm supposed to
live, you say! Live *this* life? Tell me exactly why: for whom?
For what?

THE OTHER: For yourself! For life itself! Your road is waiting. And
every so often there are lights. Are you such a coward that
you're afraid of the darkness between them? Do you want
only lights? Come, then, Beckmann, go now to the next
light.

BECKMANN: Listen to me now: I'm hungry and it's cold—understand? I can't stand up anymore, I'm exhausted. Open a door
somewhere. I'm hungry. The road's dark and all the doors
are shut. Optimist, save your breath for somebody else: I'm
homesick. Yes—even for my own mother, for black bread.
It doesn't even have to be those old special dinner biscuits
—that's not necessary now. My mother would have had a
piece of black bread for me, and warm socks. And then I
would have sat myself down, cozy and full, right next to
the Colonel—and I would have sat there and read Dostoievsky. Or Gorky. It's wonderful when one's warm and full

to read about the misery of other people, and sit there so sympathetically, sighing. But unfortunately my eyes keep shutting on me; I'm dogtired. And I want to yawn like a dog—yawn my whole head off. And I can't go on. I'm tired, I'm tired. There's no going on—do you understand me? I won't and I can't. Not even an inch. Not even—

THE OTHER: Beckmann, don't give up. Come, Beckmann, life's waiting, Beckmann, come!

BECKMANN: I don't want to read Dostoievsky, I'm afraid enough as it is, all by myself. I'm not coming. No. I'm tired. No, I'm not, I'm *not* coming. I want to sleep. Here in front of my door. I'll sit down on the steps in front of my door, and then I'll sleep. I'll sleep—sleep until some day the walls of the house begin to collapse from old age. Or until the next mobilization. I'm as tired as the rest of this whole yawning world!

THE OTHER: Don't tire, Beckmann. Come. Live!

BECKMANN: This life? No, this life is less than no life at all. I won't do it. Don't you know what you're saying? "Come on, everybody; the show has to keep going until it's over. Who knows in what dark corner we shall lie or on which sweet bosom by the time the curtain finally, finally falls." Five gray, rain-drenched acts.

THE OTHER: Get on with it then, Beckmann, be alive with life!

BECKMANN: Be quiet. Life is as follows:
Act I: Gray skies. Somebody is hurt.
Act II: Gray skies. Somebody hurts back.
Act III: It gets a little darker and it rains.
Act IV: It gets much darker. Somebody sees a door.
Act V: It is night, the dead of night, and the door is shut. A man stands outside—outside that door. He stands by the Elbe, by the Seine, by the Volga, by the Mississippi. He stands there thinking, cold, hungry and damned, damned tired. And then suddenly there's a splash, and the waves make neat little round circles, and the curtain falls. Worms and fishes burst into noiseless applause.—And that's the way it goes. Is that really anything more than nothing at all? I—I, at any rate, won't go on with the show anymore. My yawns are as enormous as the whole wide world.

THE OTHER: Stay awake, Beckmann! You must go on.

BECKMANN: What was that?—You suddenly sound so muted to me . . .

THE OTHER: Get up. Beckmann, the road is waiting.

BECKMANN: The road will have to survive without my weary tread. But why are you so far away suddenly? I can hardly—hardly —under—stand . . . (*He yawns.*)

THE OTHER: Beckmann! Beckmann!

BECKMANN: Hmmmmm . . . (*He falls asleep.*)

THE OTHER: Beckmann, you're asleep!

BECKMANN (*In sleep*): Right—I'm asleep.

THE OTHER: Stop that right now—you have to live!

BECKMANN: No thanks—I wouldn't think of waking up. I'm dreaming now. I'm dreaming a wonderful dream.

THE OTHER: No more dreaming, Beckmann—you have to live.

BECKMANN: Live? No, never; I'm dreaming right now that I'm dying.

THE OTHER: Stand up, I'm telling you—live!

BECKMANN: No. I don't ever want to get up again. I'm having such a wonderful dream. I'm lying in the road and I'm dying. My lungs won't go on, my heart won't go on, and my legs won't go on, either. The entire Beckmann won't go on, in fact, do you hear? Rank disobedience, that's what it is. Sergeant Beckmann says he won't go on—now isn't that just wonderful?

THE OTHER: Come, Beckmann, you must keep on going.

BECKMANN: Keep on going? Keep on going, you mean, keep on going downward! A *bas*, as the French say. It's really quite delightful to die, you know, I'd never have thought it. I'm getting the idea that death must be quite tolerable after all. After all, nobody's come back because he couldn't stand death, has he? Perhaps death's quite nice, perhaps much nicer than life. Perhaps— Do you know, I actually believe I'm already in heaven. I can't feel anything any more—and isn't

that just like being in heaven, not to feel anything anymore?
And here comes an old man looking rather like God. Yes,
almost like God himself. Except that he looks a little too
theological, come to think of it. And he's in tears. Can that
possibly be God? Good evening, old man. You're not God,
are you?

GOD (*tearfully*): I'm God all right, my poor dear boy.

BECKMANN: Oh, so you're God, are you. Who actually called you
that, God? Mankind? Well? Or is that what you call yourself?

GOD: Mankind calls me God, "dear God," in fact, usually.

BECKMANN: Odd, they must be very unusual men to go around
calling you that. They must be the Contented, the Satisfied,
the very Lucky ones—or, of course, those who are afraid of
you. Those who walk in the sunshine of life, those in love,
or satisfied or contented in general—or else those who are
frightened at night. Yes, they say: God! Dear God! But I
don't say dear God, understand, because I don't happen to
be acquainted with any "dear God."

GOD: My child, my poor—

BECKMANN: When exactly are you dear, dear God, anyway? Were
you dear when you let my little son, my little son who was
exactly one year old, get torn to pieces by a screaming bomb?
Were you dear when you let him get murdered that way,
dear God?

GOD: I didn't have him murdered.

BECKMANN: Right, exactly right. You only *let* him get murdered.
You didn't bother yourself when he started screaming and
those bombs started exploding. Where were you actually,
when those bombs were exploding, dear God? And were you
dear, when one night eleven men from my patrol were missing? Eleven men shot, dear God, and you weren't there
either, dear God. Those eleven men must have screamed
awfully loudly in that lonely wood, but you weren't there,
dear God, you simply weren't there. Were you dear in Stalingrad, dear God, were you dear there? Well? Well? When in
fact were you dear, then, God, when? When have you ever
bothered yourself about us, God?

GOD: No one believes in me any more. Neither you nor anyone else. I am the God no one believes in any more. No one bothers himself about me any more. No—not a single one of you cares about me any more.

BECKMANN: Has God been studying theology too? Who's supposed to care for whom, you want to know? Oh, you're old, God, all right, you're old-fashioned; you can't just cope with our long lists of the dead, with our agonies now. We really don't know you any more, you're a fairy-tale God. Today we need a new one. One for our own misery and our own particular fear. A completely new one. Oh, we've searched for you, God, believe me, in every shell hole, during every passing night. We've called for you, God! We've roared for you, wept for you, cursed for you. And where were you then, dear God? Where are you this very evening? Have you turned away from us? Have you completely walled yourself up in those picturesque, lovely old churches of yours? Can't you hear our cries through the shattered windows, God? Where are you?

GOD: My children have turned away from me, not I from them. You from me, you from me. I am the God whom nobody believes in any more. You have turned away from me.

BECKMANN: Go away, old man—you're spoiling my death. Go away, you're just one more tired, pitiful old theologian. You play around with phrases: who cares for whom? Who's turned away from whom? You from me? We from you? You are dead, God. Live—live with us, live with us at night when it's cold and lonely and when we can hear our stomachs in the silence—live with us then, God. Oh, go away, you ink-blooded theologian, just go away. You pitiful, pitiful old man.

GOD: My boy, my poor, poor boy. I can't help it! I just cannot, cannot help it.

BECKMANN: Yes, that's it, God. You just can't help it. And we're not afraid of you any more. And we don't love you any more. And you're too old-fashioned. The theologians have let you grow old. Your pants have patches in them, your shoes are worn through, and your voice has become a squeak—a squeak against the thundering of our time. We just can't hear you any more.

GOD: No, no one hears me any more, ever. You're all too loud!

BECKMANN: Or are you too quiet, God? Have you too much ink in your blood, God, too much thin theologian's ink? Go away now, old man, you've walled yourself up there inside your fine old churches, we can't hear each other any more. Go—and before total darkness falls make sure that you find yourself a little out-of-the-way hole somewhere, or a fine new suit, or dark forest to hide in; otherwise they're sure to stick you with the blame when everything's finally fallen completely to pieces. And don't slip in the dark, old man, the road is steep, and strewn with skeletons. Hold your nose, God. And then sleep well, old man, which is only to say: sleep as well as you always do anyway. Good night!

GOD: A new suit or a dark forest? My poor, poor children. My dear, dear boy—

BECKMANN: Just go! Good night now!

GOD: My poor, poor . . . (*He goes off.*)

BECKMANN: Old people have it the hardest of all these days; they have difficulty adjusting to new conditions. We're all outside. Even God's outside here, and no one opens any doors, even for him. Only death, only death has a door left for us. And that's exactly where I'm headed.

THE OTHER: You musn't just wait for the door death opens. Life has a thousand doors. Who promised you that behind death's door anything exists but emptiness?

BECKMANN: And what's behind the doors that life opens for us?

THE OTHER: Life! Life itself! Come, you must go on.

BECKMANN: I can't, I can't. Just listen to the way these lungs of mine are wheezing—(*he coughs unconvincingly*)—wheeze— wheeze—wheeze! See? I just can't.

THE OTHER: You can. Your lungs are *not* wheezing.

BECKMANN: My lungs are *so* wheezing. What could be wheezing if not my lungs? Listen: wheeze—wheeze—wheeze! What else?

THE OTHER: A street-cleaner's pushbroom! Look, there's one coming now. He's coming past us, and his pushbroom's scratch-

ing down the street like asthmatic lungs. See—your lungs
weren't wheezing at all. It was just the pushbroom—see? Hear
it: whisk—whisk—whisk!

BECKMANN (*bitterly*): Yes, that's right, the sounds of the lungs
of a man in his death rattle sound like a street-cleaner's
broom. And look—that street cleaner has red stripes down
his trouser legs. He's a street cleaner general. A member of
the High Command of the street cleaners. And when he
pushes that broom of his, lungs in their death-rattlings go
wheeze—wheeze—wheeze. Hey, street cleaner!

STREET CLEANER: I am *not* a street cleaner.

BECKMANN: You aren't a street cleaner? What are you then?

STREET CLEANER: I'm an employee of the Rubbish, Refuse, and
Remains Interment Institute.

BECKMANN: You're Death? And you work as a street cleaner?

STREET CLEANER: Today a street cleaner; yesterday a general. Death
isn't particularly choosy, you know. The dead are everywhere,
right? And lately they actually lie all over the sidewalks and
streets. Yesterday they lay on the battlefield—then Death was
a general and the accompaniment an xylophone. Today they
lie all over the streets and the pushbroom of Death goes
wheeze—wheeze.

BECKMANN: And the pushbroom goes wheeze—wheeze? From
general to street cleaner. Are the dead so devaluated?

STREET CLEANER: They're going down all right, they're going down.
No salute. No tolling bell. No funeral oration. No war memorial. They're going down. And the pushbroom goes wheeze
—wheeze!

BECKMANN: Must you go so soon? Stay here a moment, won't
you? I mean—take me with you. Death, Death, you're for-
getting me— Death!

STREET CLEANER: I forget no one. My xylophone plays "The Old
Comrades," and my pushbroom goes wheeze—wheeze—
wheeze! I forget no one.

BECKMANN: Death, Death, leave the door open for me. Death,
don't shut your door. Death—

E

STREET CLEANER: My door is always open. Always. Morning, afternoon, and night. In light and in darkness. My door is always
open. Always and everywhere. And my pushbroom goes
wheeze—wheeze. (*The noise grows softer as Death moves
off.*)

BECKMANN: Wheeze—wheeze. Do you hear how my lungs are
wheezing? Like a street-cleaner's broom. And the street
cleaner leaves his door wide open. And the street-cleaner's
name is Death. And his pushbroom sounds just like my
lungs, or like a tired, rusty old clock: wheeze—wheeze . . .

THE OTHER: Beckmann, stand up now, there's still time. Come,
breathe, breathe yourself well again.

BECKMANN: But my lungs sound just like—

THE OTHER: Not your lungs, not your lungs. Just an old broom,
Beckmann, a civil servant's pushbroom.

BECKMANN: A civil servant?

THE OTHER: Yes, and now he's far, far away. Come, stand up
again, breathe. Life is waiting with a thousand lights and a
thousand open doors.

BECKMANN: Just one door, just that one would be enough. And
he's leaving it open for me, he said, always and anytime.
One door.

THE OTHER: Stand up, you're dreaming a deadly dream. You'll
die of your dream. Stand up.

BECKMANN: No, I'll stay here. Here in front of the door. And the
door is open—that's what he said. Here I'll stay. Am I really
supposed to stand up—when I'm having such a wonderful
dream? I'm dreaming, dreaming that it's all over. A street
cleaner came by and identified himself as Death. And his
broom whisked along just like my lungs. A dead ringer for
them. And he promised me a door, an open door. Street
cleaners can be really delightful people. Delightful as death.
Yes, he was really quite, quite delightful.

THE OTHER: You're dreaming, Beckmann, you're dreaming an
evil dream. Wake up, live!

BECKMANN: Live? I'm lying here in this street and it's all over now, all, all over. I'm unquestionably, indisputably dead. It's all over and I'm dead, beautifully dead.

THE OTHER: Beckmann, Beckmann, you must live. Look—everyone's alive. Beside you. To the left, to the right, in front of you: all the others. And you? Where are you? Live, Beckmann, everyone's alive.

BECKMANN: Everyone? Who's everyone? The Colonel? The producer? Mrs. Kramer? Live along with them, you mean? Oh, I'm so wonderfully, wonderfully dead! All those people are far, far away, and I never want to have to see them again. Those people are murderers.

THE OTHER: Beckmann, you're lying.

BECKMANN: I'm lying? Aren't they all evil? You mean they're good?

THE OTHER: You don't know people. They're good.

BECKMANN: Oh, they're good, all right. And in all goodness they've killed me. Laughed me to death. Shown me the door. Chased me away. In all human goodness. They are hardened even when they dream. Hardened even in the depths of their deepest dreams. And they casually pass by my corpse—hardened even in sleep. They laugh and chew and sing and sleep and digest their way casually past my corpse. My death is nothing.

THE OTHER: You're wrong, Beckmann.

BECKMANN: No! Optimist, face it: these people do, quite casually, pass by my corpse. Corpses are, after all, unpleasant and boring.

THE OTHER: Mankind does not casually pass by your death, Beckmann. Mankind has a heart. Mankind mourns your death, Beckmann, and your corpse lies in their way when they want to fall asleep at night. They don't pass casually by.

BECKMANN: Oh yes they do, optimist. Corpses are most unsightly, most unpleasant. They just go by as fast as possible holding their noses and shutting their eyes.

THE OTHER: They do not! Their hearts contract at every corpse!

BECKMANN: Look—here comes somebody now. Do you remember him? It's the Colonel who wanted to make a new man out of me by letting me have his old suit. Colonel! Colonel!

COLONEL: Merciful heavens—beggars again! It's just like old times.

BECKMANN: Exactly, sir, exactly. Just like old times. From the same background, the same beggars. But I'm not actually a beggar, sir, to tell the truth. I'm a drowned corpse. I'm a deserter, sir. I was a very tired trooper, sir. Yesterday I was Sergeant Beckmann, sir, do you remember? Beckmann. I was rather on the soft side, wasn't I, sir, remember? Yes, and tomorrow evening I shall drift dumb and numb and bloated onto the beach at Blankenese. Awful, isn't it, sir. And you'll have me on your account then, Colonel. Just awful, right? Two thousand and eleven plus Beckmann makes two thousand and twelve. Two thousand and twelve ghosts a night, brr!

COLONEL: Never seen you before in my life, my good man. Never heard of any Beckmann. What rank did you hold?

BECKMANN: But, sir! Surely you must still remember your last murder! The one with the gas-mask glasses and the convict's haircut and the game leg! Sergeant Beckmann, Colonel!

COLONEL: Yes—of course! *That* character! Just goes to show: you can't depend in the least on these lower ranks. Imbeciles, guardhouse lawyers, pacifists, hari-kari candidates. So you finally drowned yourself, eh? Yes, that's right, you were the type that got a little tangled up, a little overly upset during the war; yes indeed, utterly lacking in military qualities. A truly unfortunate sight, a thing like that.

BECKMANN: Yes, isn't it, Colonel, a truly unfortunate sight indeed, all these soft, white corpses in the water nowadays. And you're the murderer, sir, you! Can you really stand it, Colonel, being a murderer? How does it feel to be a murderer, sir?

COLONEL: What's that? What do you mean? Me?

BECKMANN: Yes, Colonel, you laughed me to death. Your laughter sounded more dreadful to me than all the deaths in the world, Colonel. You actually laughed me to death, sir, you actually did!

COLONEL (*completely uncomprehending*): Really? Oh well. You were the type that would have ended up by going to the dogs, anyway. And now, good evening.

BECKMANN: Pleasant dreams, Colonel. And many thanks for the obituary! Well, did you hear, optimist, you great friend of man? Obituary for a drowned soldier. Epitaph of a man for a man.

THE OTHER: You're dreaming, Beckmann, you're dreaming. Mankind is good.

BECKMANN: You're beginning to sound a little hoarse, you with that optimistic obbligato of yours! Has all this begun to ruin your voice? Oh, yes, mankind is good. However, there *do* seem to be days when you keep on incessantly running into the few bad ones there are. But mankind's not really all that bad, Oh, no. And I'm only dreaming. I don't want to be unjust. Mankind is good. It's only that they're all so terribly different, right?—so incredibly, incredibly different. This man's a colonel, that man's just some lower rank or other. The Colonel's content, healthy, and goes around in nice, snug woolen underwear. And at night he has a bed and a wife.

THE OTHER: Beckmann, stop dreaming! Stand up now and live. You're dreaming everything wrong.

BECKMANN: And the other man—he starves, he limps and hasn't even a shirt any more. At night he has an old deckchair as a bed, and the squeaking of asthmatic rats from some cellar takes the place of his wife's whispering. No, mankind is good. Only their representatives *do* vary—they're really quite extraordinarily different and various.

THE OTHER: Mankind is good. Only they are so, so unaware. Perpetually unaware. But their hearts, look into their hearts—their hearts are good. Only life won't allow them to show their hearts. But don't disbelieve that at bottom they're good.

BECKMANN: Oh, naturally. At bottom. But the bottom is usually so deep, so very, very incredibly deep. Yes, at bottom they're good—just different. One is white and the other is gray. One has pants and the other hasn't. And that gray one there, without the pants—that's me. Had a run of bad luck: Corpse Beckmann, formerly Sergeant Beckmann (retired), fellow creature (retired).

THE OTHER: You're dreaming, Beckmann, get up. Life! Come, see, mankind is good.

BECKMANN: And they pass by my corpse and chew and laugh and spit and digest. That's how they pass my death by, the very kindliest of your good ones.

THE OTHER: Wake up, dreamer! You're dreaming an evil dream, Beckmann. Wake up!

BECKMANN: Oh, yes, I'm dreaming a terribly evil dream, all right. And here comes our cabaret director now. Dare I engage him in a bit of conversation, answerer?

THE OTHER: Come, Beckmann! Live! The street is full of lamps. Everyone's alive! Live with them!

BECKMANN: Live with them? With whom? With the Colonel? No!

THE OTHER: With the others, Beckmann. Live with all the others.

BECKMANN: And with that producer?

THE OTHER: With him as well. With everyone.

BECKMANN: Fine. With the producer as well. Greetings to you, Mr. Producer!

PRODUCER: What's that? Yes—what's the matter?

BECKMANN: Do you recognize me?

PRODUCER: No— Oh yes, just a moment now. Gas-mask glasses, Russian haircut, soldier's overcoat. Yes—the beginner with the little chanson about marital infidelity, right? What was your name again?

BECKMANN: Beckmann.

PRODUCER: Of course. Well?

BECKMANN: You murdered me, Mr. Producer.

PRODUCER: But, my dear boy—

BECKMANN: Yes you did. Because you were a coward. Because you betrayed truth. You drove me straight into the River Elbe, because you wouldn't give that beginner a chance to begin. I wanted to work. I was starving. But you shut your door behind me. You chased me straight into the Elbe, Mr. Producer.

PRODUCER: Must have been quite a sensitive boy, running into the Elbe like that, into that damp . . .

BECKMANN: Straight into that damp, deep Elbe, Mr. Producer. And there I let myself slowly fill up with Elbe water—I was full for once, Mr. Producer, but I unfortunately died of it. Tragic, isn't it? A real killer-diller for your revue, right? A little chanson for our time: full for once, but died of it.

PRODUCER (*sympathetic, but only superficially*): That's just terrible—terrible! You were one of those overly sensitive types, I suppose. Such a mistake today, completely out of step. You were completely possessed by truth, weren't you, you little fanatic! You'd have had whole audiences skipping out on me with that song of yours!

BECKMANN: And so you slammed the door on me, Mr. Producer. And just a little further on lay the Elbe.

PRODUCER (*as above*): Yes, the Elbe. Drowned. Through. Kaput. Poor old thing. Run over by life. Overwhelmed and flattened. Finally filled up—and so finally finished off. Well, if we were all as "sensitive" as that . . . !

BECKMANN: Never fear, Mr. Producer; we're not all as sensitive as that.

PRODUCER (*as above*): No; God knows we're not, no. You were merely one of those poor miserable millions of people who have to limp through life and who are actually happy when they fall. Into the Elbe, into the Spree, into the Thames—it doesn't matter where. Until then they don't know a single moment's peace.

BECKMANN: And so you just tripped me up a little, to help me fall.

PRODUCER: Nonsense! Who ever said that? Can't you see—you were cut out for tragic roles. Your material's a knockout!

"The Ballad of a Beginner"! The Floating Body with the Gas-mask Glasses! Tsk tsk, too bad the public doesn't want that sort of thing, tsk tsk, just too, too bad . . . (*He leaves*.)

BECKMANN: Pleasant dreams, Mr. Producer! Well—did you hear? Shall I go on living with the Colonel? Go on living with the producer?

THE OTHER: You're dreaming, Beckmann, wake up.

BECKMANN: Am I really dreaming? Is it possible that I do see everything twisted and distorted through these damned gas-mask glasses? Can they really all be puppets? Grotesque, caricatured, human puppets? Did you hear the obituary my murderer dedicated to me? Epitaph for a beginner: "Just one more of the infinitely many." Did you hear that, you Other —shall I go on living now? Shall I go limping along the road? With all those others? They've all got the identical dreadfully indifferent faces. They chatter and mutter endlessly as they go—but if anyone tries to get a single "Yes" out of them they go numb and dumb, like—yes, like all humanity. And they're afraid. They've betrayed us. Betrayed us so terribly. Listen. When we were quite young they decided to make war. And as we grew older they told us stories about their war. Enthusiastically—about this they never failed to be enthusiastic. And so when we grew just a little bit older they thought they'd think up a war for us, too. And then they sent us off to fight it. They were enthusiastic, one thing they never failed to be was enthusiastic. But nobody told us exactly where we were going. Nobody happened to mention that we were going straight to Hell. Not a living soul. They made up marching songs and held celebrations. They thought up heroes' songs and initiation ceremonies for us. And then court-martial proceedings and campaigns. They never failed to be enthusiastic. And finally came the actual war. And they enthusiastically shipped us off to it. And they told us just this one thing: "Do a good job, boys!" That was the sum of their advice. And that's how they betrayed us. So dreadfully betrayed us. And now they're all sitting there— behind their doors. The professor, the producer, the judge, the doctor. But no one's shipped us off anywhere this time. Oh no, far from it. They're all sitting there behind their doors—and the doors are shut tight, very tight. And we're here, outside. And from their pulpits and from their arm-chairs they point their fingers at us. That's how they've betrayed us. Betrayed us terribly. And now they ignore their murderings, simply ignore them. Or pass them by without looking.

THE OTHER: They don't ignore them, Beckmann. You exaggerate. You're dreaming. Look at their hearts, Beckmann. They have hearts. They're good!

BECKMANN: But Mrs. Kramer ignores my corpse.

THE OTHER: No! Even she has feelings!

BECKMANN: Mrs. Kramer!

MRS. KRAMER: Yes?

BECKMANN: Do you really have feelings, Mrs. Kramer? Where were you keeping them, Mrs. Kramer, when you murdered me? That's right, Mrs. Kramer, you murdered the old Beck-manns' son. And didn't you finish off his parents as well—now honestly, Mrs. Kramer, you did "assist" them a little, didn't you? Maybe made their life just a little sour for them somehow, perhaps? And then chased their son straight into the Elbe—but ah, your feelings, Mrs. Kramer, just what do your feelings say now?

MRS. KRAMER: You with the funny glasses—you threw yourself into the Elbe? I thought something was a little odd about you, right off. You looked so sad, too, poor little thing. Yes, I might have known it. Threw himself into the Elbe! Poor baby! Imagine!

BECKMANN: Yes, because you informed me so sympathetically and truly tactfully of the passing away of my parents. Your door was really the very last one for me. And you let me go on standing outside it. And for a thousand days and a thousand Siberian nights I'd looked forward to that particular door. You did commit a little murder there on the side, now didn't you?

MRS. KRAMER (*Very vigorously, so as not to cry*): There are people who always have hard luck. You just happened to be one of them. Siberia—gas jet—Ohlsdorf. It was all just too much for you. It goes straight to my heart—but where would we be if

E*

we went around crying for everybody? You did look so gloomy, though, poor baby. Such a little boy! But we mustn't let it get at us—or even the little margarine we can afford to put on our bread these days might start tasting badly. (*Sighs*.) Well well, we certainly do see life. And people keep on throwing themselves in every day.

BECKMANN: Yes, that's right, that's right—and so farewell, Mrs. Kramer. Did you hear, Mr. Other one? Obituary for a young man by a good-hearted woman. Did you hear, Mr. Silent Answerer?

THE OTHER: Wake . . . up . . . Beckmann . . .

BECKMANN: You suddenly sound so faint . . . you seem so far away suddenly . . .

THE OTHER: You're dreaming a deadly dream, Beckmann. Wake up! Live! Don't take yourself so seriously. Death happens every single day. Should all eternity be filled with weeping? Live! Eat your bit of bread and margarine! Life has a thousand facets. Take it! Stand up!

BECKMANN: Fine—I'll stand up. For now I see my very own wife. My wife is good. No, she's got her friend with her. Still, *once* she was good. Why did I have to spend those three long years in Siberia? She did wait those three years, though, I'm sure of that. She was always good to me. It's my fault. Once she was good, but I don't know about her now.

THE OTHER: Try it! Live!

BECKMANN: Don't be afraid, dear, it's only me. Look at me! It's your husband—it's Beckmann. I've just taken my life. You shouldn't have gone and done all that, dear, with the other man. You were the only one I had. You're not listening! I know, dear, I know you had to wait too long. But don't be upset anymore, I'm fine now. I'm dead. Without you I couldn't go on. Look at me! Look at me!

(*The wife goes slowly past, arm in arm with her lover, without even hearing Beckmann.*)

But you were my wife! Look at me! You killed me; surely you can just look at me! You're not even listening to me!

You murdered me—and now you just simply pass me by? Why don't you listen at least . . .

(*Wife and friend exit.*)

She didn't hear me. She doesn't even know me any more. Have I really been dead that long? She's forgotten me and I've been dead only one day. So good, oh, mankind is so good! And you, Mr. Optimist, Mr. Cheerleader, Mr. Answerer!? You don't wish to make any comment? Oh, you're so far, far away. Shall I go on living? She was the reason that I came back from Siberia. And you say I'm supposed to go on living? Every single door, to the left as well as to the right of the roadway is now closed. All the lamps have gone out, all, to the very last one. And the only way a man can move at all forward is by falling. And you say I'm supposed to go on? Have you got another pratfall left for me to take for you? Is that it? Don't start hiding again, Mr. Silent One; haven't you got even one lamp left for me somewhere in this darkness? Tell me—you've always got so many wonderful ideas!

THE OTHER: Here comes the girl who pulled you out of the Elbe and who kept you warm awhile. The girl who wanted to kiss your silly stupid head, Beckmann. She doesn't ignore your death; she hasn't passed by your corpse. She's been searching for you everywhere.

BECKMANN: No! She hasn't been searching for me! Nobody's been searching for me! I won't go on believing it time after time. I can't fall anymore, do you understand? Nobody's, nobody's been searching for me!

THE OTHER: This girl has been searching for you everywhere.

BECKMANN: Optimist, you're torturing me. Just go away.

GIRL (*without actually seeing him*): Fish! Fish! Where are you? Little cold fish.

BECKMANN: I'm dead.

GIRL: Oh, you're dead? And I'm searching for you all over the world.

BECKMANN: Why are you searching for me?

GIRL: Why? Because I love you, poor ghost! And now you're dead? And I would so have loved to kiss you, poor cold Fish.

BECKMANN: Are we supposed to stand up and carry on just because a girl calls to us? Tell me, girl . . .

GIRL: Yes, Fish?

BECKMANN: What if I weren't dead?

GIRL: Oh, then we'd go home together, to my house. Oh do be alive again, little cold Fish! If only for me. If only with me. Come, let's be alive together.

BECKMANN: Should I live? Have you really searched for me?

GIRL: Always. You and only you. On and on. Oh my, why are you dead, poor gray ghost? Won't you be alive with me?

BECKMANN: Yes, yes, yes. I'm coming with you. I want to be alive with you!

GIRL: Oh, my Fish!

BECKMANN: I'll stand up. You're the one light left burning for me. For me alone. We'll be alive together. And we'll walk pressed close together down the dark road. Come, let's be alive together and close together—

GIRL: Yes, yes, I'm burning for you alone on the dark road!

BECKMANN: You're burning? What's that—? It's getting dark suddenly—where are you?

(*The tick-tock of the one-legged man is heard faintly again.*)

GIRL: Do you hear? The deathworm's knocking—I must go now, Fish, I must go, poor, cold ghost.

BECKMANN: Why? why? Stay here! Everything's suddenly so dark! Light, my little light! Shine for me! Who's that knocking now? Someone's knocking! Tick-tock-tick-tock! Who knocks like that? There—tick-tock-tick-tock! Louder! Nearer! Tick-tock-tick-tock! (*Screams.*) He's there! (*Whispers.*) The giant, the one-legged giant with his two crutches. Tick-tock—he's coming nearer. Tick-tock—he's coming toward me! Tick-tock-tick-tock!!! (*Screams.*)

ONE LEGGED MAN (*Quite matter-of-fact; almost detached*): Beckmann?

BECKMANN (*Softly*): Here I am.

ONE LEGGED MAN: You're still alive, Beckmann? You've committed a murder, Beckmann. And you're still alive.

BECKMANN: I've not committed any murder—

ONE LEGGED MAN: Oh yes you have, Beckmann. We are murdered every day, and every day we commit a murder. And every day we ignore a murder. You murdered me, Beckmann. Have you forgotten already? I spent three years in Siberia, Beckmann, and yesterday I wanted to go home. But my place was taken —you were there, Beckmann, in my place. And so I went straight down to the Elbe, Beckmann, yesterday evening in fact. Where else was I supposed to go, Beckmann? That Elbe was amazingly cold and wet. But I've become used to it, since my death. How could you just forget that so quickly, Beckmann! You just can't forget murder as fast as that. It pursues you, Beckmann. Yes, I know, I made a mistake. I should not have come home. There was no place for me at home, Beckmann, because you were there. I don't blame you, Beckmann. We all commit murder, every day, every night. But we don't have to forget our victims so quickly! We shouldn't completely ignore our murders, not completely. Yes, Beckmann, you did take my place from me. On my own sofa, with my wife, my wife of whom I dreamt for three years, a thousand Siberian nights! But back home there was a man who had my clothes on, Beckmann; they were far too big for him, but he had them on, and he was very warm and doing quite well there in my clothes, with my wife. And you were that man, Beckmann; it was you. And so I withdrew. Straight into the Elbe. Quite cold down there, Beckmann, but one gets used to it quite quickly. Now I've been dead exactly one day—and you've forgotten your murder already. You mustn't do that, Beckmann, you shouldn't forget your murders right after you commit them: only bad people do that. You won't forget me, Beckmann, will you? You must promise me, Beckmann—you won't forget your murder!

BECKMANN: I won't forget you.

ONE LEGGED MAN: That's good of you, Beckmann. Then I can be dead in peace, if at least one man is thinking of me, at least my murderer—just now and then perhaps—at night sometimes, Beckmann?—when you can't fall asleep! Then at least I can be dead in peace . . .

(*Exits.*)

BECKMANN (*Waking up*): Tick-tock-tick-tock!!! Where am I? Have I been dreaming? Aren't I dead? Aren't I still dead? Tick-tock-tick-tock through my whole life! Tick-tock—through my whole death! Tick-tock-tick-tock! Do you hear the death-worm? And I'm supposed to live! And every night there will be a sentry by my bedside and I'll never be free from the sound of his steps: Tick-tock-tick-tock! No!

This is life, yes, *this*. There is a man, and the man comes home to Germany, and then the man freezes. He starves, and he limps! A man comes home to Germany! He comes home and his bed is taken. A door slams and he stands outside.

A man comes home to Germany! He finds a girl—but the girl has a husband, who has only one leg and who keeps on groaning a certain name. And that name is Beckmann. A door slams and he stands outside.

A man comes home to Germany! He searches for his fellow man—but a Colonel laughs himself half to death. A door slams and he stands outside again.

A man comes home to Germany! He searches for work—but a Producer is a coward and the door slams and he stands outside once more.

A man comes home to Germany! He searches for his parents —but an old woman is there, mourning the waste of gas, and the door slams and he stands outside.

A man comes home to Germany; And finally along comes a one-legged man—tick-tock-tick—as he comes—tick-tock, and the one-legged man says: Beckmann. Says again and again: Beckmann. He breathes Beckmann, he snores Beckmann, he groans Beckmann, he screams, he curses, he prays: Beckmann. And he walks through the life of his murderer—tick-tock-tick-tock! And I am his murderer. I?—I, the murdered, I whom they have all murdered, I am the murderer? What's to keep each and every one of us from becoming murderers then? We are all murdered each day, and each day we all commit murder! And murderer Beckmann can stand it no longer, murdering and being murdered. And he screams in the face of the world: *I die!* And then he lies down somewhere in the city streets, this man who came home to Germany, and he does indeed die. Once upon a time cigarette butts, orange peels and old newspapers lay scattered around in our streets; more recently it's people, and about that most people care just as little. And then a street cleaner comes along, a German street cleaner in military regalia with bright red stripes, representative of the firm of Rubbish, Refuse, and Remains, and he finds the murdered murderer, Beckmann. Starved, frozen, abandoned. Here, in the middle decades of the twentieth century. In the street. In Germany. And people pass by his death distracted, resigned, bored, sickened or indifferent, indifferent, oh so indifferent! And the dead man deep within his deadly dream realizes that his death was like his life: pointless, insignificant, and gray. And you—you say I'm supposed to live! Why? For exactly whom? For what particular purpose? Don't I even have any right to my death, my own suicide? Shall I go on murdering and being murdered? Where shall I finally go? How shall I live? With whom? For what? Where shall we go in this world! We've been betrayed. Terribly betrayed.

Where are you, you Other one? You've always been here before! Where are you now, optimist? Answer me now! Suddenly you're just not available! Where are you, answerer, where are you, you who begrudged me my own death? And where is the old man who went around calling himself God?

Why doesn't he speak now!!

Answer now!

Why are you all so silent? Why?

Will none of you answer?

Will no one answer?

Is there no answer at all?

DR. KORCZAK AND THE CHILDREN

by ERWIN SYLVANUS

TRANSLATED BY GEORGE E. WELLWARTH

CHARACTERS

NARRATOR
FIRST ACTOR (Leader of an Elite Gestapo Squad)
SECOND ACTOR (Dr. Korczak)
ACTRESS (German Woman & Jewish Nurse)
CHILD (Jürgen & David)

SCENERY

The stage contains only three chairs, of which one is placed downstage left (audience's viewpoint) and two are upstage right.

PROPERTIES

A large box full of multicolored (particularly red) children's building blocks. A cigarette.

COSTUMES

The actors wear everyday clothing throughout.

TIME

The action of this play took place for the first time in the year 1942.

The author has not invented the events depicted in this play; he has merely recorded them. The play must be performed without intermission.

I

NARRATOR (*enters but takes no notice of the audience at first. He carries a box full of children's building blocks, puts it down on the chair at stage left, and begins to build a doorway with red blocks. Should the audience be uncertain as to whether this pantomime is part of the action of the play or not, no harm will be done. The Narrator appears suddenly to remember the audience or possibly to become aware of it for the first time*): Nice, isn't it?—this little doorway here made out of little colored blocks. It's a lot of fun, playing around with them. But—this is wartime now, and so we destroy. (*He knocks the whole structure over with one small movement of his finger.*) That's to say, it's wartime in this play we're presenting tonight. (*He sweeps the scattered blocks back into the box with one movement of his hand.*) Ah, you're startled, are you? Beginning to think of the price you paid for your ticket, perhaps? There's still time to get up and leave, you know. You're not involved yet in what we're going to show you here. (*After a long hard look at the audience.*) You're staying? Very well! (*He sits down with the box on his lap.*) This is the story of Janusz Korczak and his children and how they had to die because they were Jewish children in Poland. All of them without parents. That's the story in a nutshell. Sixteen years, fifteen years, fourteen, thirteen, twelve and eleven and ten years old. Nine, eight, seven, six, five and four years old. Three and two years old. The youngest of them hadn't learned how to walk yet. Altogether there were sixty-five boys and girls, orphans every one of them. You can still leave, you know; no one's forcing you to stay; no one forced you to come here in the first place. What's it to you what happened in Poland in 1940 and 1942? It's a long way from here to Poland. (*He peers around at individual spectators.*) So, you have decided to stay—thank you. I want to tell you now about Janusz Korczak, who always loved and never lied. He lied just once in his life—and then he did it for love. He lived a life of love, a life without lies; a life dedicated to his children and to all the children in the world. He never asked any questions about race or religion, about nationality or about private opinions. He loved and he never lied. But that's what we want to show you. Here. (*He puts the box down next to the chair and gets up.*) Onstage, please. We need two

117

men and one woman. (*He looks at the box of blocks.*) And of course the children. But we don't need actors for that, really. Yes, just ordinary, everyday children will do very nicely. We don't want them to do any acting; they need only be children. And I don't think it's really necessary to call any out just yet. And when we do, one single child can stand for all children. All right then, if you please—two actors, one actress. (*He turns away from the audience and bows slightly to the players, who have entered upstage. He moves nearer to them—during his speech he has come all the way down to the edge of the stage—but not so near that he might be able to shake hands with them. Then he half turns around toward the audience again.*) Good evening, thank you for coming.

(*The players show marked signs of discomfort at their situation, particularly the Actress, who has remained near the door with her face turned away from the audience. The Second Actor appears to be the least reluctant and is nearest to the Narrator. The First Actor appears to be uneasy and fretful and gives the impression that he wants no part of the proceedings. At all events, the players are not lined up next to the Narrator and are clearly in different states of mind about the situation.*)

II

SECOND ACTOR (*shrugging his shoulders*): Oh well, it isn't all that easy for us, you know. We've only agreed to come here at all after doing a lot of soul-searching. What we want is to play *real* parts—know what I mean? Parts you can get your teeth into. Me, for instance—I'd like a chance to play Hamlet. You know how I'd play him? I'd . . .

FIRST ACTOR: We know all about what you can do, thank you! We also know perfectly well the names of all the various stars you're supposed to have played with.

SECOND ACTOR: Do you have any understanding at all of the concept of significant characters?!

ACTRESS: Hey! Stick to the point! The point is we're not satisfied with this piece we're supposed to play in. It doesn't have any decent parts! What we want is a chance to show what we can do. If they'd only asked me to play Ophelia! I'd have shown them soon enough!

NARRATOR: But I explained what the play is all about before you came. It's about Janusz Korczak, about a Jew who's supposed never to have told a lie.

SECOND ACTOR: A problem play, in other words!

ACTRESS: Probably the audience won't even be allowed to applaud. It'll be so solemn we won't be able to act.

FIRST ACTOR: Crying for the Jews—it's become the fashionable thing to do nowadays.

ACTRESS: Good business, too!

NARRATOR: We're not talking about a play any more now.

ACTRESS: Precisely.

NARRATOR: We're talking about a man—a man named Janusz Korczak. We're not dealing with any made-up plots here; we're dealing with reality.

FIRST ACTOR: How boring!

ACTRESS: What is reality, after all?

NARRATOR: A good question!

ACTRESS: No flattery, please.

FIRST ACTOR: Well, let's get started. (*Goes to chair at left.*) The sooner we get started, the sooner we'll be through.

NARRATOR: None of you will be playing a part. You are the actor . . . (*Each time he gives the actor's real name.*) and you are the actor . . . and you are the actress . . . and that's what you'll remain all the way through. No make-up and no costumes, either.

ACTRESS: Ah, I see: high-class amateur theatricals. Well, la-di-da!

SECOND ACTOR: We don't have any say in the matter; we're just here because the producer picked this play to do.

NARRATOR: You mean you don't think this play is worthy of your talents. Well perhaps it's a matter of our all learning exactly what sacrifices we need to make.

FIRST ACTOR (*leaning on the backs of the chairs upstage right*): Let's get going and give it a try, for goodness' sakes. The audience is sitting out there waiting.

III

SECOND ACTOR: All right, I'm Janusz Korczak now. Physician. Pediatrician, to be precise. I live in Krochmalna Street in Warsaw. Everyone here knows my orphanage for Jewish children. I am a Polish Jew—or am I a Jewish Pole?

(*First Actor and Actress sit on the two chairs at the back and listen, the former with his back to the action.*)

NARRATOR: That's not an easy question to answer at all. In a certain sense it isn't a question, really. If I say to someone "You're a Jew" it's quite different from saying "You're a Pole."

SECOND ACTOR: But we're talking about me now, about me, Janusz Korczak, one particular and unique individual.

NARRATOR: You know what the situation is perfectly well yourself.

SECOND ACTOR: That's why it's so difficult to talk about it. Knowledge shuts a man's mouth. We Jews are so silent—so completely silent—because we know, we *know* the Lord Our God is One. We don't proselytize and we don't try and convince anyone. We live in our knowledge and we act this knowledge every single day of our lives—such is the law. What do we care if they curse us and despise us? It's our business to know and to obey—but the source of our strength is no secret.

NARRATOR: You are also a Pole.

SECOND ACTOR: And gladly! I love this land that is so rich in emotions, this despised and now once more divided land which is so proud of its songs and of its birds and its lakes, its sunny springs and its children. . . . Yes, of its children, who are dressed in rags, and for whom I exist.

NARRATOR: Weren't you dressed in rags too?

SECOND ACTOR: Why do you ask such pointless questions? I don't have much time. My children are waiting for me.

NARRATOR: And for death.

SECOND ACTOR: You're not going to confuse me. My children are waiting—that's the point, and nothing else. I'll tell you and you (*to the First Actor and the Actress*) and you too (*to the audience*) what you want to know in a few words. I am the son of a lawyer who became severely ill when I was eleven years old. We were very poor after that—but that's not something one can tell about. What I can tell you about is my father's watch, a little gold-plated watch which was left to us —my mother and my brothers and sisters—as something to remember him by. We lit a candle for him every evening, but the ticking of that watch meant a great deal to us. My mother pawned it to buy bread. The pawnbroker put it on display in his window.

(*To the Narrator*) Please take this watch. I'll redeem it soon. Just keep it for us for a little while. (*He gives the Narrator his watch, which he has taken out of his pocket. This and the following actions are pantomimed.*) Now you've got to step back a bit holding the watch. Like I said, the pawnbroker put it out in his window, a narrow, rather dirty one, full of sad and curious things. Everyday we went and looked at the watch there. There it lay, my father's watch—just a little, gold-plated thing. (*He peers closely at the watch in the Narrator's hand as if he were straining his eyes to see it.*) And that's when I began to understand what life was like and became a businessman, so to speak. I was a child and I understood. I ran errands and did odd jobs to earn money. My brothers and sisters did everything they saw me do. We didn't even have to discuss it.

ACTRESS: I see, I see—you're talking about coming to a spiritual crossroads in your life.

SECOND ACTOR: Wait a minute—give me time to finish what I have to say.

ACTRESS: You said . . .

SECOND ACTOR (*forcefully*): I said that every day I felt compelled to go and take a look at my father's watch, at the little, gold-plated watch in the pawnbroker's window. (*Points at the watch in the Narrator's hand.*) That's what I said. And we children went hungry and saved money secretly so we could buy the watch back. It belonged to us and to our mother, not to the pawnbroker.

(*The Narrator takes the watch over to the First Actor and remains standing behind him and the Actress, who are sitting on chairs. The First Actor pockets the watch as if it were his own.*)

Finally, when we'd got the right amount together, we went to the shop. And the watch was gone. (*During this speech he has been searching around the area where the Narrator formerly stood.*) I went in, put the money on the counter, and asked for the watch. It had been sold that morning, the very morning of the day we had come to get it back. That's what I meant when I said that I began to understand life.

ACTRESS: Did you cry?

SECOND ACTOR: I understood . . . and I valued the determination which had enabled me to save the money. But still I felt uneasy, and so I went to see our rabbi. He was a wise man and skilled in the exposition of the holy writings.

(*During this speech the First Actor has taken the watch out of his pocket again; and now he examines it closely, apparently uninterested in the Second Actor's words. He gives the watch to the Actress with a whispered explanation. She seems a little irritated, takes the watch, and then turns her back abruptly on the First Actor.*)

I found him preoccupied, contemplating the Scriptures, which were open before him. He barely looked up, but he listened to me. He listened closely. He answered me and said, "So—you want your father's little gold watch."

(*The Narrator gets the watch back from the Actress and goes back with it to his former place.*)

"Here, take my watch. Take it. It belonged to my father." (*He takes the watch from the Narrator but holds it at arm's length.*) "But now you don't have a watch yourself any more, Rabbi," I said. He became very angry at that and threw me out. I went back to him, though—I went back many times, for I understood why he had been so angry and I wanted him to forgive me. (*He sits.*)

NARRATOR: I don't understand him. (*To Actress and First Actor.*) Do you understand him?

FIRST ACTOR: No. It's over my head.

ACTRESS: Maybe the rabbi wanted to show how unimportant a little gold-plated watch was compared to the Holy Books of the Jews.

SECOND ACTOR: Perhaps only a Jew can understand the real meaning of that little incident. I don't mean to be presumptuous when I say that—but maybe that's the way it is. The rabbi saw only the truth. I had come because of the watch, but I sat now before the Book of the Law. I had a golden watch again now. It wasn't my father's watch—and yet in a sense it was our father's watch. It wasn't a cheap watch. It was the watch of a devout man who obeyed the holy laws. He was quite fond of it, probably—even a Jew is fond of things, but at that moment he had to part with it. (*He looks at the watch again.*) Otherwise he would have had to lie. Otherwise he would have had to lie to me; and a man who knows God does not lie. He was angry with me because I had been leading him toward a lie. That's why he had to be angry. (*During this speech he has put the watch back in his pocket.*)

NARRATOR: Now I understand why you've told us this story. (*During the following speech he comes to the edge of the stage again.*)

SECOND ACTOR: I made up my mind then and there to take the rabbi as a model for my future conduct: never to become angry at human weakness, only at those who would force me to lie. And I have stuck to that code.

FIRST ACTOR (*gets up and comes downstage*): I must say—this play is getting a bit too high class for me. I can hardly recognize my friend here any more. He talks as if he had invented truth all by himself.

NARRATOR: He is trying to find out what it is that goes to make up truth. He's still your friend at the same time that you're hearing the voice of Janusz Korczak speaking . . . and we . . .

FIRST ACTOR: I didn't hear the voice of Janusz Korczak: I heard the voice of the actor . . .

SECOND ACTOR: Go ahead, I don't mind. You're just suspicious because I don't lie—just as the rabbi didn't lie.

ACTRESS: Oh, let's get on with it! (*She jumps up.*) Now I'm getting interested in him!

(*First Actor tries to sit down again, but the Actress turns his chair round. She and the Narrator go toward the First Actor. Second Actor remains seated, momentarily forgotten by the others. To the First Actor:*)

All right, you say something, Mr. Big-Shot Officer. I'd like to know what kind of a uniform you're wearing. That's what I'd like to know now.

IV

NARRATOR (*to the First Actor*): I don't envy you. You don't have to mention either your name or your rank. I don't even want to know what unit you belong to and you don't have to show your uniform either—somebody might get it into his head to investigate you, after all. After all, there's a distinct possibility that you're still alive—that you came back from the war hale and hearty and found your wife and children again and built up a new existence for yourself. That's entirely possible. After all, you do have the reputation of being an industrious sort of fellow! Go ahead, straighten your back a bit more, pull your shoulders back, if you like—but you'll have everything you need to show you're a high-ranking officer in your voice alone.

FIRST ACTOR: What do you want with me? I did my duty. I knew what my orders were. We took an oath of allegiance, and our honor depended on keeping that oath. Things always look different in retrospect.

SECOND ACTOR: One must never lie—that's the main thing.

FIRST ACTOR: How can one come out on top unless—

NARRATOR: Don't be afraid, go ahead and say it—without lying.

FIRST ACTOR: No one can live without lying.

NARRATOR: Some men can. I knew one who could. His name was Janusz Korczak. He only lied at the end—at the very end he lied.

FIRST ACTOR: Okay, okay—but he *did* lie.

NARRATOR: And that's why the story we're performing here isn't just a play.

FIRST ACTOR (*forcefully*): I refuse to have my character blackened by you. It isn't right! You want to go directly into the scene that shows me acting out my orders now. Well, I protest! I'm a man too. I've got a wife that I love.

NARRATOR: And children. And a little dog named Waldi and, above all, a home. All right, let's be just. We'll show you at home on furlough. We'll show you as a man, as you put it. As the head of a family. Would you be so good as to take the part of the officer's wife, Miss . . . (*gives the Actress's real name*).

ACTRESS: I thought I was supposed to be the children's nurse. Sister Ruth, chief nurse of the orphanage in Krochmalna Street?

NARRATOR: Yes, of course. But we have to expand the play a little bit. Now then, you had a little son, didn't you?

ACTRESS: And a daughter, little Erica, born during the war.

NARRATOR: And a dog, name of Waldi. You made a collar out of little sausages for him when you got your husband's medal in the mail. Sausages were very hard to get in Warsaw in those days. Particularly hard to get in Krochmalna Street—the only kind you could get in the ghetto were made of cat's meat and dog's meat.

FIRST ACTOR: I don't want to hear all this! (*He is all the way downstage.*)

NARRATOR: No, of course you don't want to hear all this. You
don't want to have to remember. You're on furlough now,
and you want to be a husband and a father. The Poles are
no business of yours, least of all the Jews! You've got no time
to feel sorry for inferior races! This is war! We're fighting for
the future of the German people, for our thousand-year pan-
Germanic empire!

FIRST ACTOR: Those theories were not developed by me.

NARRATOR: No, but they're tolerated by you.

FIRST ACTOR: You can say what you like: we got something done
in those years.

NARRATOR: To be sure, to be sure: you got a great deal done.

FIRST ACTOR (*moving to center stage*): There you are! Now you're
admitting it yourself. Listen— Do you remember what it
was like before the Nazis took power, eh? Do you remember
those block-long lines of unemployed in every single town,
do you remember the hunger and the misery and all those
other irresponsible and disgraceful consequences of the Ver-
sailles Treaty? Nobody talks about that any more today. I was
growing up in those days, and nobody had any idea what I'd
grow up to be. My father was just an ordinary fellow who'd
got thrown off the track somewhere along the way; times
were tough for him. I know what hunger feels like, my dear
fellow! Not loud, rumbling hunger, but quiet, creeping hunger, the kind of hunger that middle-class people hide and
won't admit to having. I used to feel ashamed. I always felt
ashamed when I was a child and I still felt ashamed when I
became old enough to go to school. And when you feel
ashamed you grow softer and softer. My father was no Nazi,
but I—my God, I never had a chance to decide! I went and
joined them—one of my friends was already a member—
maybe the smart uniform made it look good to me too.
Suddenly I felt I was somebody—I could give orders and had
duties to carry out. And I learned that you have to fight in
order not to be poor; to fight against the *others*—the Reds
and the capitalists. So I joined up and took the oath. I made
quite a success of it, too. (*Leans on the back of a chair.*) Life
became fun. I didn't have any worries any more. I had my
job to do and I had my family. Everything was beautifully

arranged. I didn't have to bother about a thing except my job and my family. Same way for the others in the Party—we had it good.

NARRATOR: And the Jews? How about them? Didn't you ever think about the Jews?

FIRST ACTOR: What's the sense of asking that now? What's that got to do with it? I'm telling you about my own life.

NARRATOR: But didn't the Jews become involved with you?

FIRST ACTOR: Just think back a moment to pre-Nazi days, will you? Did the Jews behave properly? They were all over the place!

NARRATOR: We're not talking about that now; now we're talking about November, 1938.

FIRST ACTOR: Exactly. Eye for eye and tooth for tooth. Why didn't they clear out before that? Why do they always drag their feet so long? You can't deny they assassinated a German diplomat.

NARRATOR: That excuses everything that happened, eh?

FIRST ACTOR: Don't forget my job and my family. Nobody's so high and mighty that he doesn't think of his own welfare first. Nobody gave a damn about our welfare when things were going bad for us either. Don't forget the misery I had to grow up in. It makes you hard—hard and tough—having to fight against misery all by yourself.

NARRATOR: Couldn't it perhaps make you more understanding and generous instead?

FIRST ACTOR: Oh sure, go ahead and preach. (*Walking up and down.*) Life isn't like that. Christianity had plenty of time to make people different, but it wasn't able to. The Church didn't give a damn about us—nobody gave a damn about us. So we had to do it ourselves—and it was the Nazis showed us how to do it. It's easy enough to preach morality on a full belly—so first we decided to fill *our* bellies. The screams of our enemies were for us only proof that . . .

NARRATOR: The screams of your enemies . . . !?

FIRST ACTOR: Yes, that's right—you wanted to talk facts, didn't you?

ACTRESS: Cut it out, boys! There's no sense getting mad—it just makes you tired. We're not talking about complexes here, we're telling a story. Let's get on with it!

FIRST ACTOR: Right! I'm fed up with being cross-examined, anyway. I'm on furlough—on furlough from everything; and I'm going home.

NARRATOR: Do you actually feel proud about it all?

FIRST ACTOR: We've got a right to feel proud of what was accomplished in the war.

NARRATOR: Do you feel proud of what *you* accomplished?

FIRST ACTOR: Idiotic question!

NARRATOR: I mean because you're not coming from the front, after all; you're coming from Warsaw.

FIRST ACTOR: I went wherever I was ordered to go. And now, to hell with job and duty! I'm going home, to my family, and I'm going to have a good long rest! (*Wipes his brow.*) Phew! That long train trip sure takes it out of you!

NARRATOR: Sure does—even if you manage to get on a special furlough train, as you did. The Jews went east in cattle cars.

V

FIRST ACTOR: What's that? Oh yes, to be sure! And here's my house, my home, which I'm defending. (*Calls.*) Jürgen!

CHILD (*running toward him*): Daddy!

FIRST ACTOR (*embraces wife and child*): Thank God I'm back!

ACTRESS: I've been so miserable without you. Things are getting so difficult here at home.

FIRST ACTOR: Everything'll be all right again when we win the war.

ACTRESS: When . . .

FIRST ACTOR: You're much luckier than most other wives, you know: where I'm stationed there aren't any bullets flying around at least.

ACTRESS: None—at all?

FIRST ACTOR: Don't worry about it. If bullets sometimes do fly around there, we're the ones who are making them fly. (*Turning to the Child.*) Why, you've shot up like nobody's business! Wait and see what I've got you. (*Takes candy from his pocket and gives it to the Child.*)

CHILD: Hey, candy! That's great, Papa! You can't get any here any more! Chocolate . . . (*unwrapping*) and chocolate creams! (*Running around.*) Real chocolate creams!

FIRST ACTOR (*pantomimes patting the dog*): Yes, Waldi, yes, that-aboy! Good dog, good dog! See how glad he is! Isn't it touching, the way a dog remembers you? Yes, yes, Waldi, take it easy. You'll get your sausage. I'm not bringing any medal this time, but you'll get your sausage anyway.

ACTRESS: I'd much rather you came back alive, even if you don't get any more medals.

FIRST ACTOR: Shhh! Don't say that so loud.

ACTRESS: I'm just saying it to you.

FIRST ACTOR: Well, just see that the kid doesn't hear you saying anything like that! I don't want him growing up to be some kind of softy. I couldn't stand it if he made me look ridiculous. I can't stand looking ridiculous. I often had to wear shirts that didn't fit me when I was a kid. But come on now, let's go and see Erica.

(*They go toward an empty chair upstage.*)

ACTRESS: Shh. Shh. She's still asleep. Don't make any noise.

(*Both of them bend over the chair.*)

FIRST ACTOR: She's cute. It's enough to make you feel a little soft yourself.

ACTRESS: Well then, feel soft.

FIRST ACTOR: Uh-uh. Think of my position—and of the way things are around here!

ACTRESS (*seizing him by the shoulders*): Tell me, aren't we all lying just a little bit? All of us—not just us, but all of us.

The loudspeakers and the newspapers and the bulletins with their talk of "proud but heavy hearts" and so forth—and we, we . . .

FIRST ACTOR: What's come over you all of a sudden? Don't ask so many questions! Just be glad you don't have to do anything in the war effort yourself and that you're a member of a decent and privileged family.

CHILD: Look, Mummy, look what Daddy brought me. (*He displays a rather large chocolate soldier.*) Other children don't have that.

FIRST ACTOR: And guess what I brought for mummy . . .

NARRATOR: Let's cut this scene right here, if you please.

SECOND ACTOR: Quite right. I think it's high time we showed Janusz Korczak's side of the story!

VI

FIRST ACTOR: (*Turns away and paces nervously up and down stage left.*)

CHILD: Why are you going away, Daddy?

NARRATOR: The scene's over, Jürgen. We don't need you any more for the time being. You don't have to wait here; we'll call you if we need you again.

CHILD: But I want to build a big tower!

ACTRESS: If you're going to build a really big tower, then of course you can stay!

(*Child goes over to the box of building blocks at left.*)

NARRATOR: But you're changing our plot.

ACTRESS: I know I am.

NARRATOR: You seem to forget that I'm the narrator here.

ACTRESS: Let me direct the rest of the play—please!

NARRATOR: Fine—but in that case I'm just superfluous here.

ACTRESS: No, you've got to stay. We need you—we need you desperately. You can be whatever we need you to be from time to time. A part of the sky, perhaps; a chair or a picture: I don't know. Perhaps a tool, perhaps a death chamber, perhaps death itself. Wait and see: I'll throw you a cue when it's necessary. You've got to pay closer attention to what's going on than any of the others.

NARRATOR: All right, I'll try.

ACTRESS: Right. Now we've got rid of this boring narrator and gained a fellow actor instead.

VII

SECOND ACTOR: I'm scared—

ACTRESS: What do you mean?

SECOND ACTOR: I don't know. . . . I'm just scared—

ACTRESS: Janusz Korczak! I call upon you. We are in the year 1942.

SECOND ACTOR: 1942.

ACTRESS (to Narrator): You yourself are the year. Let the year speak through you.

NARRATOR: The German armies have thrust deep into the interior of Russia. They're still winning, but they don't look so good while they're at it any more. The people back home are beginning to feel the misery of war. The casualty lists in the newspapers keep getting longer, and the type they're printed in keeps getting smaller. Food is getting short. Air raids. Casualties among the civilians. The final solution of the Jewish problem is decided upon.

ACTRESS: That's enough! (To Child.) And now you—you're little David now.

CHILD (leaving the blocks instantly): Can I come along with you, Dr. Korczak? I'm sick and I'm hungry . . . and my parents are gone.

F

SECOND ACTOR: You must come along with me, little David—who else is going to bother with you? (*He draws the Child to him.*) I have sixty-five children already and you will be the sixty-sixth.

CHILD: You're good, Dr. Korczak, you're so good.

SECOND ACTOR: There, there, David.

ACTRESS (*to the Narrator*): We are in Warsaw. Let Warsaw speak through you.

NARRATOR: Once upon a time I was a proud city, beautiful to see. They called me the Paris of the East, even though I'm in Europe, right in the middle of Europe.

ACTRESS: You're just preaching now: we're not here to hear any sermons. Anyway, we can dispense with Warsaw now. Let the Ghetto speak through you.

NARRATOR: I'm beginning to freeze.

ACTRESS: Good. That's enough. And now Krochmalna Street!

NARRATOR: I am a poor street, a street of hunger, like all the streets around here. I'm just a little wider than the others, my houses are even more overcrowded, I've got even fewer birds . . .

ACTRESS: That's enough. And now the orphanage!

NARRATOR: I am a large house and very poor. For a long time now none of my children have had their own bed, for a long time now there have been even more than two children to a bed.

SECOND ACTOR (*sits down*): And that's another thing that always makes me feel like giving up. When nobody sees me I cry a bit. Of course, it never happens that nobody sees me; even when I'm asleep God sees me . . . and gives me strength again. How else could I keep the children going? We don't even have any medicine any more—I have to go out and beg for medicine. . . .

ACTRESS: There's no bread left, Doctor.

SECOND ACTOR: Sister Ruth?

ACTRESS: There's no milk left.

CHILD: Sister Ruth!

SECOND ACTOR: Then I'll have to go and beg again . . . (*gets up*) beg from those who don't have anything anyway. . . . There isn't a Jew with a full belly in all of Warsaw . . . not one single one. But there's no point begging from those who've got full bellies in Warsaw today.

CHILD: My tummy hurts!

SECOND ACTOR (*to the Child, who has remained next to him, looking at him appealingly*): You've got to try and be tough, little David! (*Strokes the Child's hair.*)

CHILD: But it hurts so much!

SECOND ACTOR: Where does it hurt?

CHILD (*indicating his right side*): Here.

SECOND ACTOR: I wonder if it could be appendicitis—or has little David got a little hernia perhaps? (*Feels the spot indicated by the Child.*) I'll find out what it is, little David, I'll find out what it is . . . and I'll help you.

ACTRESS: Do you think it might be necessary to operate?

SECOND ACTOR: I'll speak with you later. Many thanks, Sister Ruth.

NARRATOR: Well, what now? How do we go on? Who do you want me to be now?

ACTRESS: Now you are the voice of the Jews from whom Janusz Korczak tries to beg. (*To the Child.*) And you go back to your blocks now, little David.

CHILD: (*Resumes his interrupted game with the building blocks.*)

ACTRESS: Janusz Korczak knocks on a door. (*She stamps her foot.*)

CHILD: (*Knocks on the floor with one of his little blocks.*)

NARRATOR: Who's there? Who's knocking now when there's not a Jew in Warsaw on the streets. . . .

SECOND ACTOR: It's me, Sholem, me—Janusz Korczak . . . and it isn't really me, either. It's the children, Sholem, the children. Look, Sholem, look out: it's the children. Up to today there

were sixty-five; and now there are sixty-six because little David
has been added to them . . . and tomorrow he may have to
be operated on. Sixty-six children . . . and Sister Ruth has
to have something to eat too . . . Sister Ruth and the other
nurses too . . . and . . . and . . .

ACTRESS: Hold it! We can't go on this way! We'll just have to
cut the begging scene.

SECOND ACTOR: But I just had to have a crack at it!

ACTRESS: This would be a good place to play the scene with the
dog, the one we mentioned before—the scene with the dog
Waldi . . . during his master's furlough. We can go back
and run through that part again.

FIRST ACTOR: (*Makes a gesture of rejection and shakes his head
vigorously.*)

NARRATOR: Not the whole scene all over again!

FIRST ACTOR: I don't want to do it again! (*He straddles his chair,
leaning his chin on the back, and observes the proceedings
unwillingly.*)

VIII

NARRATOR: In that case Jürgen . . . I mean little David . . .
will have to take over. . . .

CHILD (*leaves the blocks and runs over to the Actress*): I . . .
What's a dog, Sister Ruth?

ACTRESS: Ah, David, little David . . . a dog . . . a dog is. . . .
You don't know what a dog is?

CHILD: Oh yes, I've seen them in picture books.

ACTRESS: Well, you see, back when people still had enough to eat
those brown and white and yellow animals were alive; now
you only see them in picture books any more. Of course all
that was a long time ago, a very long time ago—so long ago
that our little David can't possibly know what dogs are and
how they bark and play with little children. It's a long, long
time ago.

CHILD: When Dr. Korczak comes back with something to eat, will he bring a dog back too?

ACTRESS: Perhaps. Until then we can play or we can sleep. (*She takes the Child to the back, where they sit down with their backs to the audience and softly sing a nursery rhyme.*)

IX

NARRATOR (*standing*): I am the night over Warsaw . . . a bright, dark, sparkling night . . . I am the sky over Warsaw and I know and see what goes on below . . . and I am the despair in the streets of the Ghetto. . . . I see an old man below me, an old man of whom it is said that he never told a lie. I see Janusz Korczak . . . and he got nothing with all his begging: a pound of roots perhaps, old, half-rotten roots, and that's all . . . far less than usual . . . as good as nothing. He imagines the eyes of his children . . . and yet he has to go back and tell them . . . he has to go back . . . whether he lies now or not . . .

CHILD (*escaping from the Actress*): I want Dr. Korczak to come back!

ACTRESS: He's coming, he's coming and he'll bring you something to eat.

NARRATOR (*sits*): And now I am a curbstone . . . an old and weather-beaten curbstone in Krochmalna Street. The steps of many Jews have worn me away—the steps of countless generations of Jews. And only children have sat upon me up to now—laughing children who told each other little secrets . . . and dogs—dogs came too . . . the children used to stroke me—yes, that happened too . . . and now friend Korczak, of whom the children used to speak, has come. I hear friend Korczak speaking—

SECOND ACTOR: Ah, my well-beloved stone—what memories you bring back! I feel that you are part of me, for God is in you too. And then, I envy you a little too, for you can rest forever here and be devout. Can you understand how much I long to be allowed to rest like you? To rest and simply be?

But times are evil now and full of lies. You and I, of course, will try to stay as honest with one another as we were. But perhaps they won't let you remain in peace much longer either.

NARRATOR: I lie here now, trod down by many generations, for more than one hundred years. Have I become too old?

SECOND ACTOR: No, no, you have not become too old. It's just that they were Jewish feet that trod on you . . . and now perhaps they'll force you to share our fate—

NARRATOR: What fate, friend Korczak?

SECOND ACTOR: To be pursued and persecuted and perhaps destroyed. . . .

NARRATOR: And why is that, friend Korczak?

SECOND ACTOR: Perhaps because God promised the fullness of his blessing unto the seed of Abraham, perhaps . . . but now I have to go and face a hard, hard task. It would be easier for me to die than to go back to my children without bread. (*Faintly and fitfully the sound of the nursery rhyme is heard.*) Do you hear them sing? Oh, it's just the wind, you'll say. It is the wind and it is also not the wind. It is a dirge and perhaps a complaint as well. I must fight on . . . for them. And give . . . and give . . . when God demanded it of him Abraham offered up his only son, whom he loved . . . he offered him blindly and unknowingly . . . and he was blessed. What do you want of us, O God? What shall we offer up? Ask us for everything—

X

NARRATOR (*rises*): And now I have become another day. The early morning fog lies over Warsaw. In the orphanage on Krochmalna Street the children are crying with hunger. Janusz Korczak has been awake almost all night. His eyes are staring and feverish and very, very sad. A military vehicle stops in front of the door. A perfectly ordinary military vehicle. The bell rings.

FIRST ACTOR (*to Second Actor*): Dr. Korczak?

SECOND ACTOR: Yes, that's me.

FIRST ACTOR: I've been ordered to inform you that this orphanage is being disbanded.

SECOND ACTOR: Disbanded—?

FIRST ACTOR: That's what I said. The worldwide fighting front of the pan-German struggle for freedom requires that a certain amount of action be taken in order to accomplish some important simplifications within the conquered territories. The German people offer sacrifice for sacrifice. . . . But it isn't my business to come and give you reasons for our actions.

SECOND ACTOR: Disbanded . . . that is to say, surely, evacuated . . . probably out into the country. We are all out of supplies, Major. I have already informed the Ghetto Committee. My Jewish comrades in the Ghetto here are dying of hunger themselves—they simply can't give any longer—

FIRST ACTOR: Am I to take that as a complaint? A criticism, perhaps?—or possibly even an accusation?

SECOND ACTOR: It is a statement of fact.

FIRST ACTOR: Let's keep this brief. Your orphanage is being evacuated. Not in the way you think, though. It's being evacuated to a concentration camp.

SECOND ACTOR: To a concentration camp? What's that supposed to mean?

FIRST ACTOR: You know perfectly well, Dr. Korczak, that for some time now consignments of Jews have been put together here in the Ghetto.

SECOND ACTOR: I know it. Rumor says they're being resettled.

FIRST ACTOR: That's the way the rumor goes, to be sure. We're trying to avoid any kind of *tzores*. That's the way you say it, isn't it?

SECOND ACTOR: But the German authorities explained it all very clearly to the Ghetto Committee.

FIRST ACTOR: Dr. Korczak, you're an intelligent man. You know what happens to those consignments. You're a doctor, after all.

SECOND ACTOR: I know what the German authorities told the Ghetto Committee. And I know that it is wrong to lie. I was brought up never to lie. A rabbi taught me that once, and it was a painful lesson.

FIRST ACTOR (*flaring up*): That's enough, now. You're getting insolent. We can handle this in other ways too, if that's the way you want it.

SECOND ACTOR: My children are hungry, Major. We need food desperately . . . desperately. . . . Do you understand—?

FIRST ACTOR: I understand you perfectly—and pretty soon you'll be understanding me. Your children won't be hungry much longer.

SECOND ACTOR: Thank you. I will pray for you.

FIRST ACTOR: Spare me your prayers. Doesn't anyone in the Ghetto talk about what happens to those transports we ship out of here? I mean, don't the members of the Ghetto Committee talk about it, even?

SECOND ACTOR: People say all sorts of things . . . and they await the first news from the people who have been taken away.

FIRST ACTOR: What kind of news?

SECOND ACTOR: They're waiting for the evacuees to write and say how they are.

FIRST ACTOR: Well, they'll have a nice long wait.

SECOND ACTOR: What do you mean? My uncle is one of the evacuees—and so is my friend Solomon . . .

FIRST ACTOR: Sure, and so's Rebecca and Jakey and Eli and Judy. You don't have to draw up a list of the whole bunch for me. They're in fine shape. Oh sure, they're in very good shape. And those brats in there will be in fine shape pretty soon now, too. Get me, mister?

SECOND ACTOR: Why do you talk to me that way?

FIRST ACTOR: Aha! You're getting sensible. Okay, now listen carefully: you're personally going to get out of this alive—that's a promise. I'm going to show you how to save your skin, so to speak. How's that, eh?

SECOND ACTOR: Do you mind telling me once and for all precisely what you're talking about?

FIRST ACTOR: About your escape, you blockhead!

SECOND ACTOR: I thought we were talking about how to get food for the children . . .

FIRST ACTOR: That's enough, now! I didn't come here to jabber with you all day. I suppose you think I don't have any nerves? All I'm doing is passing some orders along to you; I've got nothing to do with making them up. It isn't my fault. All right? All right, now listen carefully: you'll receive a shipment of milk and bread today.

SECOND ACTOR: Thank you. thank you!

FIRST ACTOR: Shut up! I told you to listen, and listen carefully. You'll divvy up the milk and bread. While you're doing that you'll have them pack up their belongings. Every child will make a small package of everything it owns with the exception of what it's wearing. Everything—even the toys—will be packed up. Your nurses can help the kids do it properly.

SECOND ACTOR: But, Major . . .

FIRST ACTOR: Will you stop interrupting me all the time! You'll inform the children they're going on a long journey . . . to some other place where there isn't any war, that they're going in two large buses, and that they're to put their things neatly on the stairs . . . and so on, and so forth. You'll tell them that their things will be sent on after them . . . and so on. Got it?

SECOND ACTOR: O God!

FIRST ACTOR: You can leave God out of this. He isn't on duty right now.

SECOND ACTOR: God is everywhere. You cannot show me any place where he is not.

F*

FIRST ACTOR: You'll be getting to know a place like that pretty soon now.

SECOND ACTOR: What are you talking about?

FIRST ACTOR: About a little rest camp where people stay for rather lengthy cures. About a place from which no one returns. And you, Dr. Korczak, you are going to bring your children there and you're going to see to it that they don't kick and scream and that they let everything happen quite smoothly and quietly. . . . Oh, it's quite painless, I assure you. It'll be your duty to see that none of the children get frightened; and you'll come out of it all right yourself.

SECOND ACTOR: My poor, poor children! (*After a short pause, softly:*) Are you childless, Major?

FIRST ACTOR: Me? What are you talking about? It's a question of your children now! (*Nervously.*) We know that your word carries a great deal of weight around here. (*Almost pleadingly.*) The children will believe *you*, Dr. Korczak!

SECOND ACTOR: You mean . . . you want me . . . to lie?

FIRST ACTOR: Thank goodness you've decided to be sensible about it. (*Breathes a sigh of relief.*) And anyway—what do we mean, really . . . by lying?

SECOND ACTOR (*as if sunk in thought*): and . . . so . . . on; and . . . so . . . forth. . . .

XI

SECOND ACTOR: My God, there is no comfort left for us, not even in the stones themselves! Oh, how happy I was when I could still feel life in the stones of the street and hear their voices! Jacob had a stone on which he laid his head; and as he slept the Heavens opened up unto him and the angels of Heaven descended unto him. (*He places his hands upon the stone.*) I would look up into the Heavens, as Jacob did, and ask. . . . (*Lets his arms sink.*) But even the consolations of the stones are forbidden to us. I will never more be able to find peace in this world, never more. I will have to hide myself from before Thy sight, O God. For what will happen to my children now is lowest sacrilege. These people scorn You and blaspheme Your Name. (*Goes center stage with back to audience.*) O God, look not upon this orphanage again. My children I must bring to you, I know; but look not down upon us any more. Let me expiate the sin . . . and do not curse those who do this unto us, for they are blind and foolish and know You not. But we do know You, God, even when You look not down upon us any more, for we would hide the evil from You. . . .

ACTRESS (*getting up*): One of the scenes we did before is supposed to go in here. We'll just explain it in a few words. (*She comes nearer.*)

NARRATOR (*getting up*): Now you've gone and interrupted it. Just when it was getting exciting, too—

ACTRESS (*angry and astonished*): Exciting? Maybe you even got a bit of gooseflesh out of it, eh? Well, that's not what we're doing this play for. It might be a good idea to stop now in order to sit quietly for a while and just think about all this. (*Narrator sits down again. There is an oppressive silence for a few moments.*)

XII

FIRST ACTOR: Silence. Stillness. You say you don't want any gooseflesh. But you're not bad at creating suspense, all the same. Silence . . . in preparation for the next scene, in which Janusz Korczak will once more make his demands. Everyone here knows now what that conversation with the rabbi meant for Janusz Korczak and how it altered his life. But nobody here bothers to ask what answers I got back in those days before I developed into what I am, and before this story began.

ACTRESS: Do I understand you to say that you want to make your apology, so to speak?

FIRST ACTOR: It's just that I recall a conversation I had with my mother when I was fifteen.

ACTRESS: Ah, you're banking on the fact that in this country you can always get a respectful hearing and get the sentimentalists on your side by talking about your mother.

SECOND ACTOR: I don't think we should force him to feel ashamed of himself again. Let him tell us the story; we'll listen.

FIRST ACTOR (*uncertainly*): I don't get it! Why would *you* let me talk?

ACTRESS: Can you play this scene by yourself?

FIRST ACTOR: No—I need someone to listen to me. (*Excitedly.*) Sit down over there, please. You're the only woman we've got here. Let me call you "Mother" for a few minutes.

ACTRESS: All right. (*Sits.*) Go ahead.

FIRST ACTOR: 1933. It's two years since I went to church to be confirmed. It didn't mean a thing to me at the time, although the minister was a well-known speaker and preacher. He frequently spoke on the radio, and people said he'd got 250 marks for doing a program on the Sermon on the Mount. Of course, all that doesn't have anything to do with the scene I want to play now, although, to be sure, Christ didn't take any money for his sermons. Maybe it was because I knew about those 250 marks that the whole business didn't mean a thing to me. Besides, it was just around that time that everything started to get cleaned up politically. You know, everyone had to follow the party line. The youth organizations became coordinated. The teachers' organizations became coordinated—it was pretty easy with them. All of a sudden we were told that the ancient Greeks were the direct forerunners of the Third Reich. Homer became a Prophet of Autocracy—Homer!! (*Challengingly, to the audience.*) Do you remember, gentlemen of the faculty, how you forced us to write essays on the topic, "Democracy can bring no blessings . . ."? I can still recite the whole thing for you in perfect Greek. Oh sure, all of you were able to retire with honor and a full pension when the time came as long as you kept your noses clean. But it's we—we—who are supposed to be to blame that everything went wrong. . . .

NARRATOR: We're not asking you to talk here about how or why things "went wrong." We—all of us here—are trying to find the origin of the lie.

FIRST ACTOR: The origin of the lie? What's the point of this pig-headed looking for lies all the time? Is this supposed to be a play about lying?

NARRATOR: It's a play about the lie in our time.

FIRST ACTOR: Crap! I said before we should stick to facts. I said it right at the start, when I was telling you my life story; but I should have started it earlier. I want to start with an experience I had when I was fifteen. It was right after the political coordination of the youth organizations, and I was in a Hitler Youth Camp. It was a regular camp with military rules and guards. I was a member of the third regiment. Naturally the whole thing didn't cost our parents a penny; and they were told we would be taught to be neat and orderly. The guards were members of the Hitler Youth, just like us. One night four of the fellows from our regiment decided they'd sneak out of the camp and steal some apples from a nearby field. Every kid steals apples at one time or another, after all. Later on this was known as organizing the apples, but in those days it was still stealing. Anyway, the apples were missed, and the farmer filed a complaint. The camp commandant got the whole camp together and told the farmer in front of everyone that nobody had taken his apples. The guards backed him up since they hadn't noticed anyone sneak out. The farmer insisted the apples had been stolen by kids from the camp. When the commandant started screaming and yelling at the farmer, I stepped forward and said we had stolen the apples—we'd fooled the guards and stolen them. I was fifteen years old at that time and had been confirmed the year before. I said we'd stolen them.

NARRATOR: And?

FIRST ACTOR: At last! At last you're asking a question about *my* youth! The camp commandant got white as a sheet and, as soon as he'd got rid of the farmer, had me come to his office. He asked me why I had admitted our guilt. I said, "Because it's the truth." He looked at me as if he didn't understand what I was saying. "Because it's the truth," I repeated. I didn't think much about what I was saying—I just wanted to tell the truth because the camp commandant had screamed at the farmer and because we were, after all, responsible.

Do you know what the camp commandant did? He laughed.
He laughed and laughed at me because he didn't understand me. He kept shaking his head and repeating "Because
it's the truth" whenever he managed to interrupt his laughter.
And then I was punished. My squad leader explained the
reason for the punishment to me. I had betrayed the solidar-
ity of the camp and of the regiment. My squad leader was
punished because of me as well. I told my mother about it.
(*To the Actress:*) Mother! I've been punished for telling the
truth, for admitting we were guilty. Do you hear, Mother?!

ACTRESS: I didn't get to go to college and I don't understand the
way things are nowadays. All my life I've believed in doing
the right thing and not being afraid of anyone. When I was
confirmed I was taught that . . .

FIRST ACTOR: Yes, yes. I know all about that. I was taught the
same thing; and the minister gets 250 marks over and above
his regular salary for giving a talk about the Sermon on the
Mount on the radio.

ACTRESS: You can't be sure of that.

FIRST ACTOR: But I can be sure that we stole the apples.

ACTRESS: You don't have to tell me—I'm on your side. Do the
right thing and don't be afraid of anyone.

FIRST ACTOR: You're on my side? Because I told the truth?

ACTRESS: No, because you're my son.

FIRST ACTOR: Thank you, that's as far as we need to go in this
scene. We don't have to go any further. A mother exists for
her son, a husband exists for his family, and a boy exists for
the organization he belongs to—right? And doesn't it follow
from all of that that a German exists for Germany? There's
nothing you can say against that—it's crystal-clear logic! A
Jew exists for the other Jews. Who's saying anything against
that? "Do the right thing and don't be afraid of anyone,"
my mother said. Well, I do the right thing—the right thing
for my race, for the military organization to which I belong,
and for my Fatherland. I do the right thing, gentlemen, and
I'm not afraid of anyone. Not of the capitalists, not of the

Reds, and above all not of the Jews. (*Relieved.*) There! That's that!

NARRATOR: That's that?

FIRST ACTOR: What? Oh, I see. I mean, now we can go on with the play. Now I feel easier about things. I believe in order and in authority. You've been thrown off your tracks a bit by my little German mother, eh? Come on, let's get on with it!

SECOND ACTOR: We can't avoid it now.

FIRST ACTOR: No, that you can't! Of course, I'm no longer interested in anything else you might have to say here. Go ahead—talk, talk, talk! It's a lot of nonsense! I'm waiting for action! (*Exits, slamming the door.*)

XIII

ACTRESS: Janusz Korczak has left the orphanage in Krochmalna Street. He goes to the Chief Rabbi, reputedly the holiest man in the Warsaw Ghetto, and questions him. (*To the Narrator:*) And now speak the words of the Chief Rabbi.

NARRATOR (*remains seated*): Grant, Lord, O God and God of my Fathers, that no hate rise up against us in the hearts of men—and that no hate rise up in our hearts against the children of men.

SECOND ACTOR (*goes slowly to the chair on which the Narrator is sitting*): Is that your answer, Rabbi?

ACTRESS: (*Turns to the Child again and softly sings snatches of the nursery rhyme.*)

SECOND ACTOR: You have studied the Holy Books. You sit over them and barely move. It is just as it was when I went to my rabbi about the little gold-plated watch . . . and he became angry with me. But I am not worried about any little gold-plated watch today—I am worried about sixty-six children—

NARRATOR: So you have said, Korczak.

SECOND ACTOR: Do you know what is going to happen to them? Do you know what happens to us Jews in Maidanek? Do you?

NARRATOR: It is written that we shall light memorial candles for our dead. That is what we have been taught; but no one here has candles any more.

SECOND ACTOR: You can talk like that . . . and yet you know that they'll come to fetch you tomorrow—?

NARRATOR: Read here in the Talmud: whoso shall cause a man to die, destroys a world.

SECOND ACTOR: Take your prayer shawl off your shoulders and go to the leaders of the Ghetto and tell them what is going on. People outside and abroad must know what is being done to our children.

NARRATOR: Didn't you say that they're willing to let you go?

SECOND ACTOR: If I tell a lie . . . a ghastly, horrible lie . . . !

FIRST ACTOR: (*Gets up, takes his jacket off and carefully drapes it over the back of his chair; then he sits down again as before.*)

NARRATOR: You have to decide what to do yourself . . . the Christians believe that others can take their sins upon themselves. We Jews do not. You are yourself a rabbi and a holy man. You are yourself Abraham and Moses. . . .

SECOND ACTOR: It's so hard!

NARRATOR: Do not forget our pride in ourselves!

SECOND ACTOR: These are times in which one gives up pride.

NARRATOR: No, these are times in which one must assert pride. We are talking about you. You are Abraham and Moses—you!

SECOND ACTOR (*begins to shake with agitation*): Have we all gone mad, then?

FIRST ACTOR (*coming back into the scene and speaking sharply*): Dr. Korczak, you are not permitted to leave the house!

ACTRESS: Janusz Korczak realized that for a second he had been dreaming. In that second he had visited the rabbi.

XIV

FIRST ACTOR: The moving operation will begin in three hours. I shall return at that time. There are guards in front of the house. I rely on you, Dr. Korczak!

SECOND ACTOR (*sits*): What am I going to do? I'm curious to know, really, what I'm going to do. I wonder if I really know just what my situation is. It's like a dream, a horrible dream; but I'm not dreaming—and that's more horrible yet. . . . Sister Ruth!

ACTRESS (*standing next to him*): What did that man want?

SECOND ACTOR (*quietly and hesitatingly*): Oh, it was a man, was it? Sometimes . . . one has to make an effort to remind oneself. So, that was a man . . . a man . . . born of woman. . . .

ACTRESS: What's the matter with you, Dr. Korczak? If I could only get you some coffee!

SECOND ACTOR: Coffee? I don't need coffee any more, Sister Ruth. You cannot imagine the strength I have now. (*Takes her hand.*) Listen carefully, now. The orphanage is being evacuated. You . . . you are released from your duties.

ACTRESS: You're not serious?

SECOND ACTOR: All of the nurses will be released. At seven o'clock tonight. You will be paid for the next three or four or perhaps even for the next five months in advance—it all depends on how much money we have left. But whatever it is, you must go.

ACTRESS: You're not talking sense, Doctor. You're weak from hunger.

SECOND ACTOR: I'm talking quite clearly and precisely; and I am giving you a quite clear and precise order to help the children to . . .

ACTRESS: But what are you going to do all alone with the children, Doctor? Sixty-six children, Doctor!

SECOND ACTOR: Come here to me, little David. All of you, all my children, come here!

CHILD: (*Runs to his arms.*)

SECOND ACTOR: Do you want to go with me on a long journey, a long, long journey? I won't leave you alone . . . for you are my children whom God has entrusted to me. No matter where, I shall always go with you, always. . . .

ACTRESS: We're going with you too, we nurses. . . .

SECOND ACTOR (*rises*): Sister Ruth—we have barely three hours left. (*Firmly.*) You will come to me in two hours. . . . Sing, children, sing a song in praise of God, who freed us from out of the hand of the Egyptian and who has promised us that. . . . (*He leads the Child to the building blocks and helps him pack them.*)

XV

NARRATOR (*coming to the middle of the stage*): And now I am the time which Janusz Korczak has been granted to make the children ready for their journey, the respite which has been given him so he can decide. There's a little less than three hours left, and they're running out minute by minute. Indifferent to the affairs of men, time runs out, precise, heedless, exact, and immutable in rhythm. In this short period of time how many events take place here upon this world! How many men are born, how many declarations of love are made, how many vows are broken, and how many men are killed or die a natural death! Here in the orphanage on Krochmalna Street the only thing that happens is that the children get their pitifully few possessions together and wrap them up in little bundles. Milk and bread are delivered, and the children eat their fill at last. And Sister Ruth discovers how, precisely, Janusz Korczak proposes to save her and the other nurses. And time runs out minute by minute, indifferent as the ticking of the clock. But there is yet another time, a time that does not run out minute by minute, indifferent as the ticking of the clock—and that is *real* time. Janusz Korczak already lives in this other kind of time. He looks like a prophet now;

and in the last few minutes which have been left to him from those three hours of preparation for the horror that is to come, he paces up and down alone inside his nearly empty room.

XVI

SECOND ACTOR: (*Goes slowly to the left.*)

NARRATOR: Janusz Korczak takes his prayer shawl, his old and faded prayer shawl, with whose fringes he has touched the Scrolls of Law a thousand times, as is the custom when the Holy Jewish books are carried around the synagogue. (*The Second Actor pantomimes the action of putting on the prayer shawl.*) He has put a covering on his head and, wrapped in the symbols of his faith, is ready now to step before his God. Every Jew wraps these symbols of his faith around him whenever he steps before his God, for this is how Moses himself appeared when God spoke unto him. And Janusz Korczak begins to sing. He sings the ancient Hebrew psalms. (*The Second Actor sings softly to himself during the rest of the speech.*) At the same time the German officer gets ready to do *his* duty. (*The First Actor comes to the center of the stage and then goes toward the right.*) He puts the leather belt with the revolver holster round his waist and his uniform cap on his head. (*First Actor pantomimes the action.*) He doesn't feel quite right about things, so he laughs a little; suddenly he even begins to whistle. (*First Actor whistles or sings softly a German soldier's song.*) His laughter sounds harsh. He goes into his commanding officer's room and salutes. (*First Actor takes two steps forward and gives the Nazi salute.*) The commanding officer is sitting at a desk with a picture of the Führer hanging behind him. At precisely the same time Janusz Korczak is singing and praying with all his strength. His face is turned toward the east and he mourns, as all devout Jews do. He mourns for the destruction of the Temple of Jerusalem and for the Holy of Holies which it contained. It is now almost nineteen hundred years since the Temple was destroyed, but the Jews still mourn for it as if it had happened just the other day. And indeed it is possible that they are right and that it did happen just the other day. And now Janusz Korczak is alone—quite, quite alone—together with his God. (*Second Actor goes all the way to one side of the stage.*) He stands before his God not only in heart and in spirit, but as a complete human being; and his body moves and trembles and his voice rises up, for he is unable to control his emotion. He brings unto his God all his fear and distress; and his body sways with ever greater agitation as he sings and prays. (*Second Actor sways the upper part of his body back and forth in the manner of praying Jews.*) The officer stands at attention and hears his orders repeated. He sees the picture of the Führer hanging behind his commanding officer and his mind becomes cleansed of everything but his orders. The orders are his conscience—the only conscience that he possesses. He raises his hand and says:

FIRST ACTOR: Heil Hitler! I am ready. We follow and obey.

NARRATOR: And as he speaks these words, indifferently exchanging his humanity for the orders he has been given, he hears his comrades singing, "Forward, forward, ever forward, till the world shall crumble beneath our feet." At the same time Janusz Korczak stops his singing and praying and says:

SECOND ACTOR: O God and God of my Fathers, I would keep Thy commands now and always and grow not weak; for I am one of Your people. I am ready and I obey.

NARRATOR: And as he says these words it seems to him as if he can hear his brothers singing in the synagogue these words: "I lift up my eyes to the mountains from whence my Savior shall come!" And as Janusz Korczak leaves his room—and as the officer leaves his commander's room—each says once more softly to himself:

FIRST AND SECOND ACTORS (*meet in the middle and say simultaneously*): I am ready.

XVII

FIRST ACTOR: I take it you have made your decision, Dr. Korczak. I see you've had the children's bundles put on the staircase.

(*Looks at the box of building blocks.*) Very good. What's the matter with you?

SECOND ACTOR: I have decided to accompany the children. I will see to it that they will neither cry nor scream. I will go with them and remain with them . . . to the end . . . to the very end.

FIRST ACTOR: Are you sure you know what you're talking about?

SECOND ACTOR: No one except myself would be able to keep these children quiet and stop them from screaming and crying. And so I will remain with them and not forsake them. I will go with them to whatever death awaits them. I will think of how the Red Sea was parted for the Children of Israel; and how the Red Sea became the way to safety for them. I will think of that and I will not forsake the children, just as Moses did not forsake his people. I will think of the promise that God has made us; I will think of that to the very end. I will lie—and yet I will not lie. You, Major, of course are incapable of understanding me.

FIRST ACTOR: No. I do not understand you. So—you want to die? (*Pause.*) So much the better!

SECOND ACTOR: It's not that simple. I'm offering my life in exchange.

FIRST ACTOR: What for?

SECOND ACTOR: I offer my life . . . so that the nurses may live.

FIRST ACTOR: That is contrary to my orders!

SECOND ACTOR: If I accompany the children to the end . . . to the very end . . . that too will be contrary to your orders. I have already told my four nurses that they must remain here—here in Warsaw, in the Ghetto. . . .

FIRST ACTOR: I'm not a shopkeeper. I don't bargain. I am permitted to free *one* person . . . so pick one nurse.

SECOND ACTOR (*with unshakable calm*): I have nothing more to say.

FIRST ACTOR (*wiping his forehead*): Get moving! The nurses are to stay here! (*Harshly.*) Come on, come on, get moving!

SECOND ACTOR: One moment more, Major.

FIRST ACTOR: Not another moment more . . . not one single one —let's go!

SECOND ACTOR: The bundles are lying wrapped neatly out there . . . the sixty-six bundles belonging to the children. . . .

FIRST ACTOR (*impatiently*): I've already said that I've checked them.

SECOND ACTOR: They contain the children's clothes and toys.

FIRST ACTOR: Correct—as ordered!

SECOND ACTOR: This little bundle here is the sixty-seventh. It's mine. That's all I wanted to say.

FIRST ACTOR (*shortly and reluctantly*): What's that supposed to mean?

SECOND ACTOR: Everything must be done in an orderly manner, Major. I learned that when I served in the German Army.

FIRST ACTOR (*amazed*): You served in the German Army?

SECOND ACTOR (*very calmly*): You didn't know that? It must have been somewhere around the time you were born. During the First World War I served as a Health Officer for the Germans since I used to live in the western part of Poland. . . .

FIRST ACTOR (*harshly*): There's no such thing as a western and an eastern Poland—in fact, there's no such thing as Poland anymore. These provinces have once more become part of the Reich—our Reich . . . that's the long and the short of the matter now. . . .

SECOND ACTOR (*always with the same calm*): The sixty-six children's bundles contain clothing and toys. My bundle contains my clothing . . . and my decorations. Everything must be done in an orderly manner.

FIRST ACTOR (*very surprised, peering closely at the "bundle" on the floor*): The Iron Cross . . .

SECOND ACTOR: . . . First Class. Yes, that is one of my medals.

FIRST ACTOR: This is impossible! You've swindled these from someone!

SECOND ACTOR: It is of course easier for you in your position to suspect a swindle on my part, Major. It is always much easier anyway to think of other people as being no good.

FIRST ACTOR: (*flaring up*): Dr. Korczak! (*With weary stubbornness.*) Orders are orders and obedience is obedience.

SECOND ACTOR (*with unearthly calm*): And what is reality?

FIRST ACTOR: My orders!—and they're going to be carried out now, without any further delay.

SECOND ACTOR: I merely wanted to point out that my military decorations would remain here . . . my German medals. Actually I never wore them . . . except on special occasions—and then not with any particular pride—

FIRST ACTOR (*harshly*): Have the decency not to insult the Iron Cross!

SECOND ACTOR (*looking up*): I?

FIRST ACTOR (*bending down hastily*): Nobody will find out about it. (*Pockets the medals in pantomine.*) I'll take care of these medals.

SECOND ACTOR: I've already destroyed the Polish ones. It never bothered me much to leave medals. I also leave my writing, which no one can destroy—

FIRST ACTOR (*slyly, almost as an aside*): You just leave that to us!

SECOND ACTOR: And I leave also the memory of a children's doctor who was a Pole and a Jew—both gladly and faithfully—and who stayed with the children entrusted to him till the end—

FIRST ACTOR (*harshly*): I simply can't afford to lose any more time. I'll expect you outside the house—you and the children. (*Goes aside.*) Won't I ever be able to get rid of this feeling of being ashamed? It's just like it was when I had to wear shirts that didn't fit because they were cut out of my father's old ones. This goddam Jewish swine. . . .

SECOND ACTOR: Sister Ruth, have you packed your things?

ACTRESS: Yes.

SECOND ACTOR: Good-by, Sister Ruth.

ACTRESS: Yes, I'm going, Dr. Korczak. I've sat there and thought about it for a long time. I wanted to go with you. I wanted to stay with you and show myself worthy of you. But now I'm going. I can't look at you any more, I can't! You're not really here any more! But I must live—I can and I will live! (*Looks around nervously and leaves quickly.*)

SECOND ACTOR: (*Takes the child's box under his left arm and grasps the child's hand with his right.*)

NARRATOR: And as Janusz Korczak gave the children a sign to move, the officer spoke so that no one else could hear him.

FIRST ACTOR (*addressing the heavens*): You fool and prophet, you prophet and fool! What use is any promise that we give You? What value has it? So the nurses will be shoved into the next transport after this one. Or what if I let them go, just simply let them go? Let them run out the back door? Sooner or later their fate will catch up with them anyway. And then, of course, it won't be my fault. It isn't my fault in any case. Heaven is my witness: it wasn't my fault. (*He turns away, comes all the way downstage, and peers at the audience.*)

XVIII

NARRATOR: But Janusz Korczak said to the children:

SECOND ACTOR: We're going to go through the Red Sea—through the Red Sea, about which I've already told you so many stories (*addressing the child didactically*)—into the Promised Land.

NARRATOR: And as the children heard this, they began to sing and climbed into the truck. For they had been fed that day. And the truck took them all the way to Camp Maidanek, right up to the door of the shower room.

FIRST ACTOR: (*Lights a cigarette.*)

SECOND ACTOR: (*Goes slowly in a circle round the stage with the Child. The sound of the nursery rhyme being sung comes softly from backstage.*)

NARRATOR: And then they descended from the truck. No one noticed that Janusz Korczak was crying. He told the children

to undress, and then he undressed himself and felt no need
to be ashamed. There were sixty-six children, boys and girls,
all Jewish orphans. They were sixteen years old, fifteen, fourteen, thirteen, twelve, and eleven and ten years old. Nine, eight,
seven, six, five and four years old. Three and two years old.
The youngest ones had to be carried. And now they were all
naked together, and the older children did not like it and
were embarrassed. But they took the younger ones by the
hand, and they followed Janusz Korczak. And they began to
sing again. And the door closed tight behind them. (*The
singing is broken off suddenly.*)

SECOND ACTOR: (*Exits slowly with the Child.*)

NARRATOR: And that is how it happened. And the bundles with
the rags and the toys were taken away from Krochmalna
Street. The officer let the four nurses go. He made up his
mind, also, to increase his consumption of alcohol quite a
bit that day. He did not feel at all well. Nine days later the
Chief Rabbi, to whom Janusz Korczak had wanted to go, was
taken away by night. The officer went with him all the way
to the entrance gate of the camp. But that's as far as he went.
Because he didn't want to have anything to do with it. He
had only obeyed his orders. He handed the Chief Rabbi over
to the guards there. Then he turned round, and, before he
left, he looked over his shoulder and said to the Chief Rabbi:

FIRST ACTOR: I've already forgotten your name. So what? You're
a Jew and they say that you're a Holy Man, so to speak. In
other words, you're a particularly dangerous Jew. You shel-
tered the nurses for one night, and you passed on word of
what they told you. You're guilty of fomenting rebellion, in
other words. It was forbidden to speak of it. We'll catch up
with the nurses yet, you can rely on that. You we caught right
away, and I personally saw to it that you got here. I brought
you right up to the gate of the camp—because I acted against
my orders when I let the nurses go. That will not happen
again. As for you, I'm handing you over here. You'll go the
same way the children went and that Janusz Korczak went
and that countless Jews went before you and countless ones
will yet go after you—until the day the world is free of you
and knows your name no more. (*Without turning around
again, he exits.*)

XIX

NARRATOR: (*Alone; goes slowly to the middle of the stage and stops there for a moment, as if thinking about the events of the play. Then he suddenly seems to crumple up and become smaller; one has the impression that he has become a totally different person.*) A poor rabbi—and I must be destroyed. My bones will be laid next to the other Jewish bones. Janusz Korczak died here; and his children died here with him. He told them that he would lead them through the Red Sea. And Janusz Korczak will keep his word. This is a landscape of death; but I know that it is also a landscape of life. For I know that the prophet Ezekiel saw the truth; and what he saw will be fulfilled in us. (*As if he were seeing a vision he raises his hands and holds them a few inches before his face so as to hide his eyes from the audience. It is as if he were reading the vision in his hands.*)

"The hand of the Lord was upon me, and carried me out in the Spirit of the Lord, and set me down in the midst of the valley which was full of bones,

And caused me to pass by them round about: and, behold, there were very many in the open valley; and, lo, they were very dry.

And he said unto me, Son of man, can these bones live? And I answered, O Lord God, thou knowest.

Again he said unto me, Prophesy upon these bones, and say unto them, O ye dry bones, hear the word of the Lord.

Thus saith the Lord God unto these bones; Behold, I will cause breath to enter into you, and ye shall live:

And I will lay sinews upon you, and will bring up flesh upon you, and cover you with skin, and put breath into you, and ye shall live; and ye shall know that I am the Lord.

So I prophesied as I was commanded: and as I prophesied, there was a noise, and behold a shaking, and the bones came together, bone to his bone.

And when I beheld, lo, the sinews and the flesh came up upon them, and the skin covered them above: but there was no breath in them.

Then said he unto me, Prophesy unto the wind, prophesy, son of man, and say to the wind, Thus saith the Lord God; Come from the four winds, O breath, and breathe upon these slain, that they may live.

So I prophesied as he commanded me, and the breath came into them, and they lived, and stood up upon their feet, an exceeding great army.

Then he said unto me, Son of man, these bones are the whole house of Israel: behold, they say, Our bones are dried, and our hope is lost: we are cut off for our parts.

Therefore prophesy and say unto them, Thus saith the Lord God; Behold, O my people, I will open your graves, and cause you to come up out of your graves, and bring you into the land of Israel.

And ye shall know that I am the Lord, when I have opened your graves, O my people, and brought you up out of your graves,

And shall put my Spirit in you, and ye shall live, and I shall place you in your own land: then shall ye know that I the Lord have spoken it, and performed it, saith the Lord."

INCIDENT AT TWILIGHT

by FRIEDRICH DÜRRENMATT

TRANSLATED BY GEORGE E. WELLWARTH

CHARACTERS

THE AUTHOR
A VISITOR
THE SECRETARY
THE HOTEL MANAGER
YOUNG WOMAN
SECOND YOUNG WOMAN

THE AUTHOR [this speech can be treated simply as a stage direction, or it can be read as a series of marginal comments]: Ladies and gentlemen, I consider it my duty, at the very outset, to describe to you the setting of this possibly somewhat peculiar but, I assure you, entirely true story. To be sure, there is a considerable element of danger in telling true stories—someone from the police or possibly even the district attorney might be among those present, even though they might not be here in their official capacity. Nonetheless I can allow myself to take the risk because I know perfectly well they won't believe my true story—at least not in their official capacity. In reality—that is to say, *unofficially*—all of you of course, including the district attorney or policeman who may or may not be among us, know very well that I *only* tell true stories— scout's honor! Well then: might I ask you to concentrate for a moment? Imagine yourselves in the drawing room of a Grand Hotel suite—the kind where the bill will look as if it had been added up by highwaymen. Modern furnishings. Looks as if it's meant to be lived in. Get the picture? On your left (just close your eyes and you'll see the room distinctly— don't get discouraged, now; you've got imagination just like everyone else, even if you don't think so), on your left you can see a number of assorted tables, all pushed together every which way. Are you interested in taking a look at an author's study? Very well then, step up a little closer. Disappointing, isn't it? But believe me, it's true—even studies where *minor* authors work can look something like this. Piles of papers, a typewriter, manuscripts covered with closely written corrections in various colors, pencils, ballpoint pens, erasers, a large pair of scissors. Glue. A dagger—hmm. Oh well, that got there by mistake. . . . (*He clears his throat.*) Back of this mess there's a small improvised bar—brandy, whisky, absinthe, red wine, and so forth. That doesn't tell us anything about the quality, the genius, or the greatness of the author we're dealing with here either. Doesn't tell us anything to his advantage, but then, on the other hand, it doesn't tell us anything to his disadvantage either. However, you can reassure yourselves, ladies and gentlemen: on the right side of the room you'll find everything neatly in place. Well, almost everything anyway—I'll just get rid of this—er— well, this piece of female clothing—just throw it in the corner here and—oh, yes!—might as well put this revolver away in the desk drawer. Large, soft, comfortable sofas made to the latest designs, books scattered all over the place; on the walls you can see photographs and paintings of—well, I'm sure you'll be able to figure that out for yourselves. The nicest thing, though, is the background to the whole thing. A large, open door, a balcony, an enchanting view (quite in accordance with the price charged), a sunlit lake which was covered only a few weeks ago with red and white sails but is smooth as deep blue glass now. Behind that, hills, woods, and the foothills of the mountains. Twilight, the lake shore deserted—all in all, a late autumn orgy of red and yellow. Ah, there's still a little life on the tennis courts, and you can hear the tick-tock of the ping-pong players. Do you hear it? All right, let's come back into the room and take a look at the two leading characters of our play. Let's start with me—oh yes, you heard right: *me*. I'*m* one of the leading characters. I'm sorry about it, really, but that's the way it is. All the same, I'll try not to startle you by appearing to you too suddenly. I'll just saunter unobtrusively into the room from the right—I'll be coming from the bedroom, where I've obviously been—oh well, never mind, it's nobody's business really what I've been up to in there. It'll all be written up in certain newspapers, anyway; in the evening paper or in the tabloids—after all, what is there about me that you *can't* read in certain newspapers? My life is a mess—confused, crazy, full of one scandal after another. There's no point in denying it—all I have to tell you is my name and you'll have it in a nutshell: Korbes. Yes indeed, you heard right once again! I am Maximilian Frederick Korbes, novelist, Nobel Prize-winner, etc., etc.—portly, suntanned, and unshaven—all topped off with a big bald head. As far as my personal characteristics are concerned, I'm brutal, I get what I want, and I'm a hard drinker. You see I'm honest with you, even if I'm just summing up the general impression everyone has of me anyway. Maybe it's true, that general impression; and maybe I really am the way I've described myself to you—exactly the way, ladies and gentlemen, you know me through the picture papers and the newsreels. The Queen of Sweden, at any rate (on the occasion of the presentation of the aforementioned Nobel Prize) was of the opinion that I fitted the description exactly. Rather strange, too, because I was all dressed up in white tie and tails at the time. To be sure, though, I did manage to spill a glass of Bordeaux on the royal evening gown—quite by mistake, of course. Still, who knows anyone, least of all himself? There's no point in kidding oneself. I, at any rate, know myself only fleetingly. And no wonder. The opportunities for getting to know oneself are few and far between. In my case, for instance, one of them occurred while I was zooming down a sheet of ice on Mount Kilimanjaro, another at the moment I was being cracked over the head by the well-known, er—oh well, you know whom I mean—a real "Gothic Madonna"!— no, not the one in the bedroom next door—some other one. Hmm, well, that's something you can imagine for yourselves, and pleasant dreams to you while you're at it, too! And now a word about my clothes. Here, too, I must apologize, above all to the ladies in the audience. I've got pajama bottoms on and an open dressing gown, through which my chest, covered with white hair, is dimly visible. None of this can be concealed, I'm afraid. In my hand: an empty glass. I'm on my way to the bar, but I stop short when I observe that a visitor seems to have found his way into my study. The fellow is soon described. Small, thin, very middle class, carries a brief case under his arm, looks a bit like an old traveling insurance salesman. There's really no need to describe him more closely in view of the fact that he will be removed from the scene of action in a perfectly natural manner once our story has run its course—and consequently will then be of no more interest. But that's enough for now. The visitor begins to speak. We're ready to start.

THE VISITOR (*nervously*): I feel honored to find myself in the presence of the world-famous writer Maximilian Frederick Korbes. . . .

AUTHOR (*roughly*): What the devil are you doing in my study?

VISITOR: Your secretary let me in. I've been waiting over an hour.

AUTHOR (*after a short pause, somewhat more mildly*): Who are you?

VISITOR: My name is Hofer. Feargod Hofer.

AUTHOR (*suspiciously*): That sounds vaguely familiar. (*Remembers suddenly.*) Oh, you're the fellow who's been bombarding me with letters?

G

VISITOR: Quite correct. Ever since you've been taking the baths here. Besides that, I've had a chat with the doorman every morning. Not that that did me any good! Finally I managed to ambush your secretary. A very severe young man.

AUTHOR: Theology student. Poor as a church mouse. Working his way through seminary.

VISITOR: It was only my unwavering persistence that convinced him finally this meeting would be of the greatest significance for *both* of us, honored master.

AUTHOR: Korbes is the name. You can skip that "honored master" stuff.

VISITOR: Honored Mr. Korbes.

AUTHOR: Since you're nearer the bar, you might just pass me the whisky bottle—it's the one on the far left.

VISITOR: Certainly.

AUTHOR: Thank you. (*He pours.*) Care for one yourself?

VISITOR: I'd rather not, thank you.

AUTHOR: Absinthe? Campari? Something else?

VISITOR: No, thanks.

AUTHOR (*distrustfully*): You a teetotaler?

VISITOR: No, just careful. I am, after all, in the presence of a mental giant. I feel a little like St. George just before his fight with the dragon.

AUTHOR: Catholic?

VISITOR: Evangelical.

AUTHOR: I need another drink.

VISITOR: You ought to take care of yourself.

AUTHOR (*harshly*): You can keep your advice to yourself.

VISITOR: I'm from Switzerland, Mr. Korbes. May I take a closer look at the room in which the poet creates his works?

AUTHOR: Writer.

VISITOR: In which the writer creates his works? Ah, books and manuscripts everywhere. May I take a look at the photographs on the wall? Faulkner. Personally inscribed: To my dear Korbes. Thomas Mann: To Korbes, with admiration and respect—Thomas. Hemingway: To Korbes, my best friend—as ever, Ernest. Henry Miller: To my soul mate, Korbes. It's only in love and in murder that we still remain sincere. And now the view. What a superb sight—the lake with the mountains behind it and the ever-changing clouds above it! And the sun just going down. Glowing red. Impressive.

AUTHOR (*suspiciously*): You write too, eh?

VISITOR: I read. Know your complete works by heart.

AUTHOR: Teacher?

VISITOR: Bookkeeper. Retired. Used to work for Oechsli, Trost, and Co. in Ennetwyl, near Horck.

AUTHOR: Have a seat.

VISITOR: Thanks very much. I'm a little scared of these ultramodern chairs. A very luxurious apartment.

AUTHOR: They charge enough for it.

VISITOR: I can imagine. This is an expensive spa. Absolutely catastrophic for my means, even though I live in the cheapest possible manner at the Seaview Rooming House. (*He sighs.*) It was cheaper in Adelboden.

AUTHOR: In Adelboden?

VISITOR: In Adelboden.

AUTHOR: I was in Adelboden too.

VISITOR: You were at the Grand Hotel Wildstrubel there; I was in the Pro Senectute Rest Home. Our paths have crossed several times. For example, at the ski lift in St. Moritz and on the Promenade in Baden-Baden.

AUTHOR: You were in Baden-Baden too?

VISITOR: I was.

AUTHOR: At the same time I was there?

VISITOR: At the Siloah Home for Christian Men.

AUTHOR (*impatiently*): I have to schedule my time pretty closely. I have to keep working like a slave, Mr. . . . ?

VISITOR: Feargod Hofer.

AUTHOR: Mr. Feargod Hofer. I have to deal with hundreds of thousands of people in my lifetime, and so I can only spare a quarter of an hour for you. Tell me what you want, and make it short.

VISITOR: I've come with a very definite purpose in mind.

AUTHOR (*getting up*): You want money, eh? I have none to spare for just anybody that comes along. There's such an enormous number of people who are not writers and who are perfectly easy marks, that I wish people would leave members of my profession in peace. Besides, the amount of the Nobel Prize is greatly exaggerated, anyway. And now, if you please, we'll say good-by.

VISITOR (*getting up*): Honored master . . .

AUTHOR: Korbes is the name.

VISITOR: Honored Mr. Korbes . . .

AUTHOR: Get out of here!

VISITOR (*in despair*): You misunderstand me. I didn't come to you because I need money, but because—(*determinedly*)—because ever since I retired I have been employed in detective work.

AUTHOR (*with a sigh of relief*): Oh, I see. That's a different matter altogether. Let's take a seat again. This is a great relief for me. Well then, so you're employed by the police now?

VISITOR: No, honored . . .

AUTHOR: Korbes is the name.

VISITOR: Honored Mr. Korbes. I'm a private detective. Even when I was still a bookkeeper there were all sorts of things that I uncovered. I was honorary auditor for several companies. Yes, indeed!—I even succeeded in having the town treasurer of Ennetwyl sent to jail for embezzling the orphanage funds. And so, when I had retired and the savings of a lifetime were at my disposal, my wife having died childless, I made up my mind, under the influence of your books, to devote myself entirely to my hobby.

AUTHOR: My books?

VISITOR: Your immortal books! They kindled my imagination. I read them with feverish suspense, absolutely overcome by the magnificence of the crimes you wrote about. I became a detective somewhat the way a person in the religious field, inspired by the masterful way in which the devil does his work, might become a priest, even though everything he might do calls forth an equally powerful reaction. And now, Good Heavens!—here I am sitting next to a Nobel Prize-winner, the sun going down behind the mountains, and you drinking whisky. . . .

AUTHOR: You have poetic inclinations, my dear Feargod Hofer.

VISITOR: Entirely due to reading your books.

AUTHOR: I'm sorry to hear it. You're wearing rather cheap clothes. Your new profession doesn't seem to have turned out very well for you.

VISITOR: It's true that life isn't exactly a bed of roses.

AUTHOR: The local district attorney is a friend of mine. I'll put in a good word for you with him. What particular branch of criminology are you specializing in? Espionage? Divorce? Narcotics? The white-slave traffic?

VISITOR: Literature!

AUTHORS (*getting up*): In that case, I must ask you for the second time to leave this room at once!

VISITOR (*getting up*): Honored sir!

AUTHOR: You have become a critic!

VISITOR: If you would only permit me to explain . . .

AUTHOR: Get out!

VISITOR (*in despair*): But I've only analyzed your works with respect to their *criminological* aspect.

AUTHOR (*calming down*): Oh, I see. In that case you can stay. Be seated.

VISITOR: Thank you.

AUTHOR: I have been interpreted from psychoanalytic, Catholic, Protestant, existential, Buddhist, and Marxist viewpoints, but never from the viewpoint which you have adopted.

VISITOR: I owe you an explanation, honored master . . .

AUTHOR: Korbes is the name.

VISITOR: Honored Mr. Korbes. I read your works because of a certain theory which I had formed. Whatever exists in the world of fiction—in your novels—must also exist in reality, because it seems to me impossible to invent something which does not exist somewhere in reality.

AUTHOR (*hesitantly*): A fairly reasonable conclusion.

VISITOR: As a result of this conclusion I began to look *in real life* for the murders described in your novels.

AUTHOR (*electrified*): You assumed that there was some sort of connection between my novels and reality?

VISITOR: Exactly. I proceeded to use razor-sharp logic. First I subjected your work to a searching analysis. You are not only the most notorious and newsworthy writer of our time, a man whose divorces, love affairs, alcoholic excesses, and tiger hunts are written up in all the newspapers and scandal sheets—you are also known as the creator of the most beautiful murder scenes in world literature.

AUTHOR: I have never glorified murder *per se*. I have always tried to show man as a whole. Part of that whole, of course, is the fact that he is capable of committing murder.

VISITOR: Speaking as a detective, I was not interested so much in what you tried to do as in what in fact you did do. Before you, murder was universally considered something horrible, but you have managed to bring magnificence and beauty even to this dark side of life—or, rather, of death. You are universally known as "Old Sudden Death and Homicide."

AUTHOR: That's just a mark of my popularity.

VISITOR: And of your skill in creating genuine master murderers whose identity no one can even guess at.

AUTHOR (*curiously*): You're referring to my—idiosyncrasy—of letting the criminal escape unmasked?

VISITOR: Exactly!

AUTHOR: Hmm! In other words, you read my novels as if they were police reports.

VISITOR: As if they were homicide reports. Your heroes murder neither for profit nor because of thwarted passion. They murder for psychological gratification, for pleasure, to display their skill, or to increase their range of experience—all of them motives not recognized by traditional criminological theory. You are quite literally too deep, too subtle for the police or the district attorney. Consequently they don't even suspect that a murder has been committed since as far as they are concerned, where there is no motive there is no crime. If one assumes, then, that the murders which you describe *really* took place, it follows that they must have appeared to the public to be suicides, accidents, or even natural deaths.

AUTHOR: Yes, that follows—logically speaking.

VISITOR: Exactly what they appear to be to the people in your novels.

AUTHOR: Exactly.

VISITOR: At this point in my investigations I seemed to myself to be somewhat like that Spanish knight—what's-his-name . . . Don—

AUTHOR: Don Quixote.

VISITOR: Don Quixote, whom you frequently mention in your novels. He sallied forth as he did because he took the knightly romances for reality; and I determined to take your novels for reality. But I did not let myself become frightened off by anything. My motto has always been "Forward!—even though the world be full of devils!"

AUTHOR (*enraptured*): Marvelous! What you've undertaken is absolutely marvelous! (*He rings.*) Sebastian! Sebastian!

SECRETARY (*enters*): Sir?

AUTHOR: We'll have to work all night. Offer Mr. Hofer a cigar. Surely there must be something we can give him a little pleasure with. Brazil? Havana?

VISITOR: No, no, no. I'll smoke one of my own if you don't mind.

AUTHOR: Certainly, certainly. You can go now, Sebastian, and take this dagger with you. I don't need it right now, after all.

SECRETARY: Certainly, honored master. (*Exits.*)

VISITOR: A beautiful piece! I noticed it some time ago, honored . . .

AUTHOR: Korbes is the name.

VISITOR: Honored Mr. Korbes. One push—and somebody's dead. It's extremely well honed.

AUTHOR: A light?

VISITOR: Nothing I enjoy so much as a good smoke.

AUTHOR: Enjoy it, my dear Hofer, enjoy it. But above all, do go on with your story.

VISITOR: It wasn't easy for me to arrive at a solution. I was obliged to perform some extremely detailed analysis. First I sifted through your novel *Rendezvous Abroad*.

AUTHOR: My first novel.

VISITOR: Published eleven years ago.

AUTHOR: Awarded the Bolling Prize and made into a movie by Hitchcock.

VISITOR: All I can say about it is, "What an achievement!" A French adventurer—fat, tanned, unshaven, with a big, bald head; dissipated, gifted, and a hard drinker—meets a woman, the wife of a German diplomat. Extraordinarily delicate way he has of expressing himself! He entices her to go with him to a run-down hotel in Ankara, a filthy hellhole of the worst sort, where he seduces her. Then, talking through his alcoholic haze like a Homer, a Shakespeare, he convinces her that the highest happiness is in a suicide pact. She believes in the passion that she's experiencing, hypnotized by his outbursts —and kills herself in a sexual ecstasy. But he doesn't kill himself. No, indeed!—he just lights up a cigarette and walks out. Then he takes a stroll through the slums, beats up a preacher of the Christian Mission to the Turks, robs its poor box, and makes off for Persia as the dawn comes up. There he goes prospecting for oil. Possibly the *Swiss Review of Books* is right in calling this a trivial plot. Nonetheless it leaves Hemingway miles behind in brevity and conciseness.

AUTHOR (*amused*): Surely you're not going to tell me that you took your investigations all the way to Turkey in order to verify this story, my dear Hofer?

VISITOR: I had no alternative. I went to considerable expense to obtain the Ankara newspapers for 1954, the year in which your novel takes place, and got a Turkish exchange student at the Federal Technological Institute to go through them for me.

AUTHOR: And the result?

VISITOR: It was the wife of a Swedish diplomat rather than a German who committed suicide. A blond, somewhat reserved beauty, she was found in a hotel of the worst type. No reason for the suicide was discovered, precisely as I predicted.

AUTHOR: And the man with whom she went to this—er, hotel?

VISITOR: Unknown. The evidence of the desk clerk, however, indicates that we're dealing here with a German-speaking individual. I have also established that one of the preachers of the Christian Mission to the Turks was indeed beaten up. He was, however, injured too badly to give any evidence about his assailant. After this I examined *Mr. X Is Bored*.

AUTHOR: Churchill's favorite novel.

VISITOR: Your second book. A masterpiece. Mr. X, formerly a good-for-nothing, but now an established and popular writer, moderator of the American Pen Club, meets a sixteen-year-old girl in St. Tropez. He is enchanted by her beauty and simplicity. The intensity of nature, the reflection of the sea, the merciless sun—all combine to bring out his primitive instincts. The result: rape and murder in the pouring rain of a tremendous thunderstorm. Surely the most beautiful and at the same time most horrible pages ever written. The dialogue seems merely sketched out but is actually as clear and precise as can be. Then there's the description of the police procedure—the motorcycles, the radio cars with their screaming sirens, the hunt for the killer, and the suspects, who seem to include everyone except the actual murderer—he's too famous and too admired to arouse the slightest suspicion. On the contrary: before he leaves for London in order to accept the Lord Byron Prize, Mr. X attends the funeral, with a description of which the book ends like an ancient Greek tragedy.

AUTHOR (*smiling*): Your powerful imagination is getting the better of you, my dear Hofer.

VISITOR (*insistently*): Ten years ago—in 1957—a sixteen-year-old English girl was raped and murdered in St. Tropez.

AUTHOR: And the murderer?

VISITOR: Unknown.

AUTHOR: Just like the Swedish woman's murderer, eh?

VISITOR: Exactly so—(*hesitating*)—despite an extremely efficient police force.

AUTHOR (*proudly*): Exactly so.

VISITOR: The authorities don't have the slightest clue.

AUTHOR: Did you make any further discoveries?

VISITOR: If you would be so good as to glance at this piece of paper—it is a list of all the people whose connection with characters in your novels I have established.

AUTHOR: There are—let me see—twenty-two names on this list.

VISITOR: Precisely the number of novels you have written.

AUTHOR: All of these people are dead?

VISITOR: Some of them committed suicide; some of them died because of unexpected accidents—with the exception of the young English girl who was raped and murdered, of course.

AUTHOR: Why is there a question mark next to the name of the Argentinian millionairess Juana?

VISITOR: She corresponds to Mercedes, who is strangled by the hero of your novel *Evil Nights*. As a matter of fact, however, the multimillionairess died in Ostend of natural causes.

AUTHOR: Hmm—this is a—very valuable list.

VISITOR: The result of ten years' criminological investigation. And that isn't all, either. Wherever these accidents and suicides occurred, you, my dear sir, were present.

AUTHOR (*somewhat like a schoolboy caught in the act*): Is that a fact?

VISITOR: You were in Ankara when the Swedish woman died, you were in St. Tropez when the English girl died, you were in all the twenty other places when the twenty other people on that list died. I need only mention the Parliamentary Secretary von Wattenwil in Davos, Countess Windischgrätz in Biarritz, Lord Liverpool in Split. . . .

AUTHOR: Everyone on this list, in other words.

VISITOR: Everyone.

AUTHOR: You've been on my track, eh, Mr. Hofer?

VISITOR: I *had* to follow your tracks if I was going to be a professional detective and not just a dilettante. From one resort to another, from one expensive spa to the next.

AUTHOR: So you were not merely in Adelboden and Baden-Baden with me?

VISITOR: Wherever you were, I was.

AUTHOR (*inquisitively*): Wasn't that extremely expensive for you?

VISITOR: Ruinously. Not to mention the fact that my means were extremely limited, my pension, considering the enormous profits of Oechsli, Trost, and Co., being laughably small. I had to economize, I had to deprive myself of things. Some of my trips, honored . . .

AUTHOR (*admonishingly*): Korbes is the name.

VISITOR: Thank you. Some of my trips literally meant starvation for me. The only one I wasn't able to swing at all was the one to South America seven years ago, and of course your annual excursions to the African or Indian jungle. . . .

AUTHOR: Quite unnecessary, my dear Hofer. I only hunt tigers and elephants there.

VISITOR: At all other times I stuck to you.

AUTHOR: That's beginning to be obvious.

VISITOR: And wherever we stayed—you in a five-star hotel, me in a shabby rooming house—an accident, which you later wrote up as a murder, occurred.

AUTHOR: My dear Hofer, you are the most remarkable man I have ever met.

VISITOR: The next question I was faced with—naturally!—concerned the manner in which this correspondence between your works and reality had come about.

AUTHOR: Naturally!

VISITOR: Two possibilities presented themselves to me after I had performed the necessary logical examination of the facts. Either you modeled your characters on people you had observed in real life, or your plots actually occurred in reality precisely the way you described them.

AUTHOR: Granted.

VISITOR (*portentously*): If we assume that this second theory is true, then your plots, which are universally admired as the products of your inexhaustible imagination, are nothing more nor less than factual accounts. I hesitated a long time before I permitted myself to subscribe to this theory, but now I know it is the only possible one. This brings up a new problem, however: if your novels are factual accounts, it follows that the murders you describe are also factual. And that brings us ineluctably to the question: who are the murderers?

AUTHOR: And what have you discovered?

VISITOR (*in a steely voice*): That we must look upon the various murderers as *one* murderer. All of your protagonists clearly possess characteristics common to *one* particular person. They are all powerful men with large bald heads, usually bare chested in the critical murder scene; larger than life in their gestures, they rush through the baroque sea of your prose in a permanent state of semi-intoxication. (*Pause.*) *You are the murderer!*

AUTHOR: In other words, you are saying that I have several times . . .

VISITOR: Twenty-one times.

AUTHOR: Twenty-two times.

VISITOR: Twenty-one times. The Argentinian multimillionairess constitutes an exception.

AUTHOR: All right, all right—you're saying, in other words, that I have murdered almost twenty-two people?

VISITOR: That is my firm and immovable conviction. I am in the presence not only of one of the foremost writers, but also of one of the foremost murderers of all time.

AUTHOR (*pensively*): Twenty-two . . .

VISITOR (*stubbornly*): Twenty-one times.

AUTHOR: Twenty-one times, then. When you hear a thing like that . . .

VISITOR: . . . it makes one think, honored master. (*Pause.*)

AUTHOR (*smiling*): Well now, what do you really want from me, my dear Feargod Hofer?

VISITOR: Now that I've told you the results of my researches, I can breathe again. I have often trembled at the thought of this moment, but I have not been disappointed. I see you calm and still amicably disposed to me, and would like to continue speaking with the same terrible frankness to you.

AUTHOR: By all means.

VISITOR: At first I only intended to hand you over to the forces of justice.

AUTHOR: And have you changed your mind?

VISITOR: I have, indeed.

AUTHOR: Why?

VISITOR: I have been observing you now for ten years. I have seen how masterfully you have pursued your passion, how carefully

you have chosen your victims, and how calmly and resignedly
you have approached your work.

AUTHOR: You admire me?

VISITOR: Immeasurably.

AUTHOR: As murderer or as writer?

VISITOR: *Both.* The more I have discovered about your criminal
activities, the more I have learned to value your literary fi-
nesse. I am ready and willing to make a supreme sacrifice to
your art.

AUTHOR: Namely?

VISITOR (*quietly and simply*): I am prepared to turn my back on
the greatest thing in life: I will sacrifice the fame and glory
that are due to me.

AUTHOR: So, you've decided not to turn me in?

VISITOR: I renounce the opportunity.

AUTHOR: And what do you expect me to give you in return?

VISITOR: A small token—of appreciation.

AUTHOR: In what form?

VISITOR: Well, you see—I'm bankrupt. I have sacrificed everything
I own for my art. I am no longer in a position to lead the
kind of life I have become accustomed to while serving the
cause of criminological science. I can't afford to roam from
one expensive resort to another any more. I shall be obliged
to return to Ennetwyl near Horck with a cloud over my head
and my life in ruins unless—unless—(*He hesitates.*) . . .

AUTHOR: Go on, go on.

VISITOR: . . . unless you see fit to supplement the pension I get
from Oechsli, Trost, and Co. with a little extra pocket money
—say, six or seven hundred Swiss francs per month—so that I
can continue to play a part in your life—oh, quite discreetly,
of course—as your admirer and confidant. (*Pause.*)

AUTHOR: My dear Feargod Hofer, I, too, would like to make a con-
fession; I, too, would like to speak with terrible frankness, as

you put it. There is absolutely no doubt in my mind that you are the greatest detective I've ever met. Your criminological talents and your razor-sharp mind have not led you astray. You are perfectly right. I confess everything. (*Pause.*)

VISITOR: You admit it?

AUTHOR: I admit it.

VISITOR: The Swedish woman?

AUTHOR: The Swedish woman.

VISITOR: The young English girl?

AUTHOR: Her too.

VISITOR: Countess Windischgrätz?

AUTHOR: Likewise. The Argentinian multimillionairess as well.

VISITOR: I'm sorry, I cannot allow you that one.

AUTHOR: But, my dear sir . . .

VISITOR: You know perfectly well that you're trying to cheat now, honored master.

AUTHOR: All right, all right, we'll omit the multimillionairess.

VISITOR: And you did murder the twenty-one others?

AUTHOR: All twenty-one of them. I'm no piker, after all. (*Pause.*)

VISITOR (*pensively*): This is the culminating moment of my existence.

AUTHOR: Very true. This is the culminating moment of your existence. In a somewhat different sense from the one you intend, however.

(*A young woman appears in the bedroom door, runs in despair across the room, and disappears again.*)

YOUNG WOMAN: I simply *must* go back to Papa, Maximilian Frederick!

VISITOR: Wasn't that the charming daughter of the English colonel in the next room flitting across here in her bare feet?

AUTHOR: To be sure.

VISITOR: Your next victim?

AUTHOR: Hardly. My next victim is going to be someone else. Despite the correctness of your conclusions, you have made one mistake, Mr. Hofer. Hasn't it occurred to you that it might be dangerous to come and tell me all about your knowledge of my—er, private life?

VISITOR: You mean—you could kill *me?*

AUTHOR: Precisely.

VISITOR: Well, naturally that occurred to me, my dear Mr. Korbes. I have examined the situation from every angle and quite quietly and calmly taken every imaginable precaution. A well-known American movie star lives in the room above yours, a colonel in the English army on your left, and a middle-class widow on your right.

AUTHOR: Excuse me—a widowed duchess.

VISITOR: Incorrect! My investigations reveal that her husband was a department-store doorman in Geneva. The room below yours is occupied by the tubercular Archbishop of Czernowitz. One cry for help from me and there'll be a scandal which will shake the world. So you'd have to kill me noiselessly—poison would be your only way.

AUTHOR: Quite so, quite so. So that's why you wouldn't take a drink.

VISITOR: Exactly. It wasn't very easy for me to refuse, either—I happen to be particularly fond of whisky.

AUTHOR: And you wouldn't smoke a cigar, either.

VISITOR: Well, after all, you got rid of the tenor Lorenz Hochsträsser with a particularly mild Havana impregnated with an Indian poison.

AUTHOR: My dear Feargod Hofer, you forget one thing—that you come from Ennetwyl near Horck.

VISITOR: Don't underestimate the place. Ennetwyl is very much in the swing of things and has an active cultural life.

AUTHOR: That's exactly what I mean. Nowadays places that have an "active cultural life" are on the other side of the moon, so

to speak—otherwise you would have been aware of the sense-
lessness of your investigations. (*He pours himself another
whisky.*) You have merely proved something that didn't need
proving. (*Pause.*)

VISITOR (*dismayed*): You mean . . .

AUTHOR: Yes, indeed. The world has known what you seem to
consider your secret for a long time.

VISITOR (*almost hysterical*): That's impossible. I've gone through
all the serious newspapers with a fine-tooth comb and haven't
found the slightest hint of it.

AUTHOR: The only place you can find the truth nowadays is in the
scandal sheets, Feargod Hofer. They're full of my murders.
Do you really suppose that the public would swallow my
works if they didn't *know* that I only describe murders that
I've committed?

VISITOR: But, honored mas . . .

AUTHOR: Korbes is the name.

VISITOR: Honored Mr. Korbes. . . . You'd have been arrested long
ago if that were true!

AUTHOR (*amazed*): But why?

VISITOR (*in despair*): Because you're a murderer, of course! A mass
murderer!

AUTHOR: Well, what of it? We writers have always been monsters,
according to middle-class morality! Look at Goethe, Balzac,
Baudelaire, Verlaine, Rimbaud, Edgar Allan Poe. But that
isn't all. No matter how horrified the world was with us at
first, it always wound up worshipping us more and more as
time passed—*precisely because* we're monsters. We went up
and up in the social scale until finally we were held in awe as
superior beings. Society has not only accepted us, it has concentrated its interest almost exclusively on our private lives.
As people who can permit themselves anything—who are
supposed to permit themselves anything—we've become wish
fulfillment figures for the millions. Our art gives us carte
blanche for our vices and our adventures. Do you really suppose I'd have been given the Nobel Prize for my novel *The*

Murderer and the Child if I hadn't been the murderer myself? Look at these letters scattered in heaps around my room.
They're from high society women, from middle-class wives,
from chambermaids—all of them offering themselves as victims for my future murders.

VISITOR: I'm dreaming.

AUTHOR: Well then, it's high time you woke up. Only critics suppose that a writer works on his literary form and on his
dialogue. Real literature has nothing to do with literary matters—its purpose is to satisfy mankind. People don't long for
new literary forms or for linguistic experiments, least of all
for philosophical revelations: they long for a life that doesn't
need hope because hope doesn't exist any more; they long for
a life overflowing with fulfillment, with tension, with adventure, and with the pleasures of the moment—a life that the
reality of our machine age can no longer offer them—and they
have to turn to art for it. Literature has become a drug—a
substitute for a way of life that is no longer possible. But in
order to manufacture this drug writers must unfortunately
lead the kind of life they describe—something which (believe
me!) is one hell of a strain, particularly after one has passed
a certain age.

(*Another young woman appears in the doorway.*)

2ND YOUNG WOMAN: Maximilian Frederick!

AUTHOR: Get out of here! (*The second young woman also disappears.*) That was the American movie star. When I was
young I concentrated strictly on style. A few provincial editors
patted me on the back—other than that nobody gave a damn
about me. Quite right, too. I gave up writing and bummed
around, prospecting for oil in Persia. I failed at that too.
That left me with only one thing to do—describe my life. I
thought I'd be arrested. The first person to congratulate me
and advance me an appreciable sum of money was the
Swedish attaché whose wife I had had an affair with. The
story of that affair became my first best seller. There—and
now do have a glass of whisky since you're particularly fond
of it. (*He pours.*)

VISITOR: Thank you . . . I'm . . . I don't know . . . thank
you . . .

AUTHOR: As soon as I realized what the world wanted, I began to furnish it with the desired commodity. From then on I wrote nothing but autobiography. I stopped paying attention to my style in order to write without it and, presto! I had style. So, I became famous, but my fame forced me to lead an ever more abandoned life, because the public wanted to see me in ever more horrifying situations so that it could experience *through me* everything that was forbidden. And that's how I became a mass murderer! From then on, everything that happened only increased my fame. My books were impounded and destroyed, the Vatican put me on the Index, and the printings became bigger and bigger. And now you show up! You with your ridiculous proofs that my novels describe the truth. There isn't a judge or jury in the world that'd pay any attention to you, because the world wants me the way I am. They'd declare you insane, just as they've declared everyone else who's tried it insane! Do you really suppose you're the first? Mothers, wives, husbands, sons have gone bursting in on the lawyers, sniffing for revenge. Every single lawsuit has been put off so far. District attorneys and ministers of justice —yes, even presidents—have successfully intervened on my behalf in the name of art. Everyone who's tried to drag me to court has wound up looking like a fool so far. You are an idiot, Feargod Hofer. You have thrown your savings away and you deserve to be punished for it. Don't expect money from me. You'd do better to expect something else. Go on, call for help!

VISITOR (*fearfully*): For help?

AUTHOR: I need a new plot.

VISITOR: A new plot?

AUTHOR: You are the new plot.

VISITOR: What do you mean?

AUTHOR: High time I got to work.

VISITOR (*horrified*): Why are you drawing a revolver all of a sudden?

AUTHOR: Haven't you figured it out yet?

VISITOR: I'm going—I'm on my way already.

AUTHOR: I didn't draw this revolver to send you on your way—I drew it to kill you.

VISITOR: I swear to you by all I hold holy that I'll leave this place at once and go back to Ennetwyl.

AUTHOR: You've given me an idea for a radio play and so now you must die, for I only write down what I have experienced, because, you see, I don't have any imagination at all—because I can *only* write down what I experience. I'll make you a part of world literature, Feargod Hofer. Millions will see you standing before me the way you are now, trembling with fright, your eyes and mouth wide open—pits into which cataracts of horror are crashing, opening up before you— you, a mug of a bookkeeper who finally wakes up after end- less self-delusion and sees truth tear away the veil.

VISITOR: HELP! (*Pause.*)

AUTHOR: Well? Do you see any people rushing in? Is the movie star or the English colonel or possibly the Archbishop of Czernowitz springing to the rescue?

VISITOR: You . . . you're the devil.

AUTHOR: I am an author and I need money. The radio play which I will write about your murder will be carried on all the networks. I *have* to kill you, if only for purely financial rea- sons. Do you think I enjoy doing this? God knows I'd a thousand times rather drink a bottle of wine with you down in the bar and then go bowling with you than spend the night writing the account of your death.

VISITOR: Mercy, honored master!

AUTHOR: Korbes is the name.

VISITOR: Honored Mr. Korbes, mercy!

AUTHOR: The practice of the literary profession does not involve mercy.

VISITOR (*staggering back on to the balcony*): Help!

AUTHOR (*in a powerful voice*): You are case Number Twenty- three!

VISITOR: No, twenty-two. . . . (*There is a loud noise; then a long-drawn-out cry, fading away.*) Heeeelllllp! (*A silence.*)

AUTHOR: Such a bungler!

SECRETARY: Mr. Korbes! What's happened, for heaven's sake?

AUTHOR: My visitor jumped off the balcony, Sebastian. He seemed to panic all of a sudden. Can't imagine why. Ah, here's the manager.

MANAGER: My dear Mr. Korbes! I am desolate! Somebody has been permitted to annoy you! He's lying smashed up among the roses down there. The doorman's been noticing him going around like a crazy person for a long time now. Thank God no one was injured by his fall.

AUTHOR: Kindly see to it that I am not disturbed.

MANAGER (*retiring*): But of course, my dear Mr. Korbes, of course.

AUTHOR: All right, let's get to work, Sebastian. But first I believe I'll light up a cigar.

SEBASTIAN: A light, sir?

AUTHOR: Use it to burn that piece of paper on the table.

SEBASTIAN: What are these names?

AUTHOR: Oh, just names. Give it here. That's the best way. Thank you. We'll have to hurry. Tomorrow we'll pack. This place has served its purpose. We'll go to Majorca.

SEBASTIAN: Majorca?

AUTHOR: A little Mediterranean scenery will do us good. Ready?

SEBASTIAN: Ready, sir.

AUTHOR: Another whisky first.

SEBASTIAN: Here you are.

AUTHOR: All right, take this down: Ladies and gentlemen, I consider it my duty, at the very outset, to describe to you the setting of this possibly somewhat peculiar but, I assure you, entirely true story. To be sure, there is a considerable element of danger in telling true stories—someone from the police or possibly even the district attorney might be among those present, even though they might not be here in their official capacity. Nonetheless I can allow myself to take the risk because I know perfectly well they won't believe my true story—at least not in their official capacity. In reality—that is to say, *un*officially—all of you of course, including the district attorney or policeman who may or may not be among us, know very well that I *only* tell true stories—scout's honor! Well then: might I ask you to concentrate for a moment? Imagine yourselves in the drawing room of a Grand Hotel suite. . . .

THE GREAT FURY
OF PHILIP HOTZ

by MAX FRISCH

TRANSLATED BY MICHAEL BENEDIKT

Characters

PHILIP HOTZ, Ph.D.
DORLI, his wife
WILFRED, a friend
CLARISSA, his wife
THE OLD MOVING MAN
THE YOUNG MOVING MAN
A SPINSTER
A REFRESHMENT VENDOR
FOUR FOREIGN LEGIONNAIRES
GERMAN AND FRENCH CUSTOMS OFFICERS (played by the same actor)

A room in an apartment building. It is empty. Hotz enters in a raincoat flung open, pale with rage, and packs a tiny suitcase.

HOTZ: Just to let you know: I'm packing now. Shirt, toothbrush, pajamas. All else, I assume, will be provided by the Foreign Legion. (*The sobbing of a woman is heard.*) I'm going as fast as I can. Just stay calm. As soon as I finish I'm going to let you right out of that closet. (*He closes the suitcase.*) You see—my suitcase is packed already. (*He stands it upright.*) All I have to do now is wreck this whole apartment. (*He looks around to see where to begin, tears down a curtain and crumples it up; then, as if awakened by the sight of the crumpled curtain, he steps downstage and addresses the audience at the edge of the stage:*) I know, ladies and gentlemen, I know that you are one and all on my wife's side. And also—I know! —that you are all of the considered opinion that marriage works—(*He takes out a cigarette.*) Now I have no intention of becoming excited. (*He smokes meditatively.*) I don't know, ladies and gentlemen, what Dorli has told you—(*The telephone rings.*) Excuse me! (*He picks up the receiver and speaks into it.*) One moment please. (*He puts down the receiver and returns downstage.*) If you too, ladies and gentlemen, like our divorce court judge and like everyone else who has not been married to Dorli, are of the opinion that we —two such worthy people as we—should try a little harder; or, as our divorce court judge phrased it: should "just try sleeping on it once again. . . ." (*He remembers the telephone.*) One moment, please. (*He speaks into the receiver.*) Hotz, yes, Dr. Hotz. No, I'm not my wife . . . No, I'm sorry I'm not . . . Yes, I'll give her your message. (*He hangs up and addresses the large, old-fashioned wardrobe standing in the room.*) You're to give your lawyer a ring as soon as you get home. (*He comes downstage once more.*) And what I told the judge was: I'd just as soon wreck our whole apartment (which Dorli doesn't believe I'll really do) and just as soon go and join the Foreign Legion. (*The doorbell rings.*) There are my moving-van men! (*Hotz goes back into the set, through it, and out the door. Sobs from the wardrobe. Enter a nervous, meek old spinster lady, who stands quietly by herself in the room, while Hotz emerges from the wings and once more steps downstage.*) I said I'd just as soon wreck our whole apartment!—but nobody is taking me seriously!

Dorli calmly strolls home with me, arm in arm; everybody doubts that I'm capable of such a thing since, after all, I'm such an educated man. . . . (*He takes a fresh cigarette and discovers he's already smoking one; he stamps out the first, lighted, cigarette on the floor.*) They'll find out what I'm really like! (*He steps backward into the set.*) Please, do sit down.

SPINSTER: I hope I'm not disturbing the gentleman?

HOTZ: Please, do sit down. (*He indicates a chair, and she sits down.*) What did my wife tell you?

SPINSTER: She told me to come back when Doctor Hotz was at home.

HOTZ: Now let's speak frankly about this! (*He finally lights the fresh cigarette.*) It's not that I deny in the least that Dorli is the more worthwhile person. And I don't need any divorce court judge or any Aunt Bertha in order to understand that I don't begin to deserve a person like my wife. . . .

SPINSTER: But Doctor . . .

HOTZ: Let me finish. (*He sits down as if for some legal consultation.*) What does the word "marriage" signify to you, Madam? (*The spinster fumbles in her handbag.*) Madam, I have taken the trouble to compute the average number of cases of adultery among my own circle of friends, who are certainly no worse than most people—only taking into account, of course, such adulteries as appear indisputable to at least three impartial observers—and I have arrived, madam, in a consideration only of men up to the age of 50—at an average in this particular locality of 5.1607 per cent. Just think of that! Not counting adulteries that have been carefully planned and which mere forces of circumstances have prevented from taking place, and relationships that to be sure may go very far indeed and even in point of fact may exceed actual adultery in emotional intensity: 5.1607 per cent. And don't forget, madam, that all these people—I shall name no names—are people who are of the opinion that marriage "works."

SPINSTER: But Doctor . . .

HOTZ: That is to say:—

SPINSTER: But . . .

HOTZ: Don't keep interrupting me! (*He has jumped to his feet.*) Since Christmas, madam, since Christmas we have been speaking nothing but the whole truth to one another, and tomorrow will be Easter, and what, exactly, have we accomplished? Aside from court costs and in addition to the bills from two lawyers. . . .

SPINSTER: But . . .

HOTZ: Aunt Bertha! (*He manages to suppress his emotions.*) I did all I could to arrange a divorce in peace and in friendship. Everything was arranged in the customary way: Mrs. Simone Dorothea Hotz, née Hauschild, sues for divorce on the grounds of her husband's adultery; and the suit has not been contested. My counter-suit specifies—in order to spare Dorli! incompatibility, which is certainly no exaggeration, since I have never understood my wife, as she herself says—and never less than I did this morning, at precisely eleven o'clock when Dorli—the little hussy!—suddenly withdrew her entire case for divorce. (*The spinster has risen to her feet.*) Sit down! (*The spinster sits down.*) My dear, beloved Aunt Bertha—

SPINSTER: You're mistaken, Doctor, you're mistaken!

HOTZ: I'm not mistaken, Aunt Bertha; unfortunately, not mistaken in the least. What made our marriage come to grief was not the few acts of adultery—that was a bit painful, I confess, and as the "fashion" it is today, I think it's disgusting—but the fact, madam, the plain and abysmal fact that I am a man, intellectual though I may be, and my wife, if you will pardon my saying so, is a woman. (*The doorbell rings.*) And in this respect, my dear, beloved Aunt Bertha, nothing will be altered if, as our judge puts it, we just try sleeping on it once again—(*The doorbell rings.*) On the contrary. (*The doorbell rings.*) Excuse me, please. (*Hotz goes to the door.*)

SPINSTER: Mrs. Hotz? Mrs. Hotz? (*She looks around to see where the sobbing is coming from.*)

HOTZ (*immediately stepping back from the wings, holding up a handsaw, and addressing the audience*): Oh no, dear ladies,

I'm not jealous. Please don't think that I'm jealous just because Dorli became involved that time—ages ago!—with that
insect, that engineering executive—although for all I know
he might have been in the export trade— Oh no, my dear
ladies, Oh no! . . . (*Two Moving Van Men enter the
room, carrying straps.*) I'll be right with you. (*He remains
where he is.*) I'm not, dear ladies, some kind of Eskimo, who
looks upon his wife as a piece of property. There is no such
thing, as far as I'm concerned, as ownership in love. It's
impossible for me to feel jealous, ladies, absolutely impossible—(*The saw held in his hand increasingly trembles and
shakes.*) However: when the moment you get into court, a
wife withdraws the suit for divorce you've worked out so
carefully together— Ladies! What's left of common understanding then? Of good faith in every circumstance? Of
mutual trust? Of comradeship between man and wife? I ask
you: what the hell does marriage mean *then*? (*He begins to
step back into the set, but turns around once more.*) She's
obviously counting on the impermanence of my rage. (*Steps
back into the set.*)

HOTZ: Gentlemen, you'll have no need of those straps.

OLD MAN: Why not?

HOTZ: I'm liquidating everything. (*The spinster has risen to her
feet.*) In a word, dear Aunt Bertha, I deplore, deplore absolutely . . . (*The spinster hands him a leaflet.*) What's this
for?

SPINSTER: It's in connection with the demonstration, Doctor.

HOTZ: You're not my Aunt Bertha? (*He turns to the Moving Van
Men:*) Have you a crowbar? And a pair of strong cutting
pliers? I expressly ordered a crowbar, a pair of strong cutting
pliers, and a good handsaw.

YOUNG MAN: We've got them.

HOTZ: And the handsaw?

YOUNG MAN: You've got it. (*Hotz sees that the saw is in his own
hand.*)

HOTZ: Fine. (*He gives the leaflet back to the spinster.*) Madam,
I have no need of a vacuum cleaner. (*He conducts her to*

the door.) We haven't much time, gentlemen—you must begin at once! Those pictures, for example. Take a carving knife or whatever you can find and cut them from the upper left-hand corner to the lower right-hand corner—like this. (*He demonstrates by slashing at the painting.*) Got it? (*The Movers look at one another.*) What's bothering you?

OLD MAN: Total destruction?

HOTZ: Excluding, of course, things that belong to the building: plumbing fixtures, the gas range, the radiators, the bathtub, light switches and that kind of thing. . . . Young man, here is an ash tray!

YOUNG MAN: What should I do to that?

HOTZ: It's for your ashes.

YOUNG MAN: Oh, I see.

HOTZ: The carpet is my wife's property. (*He goes over to the writing desk.*) Dorli! Where did we put the list of your property? (*The two Moving Men pick up the grandfather clock.*) I'll take care of the grandfather clock myself; it's an heirloom. (*The Moving Men leave the grandfather clock in the middle of the room.*) And all those ladies' things lying around everywhere, dresses and underclothes and so on, lipstick, magazines, stockings and all those pink things, brassieres, teeny-weeny little bottles, combs and so on, letters from the Argentine, slippers and so on, notes and belts and nail clippers and so on and gloves and so on, shell and wood necklaces and so on and so on, everything that can practically drive you to distraction!—don't touch any of that. My wife is very sensitive. And if you have to saw anything, Gentlemen, please do it outside in the hall. (*The Moving Men put their straps around the wardrobe.*) Stop! For heaven's sake! The wardrobe stays here—for heaven's sake! (*The Moving Men put down the wardrobe again.*) I'm sorry. (*He wipes the sweat from his brow.*) Now here's the list of my wife's property. . . . (*The Moving Men pick up an armchair and a table.*)

YOUNG MAN: Doctor, what shall we do with this?

HOTZ: Yes, yes, that's right, do it quickly.

YOUNG MAN: Do what quickly?

HOTZ: Yes—quickly: saw off the legs. (*He shows the Young Man exactly where.*)

YOUNG MAN: Right here?

HOTZ: Yes, please. (*The Young Man carries off the armchair and table.*) I said that I was sorry! (*Pause. He knocks on the wardrobe.*) Dorli? (*He puts his ear to the wardrobe.*) Why are you holding your breath? (*As he listens, the sound of sawing is heard from the hallway outside.*) Do you hear that, Dorli? I've got two workmen on the job now, don't worry. It won't take very long. (*A piece of wood falling is heard; the sawing stops.*) The first leg. (*Sawing begins again.*) Now is not the time to lose my anger! (*A piece of wood falls; the sawing stops.*) The second leg. (*He holds his hand over his face until the next thud.*) The third leg. (*He goes over to the grandfather clock and topples it with one kick.*) I mustn't lose my anger now! (*While the sawing resumes, he begins looking around for something.*) Dorli, where do we keep our screwdriver? (*He stares at the wardrobe.*) Are you out of your mind!? Dorli! (*A wisp of smoke comes from the wardrobe.*) I refuse to be responsible for this. Do you hear? It's true that I shut you up in that wardrobe, but you're over twenty-one, Dorli, and you know how dangerous it is to smoke in a wardrobe. (*Another puff of smoke.*) Do you hear? (*Another puff of smoke. Hotz comes toward the edge of the stage to address the audience.*) Now ladies and gentlemen, you can see for yourselves: she is simply depending on my guilty conscience catching up with me. (*He steps back into the set and picks up the little suitcase.*) Just to let you know what you can't see, Dorli: I'm standing here with my suitcase in hand, and whether you believe me or not. . . . (*Enter the Old Moving Man.*)

OLD MAN: How do you want the curtains, sir?

HOTZ: Curtains?

OLD MAN: Cut up or burned up?

HOTZ: Cut up, I think.

OLD MAN: In long strips or—

HOTZ: Yes, please, try strips.

OLD MAN: How wide would you like the strips?

HOTZ: Oh, the width of my hand.

OLD MAN: Four inches?

HOTZ: Yes, roughly. (*The Old Moving Man pulls a tape measure out of his trousers pocket.*) Roughly, roughly! You can cut them into triangles if you like. Whichever amuses you most, my friend, whichever amuses you most. (*The Old Moving Man picks up the curtains and walks out.*) Dorli, I'm going now. It's not right that I should always be the one to start making up first. (*Pause. In a louder voice than before:*) I said, I'm going now. . . . (*A puff of smoke comes from the wardrobe. Hotz puts down his suitcase and steps to the edge of the stage to address the audience.*) My wife is driving me into the Foreign Legion for the simple reason that she doesn't believe that I'll actually go. (*He plucks a railroad timetable from his pocket.*) Geneva, Lyons, Marseilles. (*He scans it hastily.*) I know all those eyewitness accounts describing what it's like in the Foreign Legion and, believe me, Dorli knows them too. . . . (*He puts the timetable back into his pocket.*) Take the 5:23 train to connect with the 10:07. (*He steps back into the set and picks up the suitcase again.*) For the last time, Dorli, I'm going. (*He knocks on the wardrobe.*) Hello? (*Loud sawing is heard outside.*) I've given them the list—the list of your property. Nothing that you brought into the marriage will be touched. All will be completely untouched. I'm going off with a shirt and a toothbrush, as you can see, and I'm leaving behind your India-paper edition of Goethe. . . . I have no doubt that you'll be able to find a job and support yourself very nicely. . . . Give my best regards to all your family. . . . We'll never see each other again. . . . In case any mail comes for me during the next few years—

(*The Young Moving Man comes in carrying the armchair with its legs sawn off; the seat is now about four inches off the floor.*)

YOUNG MAN: There's somebody out in the hall, Doctor Hotz.

HOTZ: I'm not entertaining any visitors now.

YOUNG MAN: He says he wants to talk to the lady. (*A puff of smoke comes from the wardrobe.*)

HOTZ: I absolutely refuse to be responsible for this!

Hotz exits, and the Young Moving Man, who has grown curious, turns the key, which is in the lock, and opens the wardrobe. Out steps Dorli, a delicate and, despite her tear-stained face, somehow charming person; in her hand she holds a cigarette.)

DORLI: Do we have an ash tray left? (*The Young Moving Man hands her an ash tray. Dorli stubs out her cigarette and, going to the telephone, dials a number.*) Hotz, yes, Mrs. Hotz. Can I speak to my lawyer. (*To the Young Moving Man:*) Thanks a lot! (*Into the receiver:*) Hello!—We've been trying for three hours now, but . . . What's that? Yes, he's doing it; he's not just saying it anymore, he's doing it. Pardon me? No, I didn't say one single word to him. After all, what can I do when he just locks me up in the wardrobe like that? (*To the Young Moving Man:*) You're my witness. (*She puts down the receiver.*) Even my lawyer won't believe me about this.

(*Men's voices are heard from outside. Dorli slips behind a curtain, while Hotz [still in his unbuttoned raincoat and holding a screwdriver] shows in a visitor who is rubbing his hands together.*)

WILFRED: Who would have believed it, Philip, who would have believed it! A few minutes ago I landed, and here I am already. And who would have believed it! I still feel a little dazed—three long years in the Argentine, three years in that climate, you just can't have any idea, three years spent doing nothing but making money, no, you just can't have any idea. . . . (*He glances about.*) Unchanged, unchanged—everything unchanged! (*Embarrassed pause.*) And you, Philip, old pal, are you still a writer? (*Wilfred laughs and slaps him on the back.*) Philip, my dear old friend!

HOTZ: Wilfred—

WILFRED: No, my friend, you can't have any idea how it feels—three years over there, and no sooner have you set foot on your own soil, no sooner have you landed, than you feel completely at home all over again.

HOTZ: Please, do sit down. (*He moves the legless armchair into position.*) Please.

(*Wilfred sits down as if all were as usual. The sawing outside is resumed. Hotz straddles the grandfather clock and begins to take it apart with his screwdriver; Wilfred takes out a cigar.*)

WILFRED: Tell me—how is Dorli? (*He lights his cigar and smokes.*) Is she still making ceramics?

HOTZ: Not at present.

WILFRED: Where is she, then? (*Hotz stands up and goes to the door.*)

HOTZ: Gentlemen, take the wardrobe out. (*To Wilfred.*) Excuse me (*To the Moving Men.*) But please don't drop it! (*The Moving Men take up their straps.*) Wilfred, my friend, what can I offer you? I don't think we have any glasses left, though. Gin? Campari? Whisky? (*The Moving Men tip the wardrobe.*) Stop! Are you out of your minds? Yes, stop that! I warned you especially about not dropping—

OLD MAN: But you see the doorway's a little too low and—

HOTZ: Then—please—take it out onto the balcony. (*He opens the door to the balcony. To Wilfred:*) Excuse me. (*He mops his brow while the Moving Men carry the wardrobe out onto the balcony.*)

WILFRED: Why don't you try taking off your raincoat, since you're so hot?

HOTZ: (*locking the wardrobe and putting the key in his pocket*): Thanks a lot.

(*The two Moving Men go out with their straps dragging behind them, while Hotz once again straddles the grandfather clock and begins to take it apart. Wilfred puffs on his cigar.*)

WILFRED: I asked how Dorli's doing these days. . . . (*Hotz detaches the pendulum and tosses it away.*) You'd tell me if I'd come at the wrong moment, right, Philip?

HOTZ: On the contrary.

WILFRED: Word of honor?

H

HOTZ: You can hold the screws for me. (*He drops the screws in his hand.*) Also you can answer a question for me. (*He removes the clockface and tosses it away.*) Do you think marriage works?

WILFRED: Which marriage?

HOTZ: Marriage in general. (*The mainspring pops out.*)

WILFRED: Hurt yourself? (*Hotz sucks his finger.*) Tell me, what actually are you doing there?

HOTZ: I'm disassembling an old clock.

WILFRED: Why?

HOTZ: Because I don't have any sense of humor.

WILFRED: Philip—!

HOTZ: Do you think I have any sense of humor?

WILFRED: No.

HOTZ: So there you are.

WILFRED: Who told you that?

HOTZ: Dorli, my consort and companion—whom you know of course. She says first of all that I'm not a man: I only talk; I never practice what I preach. Unlike you, for example. Her lawyer goes a step further, because I pay him to, and says: "Your husband is schizoid." Secondly, I have no sense of humor. Unlike you, for example. I lost my sense of humor, according to Dorli, the moment I was born. (*Wilfred can't help laughing.*) I think it's nice of you, Wilfred, to be able to laugh just the same. . . . (*The Old Moving Man brings in the legless table.*) Thanks.

OLD MAN: What's next?

HOTZ: Our wine cellar. All the bottles are to be uncorked. But I'll see to that personally; simply bring the bottles in here.

(*The Old Moving Man goes out.*)

WILFRED: Very convenient! (*He runs his hand over the low table.*) Most comfortable!

HOTZ: You think so?

WILFRED: You know, even though you haven't got any sense of humor—you know, you've got some good ideas. (*Hotz sucks his injured finger again.*) Have you ever lived in Japan? (*Hotz shakes his head, still sucking finger.*) Your own original idea? (*Hotz nods, still sucking finger.*) Three years in the Argentine, no, you have absolutely no idea how one longs for just this kind of thing—for taste, for culture and so on and so forth: for comfort and convenience.

HOTZ: To come back to our question. (*He drops a screw into Wilfred's hand.*) Do you really love her?

WILFRED: My wife?

HOTZ: Mine! (*Wilfred starts.*) Don't lose my screws now.

(*A loud noise; the Young Moving Man enters.*)

YOUNG MAN: I'm sorry, sir, but that was the only way to do it.

HOTZ: What was it?

YOUNG MAN: The innerspring mattress.

HOTZ: Fine, thanks. (*The Young Moving Man goes out.*) To come back to our question:—

WILFRED: Enough of that, now!

HOTZ: So you really think that marriage works?

WILFRED (*jumping up*):—Or I'll throw your screws straight out that window! Straight out!

HOTZ (*resuming the unscrewing*): I've always envied you your sense of humor, Wilfred. There's no need to lose it now, merely because I am unable to laugh at the fact of your having slept with my wife.

WILFRED: Philip!

HOTZ: Are you going to hold the screws for me, my friend, or aren't you? (*Wilfred stands with his back to Hotz.*) I don't understand your indignation. (*The Old Moving Man comes in and throws down some assorted sticks of wood.*)

HOTZ: What was that?

OLD MAN: The bedstead.

HOTZ: Thanks. (*The Old Moving Man goes out.*) To come back to my question. (*The telephone rings.*) Excuse me. (*He speaks into the receiver:*) Yes, it's me, Hotz—in person. (*He puts the receiver down.*) Give me those screws! (*He takes the screws from Wilfred and throws them out of the window; then he picks up the receiver again.*) Are you still there? Yes, I am—what was that again? (*He places his hand over the mouthpiece.*) Do you think that I'm making disturbing noises? (*He listens again, ear to receiver.*) I guess that must have been the grandfather clock falling over; I own only one grandfather clock, Mrs. Oppikofer, so I can promise you that it will never happen again. Pardon me? (*He tucks the receiver under his arm and searches though his pockets.*) Yes —here's the key!

WILFRED: What key?

HOTZ: You came to see Dorli—take it! She's in the wardrobe.

WILFRED: Dorli?

HOTZ: Yes—outside on the balcony there. (*He holds out the key, but Wilfred doesn't take it.*) I'll answer you as soon as you stop shouting like that, Mrs. Oppikofer. (*He places his hand over mouthpiece.*) How is your dear Clarissa? (*He speaks into the receiver.*) No, Mrs. Oppikofer, *I'm* the one who's giving *you* notice. I'm coming down at once. (*He hangs up.*) I've never had so many unpleasant things to do in one day before in my whole life. I'm even surprising myself: I'm not usually such a man of action. . . . (*He finds a comb and quickly combs his hair.*) I *mustn't* lose my anger now!

(*The Old Moving Man comes in carrying a large vase, from which he strips a layer of wrapping paper; then he turns to Wilfred.*)

OLD MAN: Is this the lady's property?

WILFRED: That—hey, what's the big idea, just unpacking it that way, without asking?—that's a genuine Inca vase.

OLD MAN: What's "Inca" mean?

WILFRED: Mind your own business.

OLD MAN: Is this for Mrs. Hotz?

WILFRED: You know I must say—you certainly . . .

OLD MAN: You certainly must say, or otherwise it'll be in pieces in a minute.

WILFRED: Mrs. Hotz and I have known each other since kindergarten—

OLD MAN: You mean it's the lady's property.

(*He puts the vase down and goes out again; Hotz has taken no notice: he has been combing his hair for his visit with Mrs. Oppikofer.*)

HOTZ: I *can't* lose my anger now!

(*He puts the comb in his pocket and goes out; Wilfred looks over at the wardrobe standing there outside on the balcony, and Dorli—behind his back—steps out of her hiding place.*)

DORLI: I must thank you—

WILFRED: Dorli!

DORLI: . . . for the lovely vase. (*He holds her by both shoulders, absolutely speechless.*) Give me a cigarette. (*Despite himself, he has to give her a cigarette.*)

WILFRED: Dorli, he knows everything.

DORLI: I know.

WILFRED: Who told him?

DORLI: I did. (*She takes the cigarette lighter from his outstretched hand, as he stares in astonishment.*) Well now—how are you?

(*Hotz emerges from the wings: he addresses the audience while Dorli addresses Wilfred:*)

HOTZ: Now, ladies and gentlemen, you will hear what I cannot hear—I'm downstairs with Mrs. Oppikofer, of course—but I can imagine it. (*He remains downstage, facing the audience.*)

DORLI: He's absolutely primitive!

HOTZ: She means me.

DORLI: He's self-centered!

HOTZ: That's me again.

DORLI: He never thinks of anybody but himself!

HOTZ: Now comes the expert opinion . . .

DORLI: He's positively schizophrenic!

HOTZ: Schizoid!

DORLI: Or whatever you call it. (*Hotz puts a cigarette to his lips.*)

HOTZ: Go on! (*He leaves it unlit, listening.*)

DORLI: Marriage as a spiritual partnership!

HOTZ: That's what I always thought it should be.

DORLI: Yes, yes—and with all other women a somewhat different kind of partnership. That would suit him just fine. Freedom in wedlock! *I* can do just exactly as *I* like. . . .

HOTZ: My wife is not my property.

DORLI: He is incapable of jealousy. What nonsense! Absolutely incapable. What nonsense! He places no blame on me whatsoever— (*Hotz slowly lights his cigarette.*) What's left to marriage then, anyway? (*Hotz smokes meditatively.*)

HOTZ: It's hopeless. I've spent seven years explaining what I mean by marriage—delivering lectures and dissertations, as my wife calls it—explaining that marriage, for me, is a partnership, a partnership in freedom and frankness. (*Dorli can't help laughing.*) A spiritual adventure. (*Dorli laughs again.*) Marriages aren't made in bed. (*Dorli can't help laughing again.*) What *I* say is that—

DORLI: If you only could hear the way he goes on—

HOTZ: A marriage founded simply on fidelity in bed—

DORLI: I know it by heart!

HOTZ: A marriage not in tune with the facts of real life—

DORLI: What nonsense. (*Dorli shouts at him:*) And is he ever jealous! (*Hotz shouts at her:*)

HOTZ: That's not so!

DORLI: He simply keeps all his feelings under control. And that's all there is to it. And so, you see, therefore I have no right to be jealous—

HOTZ (*smoking thoughtfully*): That's right: you have absolutely no right to be jealous.

DORLI: It's a mean, dirty, filthy trick, the way he controls those feelings of his!

HOTZ (*smoking thoughtfully*): No one, in fact, has any right to be jealous.

DORLI: Tomorrow morning it will be exactly a year since I first told him. About us, I mean. And today, *finally*, he shows his real anger. He's *that* introverted. Finally, *today*— (*The Young Moving Man walks in and dumps out a basketful of broken glass.*) Just look at him over there!

WILFRED: Wreckage, wreckage . . .

DORLI: Just because I withdrew my suit for divorce. Just look at him! Just because I said: "You'll never do it, Philip, I know you." (*The Old Moving Man dumps out a basketful of broken glass.*)

WILFRED: But what's the point of all this?

DORLI: Just so I take him seriously the next time he gets angry and starts insisting that our marriage isn't working— (*Dorli shakes her head.*) The curtains! The furniture! The pictures! Did you ever see anything like it!—Just because the divorce court judge told him he was an educated man. (*Dorli takes out a cigarette.*)

HOTZ: Now, finally, her amazement's beginning! (*Hotz steps back into the set and offers her a light with his cigarette lighter.*)

WILFRED: Well, will you look at that—even those beautiful glasses I gave you are there in the wreckage. . . . (*Dorli exhales a puff of smoke, and Hotz steps out of the set.*)

DORLI: And still I love him! (*Hotz is now downstage again, facing the audience, smoking.*) But I can't go running down to the station every time he decides to join the Foreign Legion and go dragging him off the steps to the train—just to convince him that I take him seriously. (*She begins to cry again.*)

WILFRED: Why did he shut you up in the wardrobe like that?

HOTZ: She knows perfectly well why.

WILFRED: Well, why?

HOTZ: Go ahead—tell him!

DORLI: Because—just because—because I simply said:— "You'll never do it—never, Philip—I know you!" (*She breaks down once more.*)

HOTZ: It strikes me as worthy of note that Wilfred, my old friend Wilfred, hasn't even thought of touching my wife since he's heard that we're getting divorced.

DORLI: Because—just because—I simply said to him:—"You'll never do it, Philip—never—you've been saying that for seven years. . . ." (*Hotz steps into the set to offer her an ash tray.*) And yet I'm so very happy in our marriage! (*Dorli puts her cigarette into the ash tray, and Hotz goes out, carrying it.*) Why do I have to get a divorce? (*Wilfred puts his arm around her.*)

WILFRED: Oh, Dorli!

DORLI: Oh, Wilfred!

HOTZ: Now he's going to work!

WILFRED: Do you love him?

HOTZ: Yes, so you have nothing to worry about. (*Wilfred strokes her hair.*) Please, please—don't mind me. (*Hotz takes out a cigarette—although he is already smoking one.*) Perhaps, ladies and gentlemen, you think it rather self-centered of me to imagine that the two of them are talking so much about me. But that's the way it is! I'm the only topic of conversation that hasn't completely died out on them. (*Hotz lights the second cigarette.*)

WILFRED: And do you think he loves you, too?

HOTZ: That's what she thinks, all right.

DORLI: Why is he always trying to impress me? He blames all our adulterous acts on himself—to spare my feelings! And I'm supposed to go on playing the Madonna. And why? Just so no mention can ever be made in court of the *thing*—the thing that makes the blood rush to his head, just so even his own lawyer can't see how jealous he is—my jealous, jealous Philip! No! He'd much rather take all the guilt on himself, he'd much rather pay alimony as the guilty party in the divorce suit and ruin himself until he's sixty—simply to impress me. . . . (*Dorli stamps her foot.*) I won't let him impress me! (*Suddenly she starts to shout.*) And I won't let him divorce me! Even if it takes the rest of my life, I'm going to stay his wife until he admits it! Until my Philip absolutely admits it!

HOTZ: What? (*Also shouting:*) Admits what!?

DORLI (*calming down again*): No primitive shouting was ever actually involved, no, none of that—but still, somehow, inwardly, it was always possible to sense it: essentially, he's behaving exactly like a cave man.

HOTZ (*shouting even louder than before*): It takes one to know one!

DORLI (*rushing up to Wilfred*): Oh, Wilfred!

WILFRED: Oh, Dorli! (*Wilfred and Dorli embrace.*)

HOTZ: Finally! (*Hotz is very embarrassed while they kiss.*) What I really meant to say before was: actually *I* can't really know what's going on up here—actually I, at this very moment, am downstairs with Mrs. Oppikofer. (*He stamps out his cigarette.*) Gentlemen, don't look! I'm not looking myself. We can easily imagine all this. And if you are ever in my position, gentlemen, I suggest to you that— (*He looks, anyway.*) How very idyllic! (*An enormous crash is heard.*)

WILFRED: What was that?

DORLI: I've no idea.

WILFRED: Gentlemen, if you don't immediately—but immediately —stop that damned commotion— (*Another crash.*) What are you doing with that genuine Bechstein grand piano—!? (*Sound in the background of a long series of snapping strings.*)

HOTZ: Division of Property: . . . (*Dorli starts to cry.*) "If the division of the property takes place during the marriage, the property formerly shared by the spouses mutually is separated into the property of the husband and the property of the wife." (*Another crash.*) Matrimonial Claims Law, Section

H*

One, Article 189. (*He buttons his collar.*) As I was saying, ladies and gentlemen, actually, at this particular moment, I'm downstairs with Mrs. Oppikofer. (*He exits.*)

WILFRED: Why did you tell him?

DORLI: He's the one who told *me*.

WILFRED: Told you what?

DORLI: About Clarissa.

WILFRED: Clarissa?

DORLI: Frankness! I can be frank too—nothing could be easier! If he wants frankness as the basis of the marriage, he can have it!

WILFRED: What has Philip to do with my wife?

DORLI: Exactly what *you* have to do with *me*. (*She wipes away the tears with her handkerchief.*) You didn't know?

(*Hotz walks out onto the stage. A sheet of paper is in his hand.*)

HOTZ (*addressing the audience*): I've given notice that, forthwith and immediately, I'm canceling our lease. (*He tears up the document.*)

WILFRED: You mean my Clarissa—?

DORLI: Don't yell.

WILFRED: My dear Clarissa?

DORLI: Do you want the whole building to hear you?

WILFRED: Women! . . . Whores! (*He exits.*)

DORLI: Now *he's* being the primitive one. (*She follows him out.*)

HOTZ (*addressing the audience*): Now I have only to bid a few final adieux. (*He calls out to the empty set.*) Gentlemen! (*The two Moving Men come out, sandwiches in hand.*) Bring the wardrobe in here immediately; it's pouring out there. (*He remains downstage, facing the audience.*) No, ladies and gentlemen, I'm not schizoid. I'll admit to you that in my thoughts and imaginings I was here, while I was downstairs terminating my lease, and I imagined what my wife and my friend were saying about me. But I know perfectly well that my wife—*in reality*—is locked up, there, in that wardrobe. I'm not schizoid! (*He steps back into the set. The Moving Men carry in the wardrobe.*) Everything going nicely? (*With mouths still full, they nod their heads.*) Is it very heavy? (*They shake their heads.*) I envy you your strength. (*They return the wardrobe to its original location in the room.*) Again, many thanks! (*The Moving Men go out, their straps dragging behind them; Hotz waits until they have left, then addresses the wardrobe.*) Dorli? Did you get a little wet out there? (*He knocks on the wardrobe.*) Dorli? (*He picks up his little suitcase.*) I'm going now, Dorli—going off to join the Foreign Legion. (*He puts his ear to the wardrobe.*) Why are you holding your breath again?! (*He stands there, very puzzled.*) I think it's disgraceful, Dorli, the way you're treating me. You've been playing at holding your breath for seven years now, and every single time you try it, you scare me out of my wits and make me think I've killed you. . . . Dorli, that's no way to run a marriage! You simply rely on the fact that I love you, and do just as you like with me! Just as you like! Just because you're weaker than I am. (*He picks up his little suitcase again.*) Listen, I'm going now. (*He looks at his wristwatch.*) I have to catch a train to Geneva at 5:23, and make a connection at Marseilles at 10:07. If you feel sorry later today for keeping silent now, Dorli, you can write to me care of *Poste Restante*, Poste de la Gare, Marseilles. . . . (*Churchbells begin to ring mutedly in the distance.*) Farewell! (*Enter the Young Moving Man.*)

YOUNG MAN: Sir? (*Hotz starts a little.*) About the radio. I'd just like to say that if you don't want to sell anything, sir, that's a great hi-fi set you have there—radios are something I know about. With a pre-amp, too. Could you tell me if it would be okay just to smash it up a little, so I can take it home and fix it later?

HOTZ: Yes, yes, of course.

YOUNG MAN: You see, sir, I'm going to get married myself and . . .

HOTZ: Yes, yes, of course. (*The Young Moving Man goes out again.*) I said "Farewell!" (*A new bell begins to ring out above the other chiming.*) Tomorrow will be Easter. . . .

Our Easter Sunday in Rome, Dorli, it was only a year ago, ah yes—but all the same, I'm going now. (*He kisses the wardrobe.*) Good luck be with you. (*Enter Dorli, her arms full of paper bags.*)

HOTZ: Dorli?

DORLI: Yes—

HOTZ: No—

DORLI: What's the matter?

HOTZ (*staring at her and digging in his pocket*): Just a moment, just a moment. (*He pulls out the key and opens the wardrobe.*) Dorli? . . . Dorli? . . . Dorli— (*He flings all the clothing inside the wardrobe outside it, until it is empty; then, pulling his head out, to Dorli:*) I never want to see you again! (*The Old Moving Man comes in carrying a violin.*)

OLD MAN: Excuse me, sir, but we have to finish up on this job now—and I was wondering whether this was the lady's property.

HOTZ: My violin?

OLD MAN: It says on this list: one antique violin, Italian, with accessories, late eighteenth century, from Aunt Bertha—but then the whole thing is crossed out again.

HOTZ: Crossed out?

OLD MAN: Right—what's that supposed to mean?

DORLI: It means that once you actually bought it from me, Philip.

OLD MAN: That's what I wanted to know. (*Hotz stares at him.*) In other words, it doesn't belong to Mrs. Hotz, right?

HOTZ: No.

OLD MAN: That's all I wanted to know. (*The Old Moving Man breaks the violin across his knee, and exits.*)

HOTZ: I never want to see you again! (*Hotz exits.*)

DORLI: Where are you going? (*She sits down in front of the low table and begins to take some food out of her paper bags.*) Are you as absolutely ravenous as I am?

HOTZ (*coming out of the wings and addressing the audience*): This time I forgot my suitcase. (*He rubs his chin.*)

(*Dorli goes on talking as if Hotz were still outside in the hall.*)

DORLI: Philip—will you have salami or will you have cheese? (*She butters some bread.*)

HOTZ (*addressing the audience*): I can't understand why she isn't in that wardrobe. I had the key in my own trousers pocket. The wardrobe was locked. It gets harder and harder to figure her out. (*He takes out a cigarette.*) Just this final cigarette! (*He lights it.*)—And then I'm off with my little suitcase.

DORLI: Your sandwich is ready now. (*She calls out in a friendly voice:*) Philip? (*She turns around, to see the two Moving Men entering.*)

YOUNG MAN: We're all finished now, ma'am.

DORLI: If you'd like a tip, my husband is outside in the hall.

OLD MAN: No, he isn't.

DORLI: Then try the landing.

OLD MAN: What if he's not there, either?

DORLI: In that case he'll be sitting around in the Café Morocco.

(*The Moving Men don their caps.*) Happy Easter! (*The Moving Men file out glumly, in silence.*) Philip? (*Hotz steps back, into the set.*)

HOTZ: I'm going now. (*He picks up the suitcase.*) Farewell.

(*Dorli looks at him incredulously.*)

DORLI: But I'm not angry with you.

HOTZ: Dorli—

DORLI: Really, Philip, why have you kept your raincoat on all day this way? (*Dorli takes a bite out of her sandwich.*)

HOTZ: Listen—I'm going now. (*He looks at his wristwatch.*) Do you happen to know the right time?

DORLI: It's exactly forty-eight minutes after four.

HOTZ (*winding up his wristwatch*): This is no way to run a marriage, Dorli. You always do just as you like with me—just because you're weaker than I am.

DORLI: But what do I do?

HOTZ: I have to catch a train to Geneva at 5:23, and make a connection at Marseilles at 10:07. If you feel sorry later today for keeping silent now, Dorli, you can write to me care of *Poste Restante*, Poste de la Gare, Marseilles.

DORLI: But I'm not keeping silent in the least.

HOTZ: But now I have to go.

DORLI: Where to?

HOTZ: Farewell. (*Pause; the sound of bells.*)

DORLI: When will you be back? (*Pause; the sound of bells.*)

HOTZ: Tomorrow it will be Easter Sunday . . . our Easter Day in Rome, ah me, that's a year ago already—but I'm going just the same.

(*Dorli butters another slice of bread as Hotz, finally, goes.*)

DORLI: By the way, I didn't buy any smoked salmon today. I guess we'll have to be pretty thrifty from now on, Philip; it's been quite an expensive day for you. . . .

HOTZ (*stepping from the wings, suitcase in hand, and addressing the audience*): If she comes out now to call me back, even if—as in recent years—she only comes out as far as the doorway—then it means she believes once again that someday, someday, I'll really go—and then it won't be necessary for me to go. (*He looks at his wristwatch.*) I hope her watch is right! (*He holds his own watch to his ear and winds it again.*)

DORLI (*after looking around the room and seeing that nobody is there; calling out*): Philip! Would you like a little pickled herring before you go?

HOTZ (*addressing the audience*): I wonder if they'll actually take me when I get to Marseilles?

DORLI (*as if answering the doorbell*): Come in! (*Enter a lady pulling off her gloves.*)

CLARISSA: I'm absolutely beside myself!

DORLI: You—

CLARISSA: He actually boxed my ears!

DORLI: Who?

CLARISSA: Wilfred, my husband.

DORLI (*clearing aside the debris of lunch*): Sit down.

CLARISSA (*throwing down her gloves*): I'd like to know just what you meant by telling my husband that I had an affair with your husband?

DORLI: Because Philip told me he had.

CLARISSA: Philip?

DORLI: Yes.

CLARISSA: I'm beside myself.

DORLI (*resuming eating*): That's one of his favorite ideas, you know—frankness as the basis of marriage.

CLARISSA (*picking up her gloves again*): We never had anything to do with one another. (*She throws down her first glove.*) Never! (*She throws down her second glove.*) Never! (*She bursts into tears.*)

HOTZ (*addressing the audience*): If Dorli hears, now, that I've never been unfaithful to her—and if she believes it—then she'll never believe anything I ever tell her again! And then I'll *really* have to leave.

DORLI: I really don't know why we women don't try to stick together. It's an absolute shame. We went all through school together, but just as soon as we became grownup, adult women, than we set our sights on only one goal: to please men, and to deceive our spiritual sisters. (*She holds out a paper bag to Clarissa.*)

CLARISSA: No, thanks.

DORLI (*taking an apple from the paper bag for herself*): And you came all the way from Argentina just to tell me it isn't true! How was the flight?

CLARISSA: Simone—

DORLI: There's no need to start getting formal now.

CLARISSA: It isn't true!

DORLI (*polishing her apple*): I asked you—how was the flight? (*Dorli bites into her apple.*)

CLARISSA: What must I do, Simone, to make you believe me?

DORLI: Nothing. (*Offering bag.*) Apples aren't fattening.

CLARISSA: Do you think I'm fat?

DORLI: Let's stick to the subject. (*Chewing her apple.*) Our subject was husbands.

CLARISSA: Mine or yours?

DORLI: Mine! (*Clarissa laughs.*) I'm *not* going to be divorced, do you hear—and certainly not on your account! (*Dorli shouts:*) Certainly not on your account!!

HOTZ (*addressing the audience*): Already they've begun to screech at one another. (*Looking at his wristwatch:*) Well, this can't last too long.

CLARISSA: It simply isn't true! I'll tell it to the whole world: it simply isn't true! We had nothing to do with one another!

HOTZ (*addressing audience*): I'm going to miss my train. (*He looks at his wristwatch.*) What the devil has it to do with the world anyway if we never had anything to do with one another—what business is it of the world's, anyway?

(*Meanwhile, the two women have resumed an exaggerated dignity and calm.*)

DORLI: Must you be going so soon?

CLARISSA: Oh! I see you've grown a bit thin.

DORLI: And you haven't answered my question yet.

CLARISSA: Very thin, in fact.

DORLI: Why isn't Philip your type? (*Clarissa shrugs.*) You really don't know my husband—

CLARISSA: That's exactly what I keep trying to tell you.

DORLI: You can say what you like against my husband, and against all men in general, but there's nobody else in the world who'd admit to an adultery that never even took place—and in public, too.

CLARISSA: Your husband is a writer; after all—

DORLI: And what do you mean by that? (*Clarissa rises.*) My husband doesn't tell lies! (*Clarissa goes over her make-up.*) Clarissa, I'll tell you something. (*Dorli puts her arm around Clarissa.*) Between sisters, so to speak.

CLARISSA: I'd rather you didn't, darling.

DORLI: Well then, stop clutching me like that! (*She releases her hold on Clarissa.*) Well, I'm going to tell you anyway:—

CLARISSA (*starting to do her lips*): Your Philip just doesn't interest me.

DORLI: Philip is the shyest man on earth. He's so shy that he does sometimes lie to me, when we're alone. He's *that* shy. But the moment he realizes somebody else can hear—he just stops dead.

CLARISSA: Oh.

DORLI: Yes, it's strange.

CLARISSA: So he doesn't tell lies—is that right?

DORLI: Right; under no circumstances; absolutely not. That's why I can't stand the things Philip writes: the moment he detects the presence of the public, he speaks truths—about marriage for example—which he would never reveal here between our

CLARISSA (*picking up her gloves once more*): In other words, you don't believe me. (*Dorli takes another apple out of the bag.*) Simone! (*Clarissa begins to put her gloves on.*) Nothing happened! I give you my word! Absolutely nothing at all!

DORLI: I don't care to hear the details . . .

HOTZ (*addressing the audience*): Now I'm going! (*He picks up his suitcase.*) And yet—I hesitate. But why? I've got my suit-
four walls.
case. . . .

CLARISSA: Happy Easter!

DORLI (*Standing, still gnawing on her apple*): Happy Easter! (*Clarissa exits.*) Have you ever seen two women who would believe one another in anything concerning the same man? (*Enter Hotz, without Dorli noticing.*) Happy Easter! (*Hotz, thinking Dorli is dismissing him, retreats downstage. Dorli tosses away her apple.*) That fat old cow!

HOTZ (*addressing the audience*): She never used to be quite that nasty. That's something new she's got there! She used to be —well, I can't exactly describe it—but she was never quite that nasty. (*He mimics her voice.*) "Happy Easter!" (*He seems radiant with hope.*) At least that's a new note she's got there! (*He steps back into the set. Dorli has sat back down at the low table and is fumbling in her paper bag.*)

HOTZ: I'm going now.

DORLI (*starting*): Good heavens!

HOTZ (*setting himself squarely in front of her*): Yes, I'm going now.

DORLI (*eyeing him*): Good heavens, I've gone and forgotten the tomatoes! (*She again fumbles in her bag.*)

HOTZ: I'm going now. (*He waits a little longer, then goes.*)

DORLI: No! they're right here! (*She extracts a tomato.*)

(*The bells in the background stop pealing. Hotz steps out of the wings, raincoat over arm, and addresses the audience.*)

HOTZ: It was a melancholy journey to Geneva—at least while I tried to keep up my anger, furious, there alone in my first-class carriage—and until I admitted to myself what total idiocy it would be to try and go on with it.

REFRESHMENT VENDOR: Cigarettes, cigares, journaux, chocolats!

HOTZ: She was right. It was too much to expect Dorli to go chasing to the station once a year, every spring, to drag me off the steps to the train like that, just to convince me that she's taking me seriously.

REFRESHMENT VENDOR: Cigarettes, cigares, journaux, chocolats!

HOTZ: But anyway, at least now I know she doesn't really take me seriously.

(*The sound of a train entering a station is heard.*)

DORLI (*standing at the telephone in the Hotz apartment*): Philip! . . . Yes, I'm at home. Hello? And where are you? In a telephone booth? Hello? Hello? I can't understand what you're saying. Where? There's so much static on the line. Hello? It's better now . . . What do you mean you're in Geneva! (*She slowly puts down the receiver, at a loss for words, while the rumble of a train is heard; then she begins dialing a number.*)

HOTZ (*addressing the audience*): What did I expect? I might have known Dorli would be sitting there at home; that bitch never even thought of— (*Enter a Customs Officer.*)

CUSTOMS OFFICER: Schweizer Zollkontrolle. Douane Suisse.

HOTZ (*as he hands him his passport*): How could I have had so much faith in her?

CUSTOMS OFFICER: Haben Sie Handelsware?

HOTZ: I'm really very annoyed with myself.

CUSTOMS OFFICER: Ob Sie Handelsware haben? (*Hotz points to his little suitcase.*) Aufmachen bitte. (*The Customs Officer holds up a shirt, a toothbrush, and pajamas.*) Vielen Dank! (*Hotz packs his suitcase again.*)

HOTZ: The only chance Dorli had left was if they had decided to go over me with a fine-tooth comb—I might have missed the train then. (*The Customs Officer has in the meantime switched caps.*)

CUSTOMS OFFICER: Bon soir, monsieur.

HOTZ: I jumped nervously.

CUSTOMS OFFICER: Votre passport, s'il vous plaît. (*Trembling and shaking, Hotz hands him his passport.*)

HOTZ: But he wasn't in the least suspicious. . . . (*The Customs Officer hands back the passport.*)

CUSTOMS OFFICER: Est-ce que vous avez des marchandises? (*Hotz points to his suitcase.*)

CUSTOMS OFFICER: Ouvrir, s'il vous plaît. (*The Customs Officer holds up the shirt, the toothbrush, and the pajamas.*) Bon voyage monsieur. (*Hotz packs again; the Customs Officer exits.*)

HOTZ: Nobody stopped or even delayed me. . . .

DORLI (*in the apartment, standing at the telephone*): Operator, can you find out for me whether that last call really came from Geneva? About five minutes ago. Thank you. (*She waits, telephone in hand.*)

HOTZ (*addressing the audience*): It was quite warm in Marseilles. . . . (*He takes off his jacket.*) I arrived exactly as taps, or reveille, or whatever they call it, was sounding—but first I went into a little bistro there for a cup of coffee—my favorite breakfast.

(*Enter a waiter, yawning.*)

WAITER: Café?

HOTZ: Au lait. (*The waiter yawns again.*) Est-ce qu'il y a des brioches? (*The waiter nods, yawns, and exits.*) My favorite breakfast. (*He turns and looks around.*) Not a sign of my wife, naturally. (*Sound of bugles in the distance.*) And then it was too late.—

FINALE

(*While blaring military music is heard, with many bugles and drums, an iron grillwork, such as encircles barracks, descends from the flies, gray and draped with a dirty tricolor. Peering through this grillwork appears Dorli.*)

DORLI: Philip! . . . Philip?

(*Marching past, the following figures appear: two dusty legionnaires with rifles and fixed bayonets; behind them, Hotz with his little suitcase and his raincoat and jacket over his arm; then two more dusty legionnaires with rifles and fixed bayonets. Hotz stops to wave to Dorli, but the legionnaire just behind him nudges him with his rifle butt to make him march on. Behind the grillwork, Dorli sinks to her knees, sobbing bitterly:)*

Philip!—that's no place for you. . . .

(The military music fades away and the barracks fence floats back up into the flies. Dorli remains on her knees—back in the apartment—and weeps, as Hotz enters and sets down suitcase, raincoat, and jacket.)

DORLI: Philip—?

HOTZ: They didn't take me.

DORLI: —there you are!

HOTZ: Too nearsighted.

DORLI *(throwing her arms around his neck)*: Philip!

(Hotz strokes her hair, while Dorli rests blissfully against his chest; then, obviously far more out of embarrassment than unfeelingness—and to make light of the situation—he asks:)

HOTZ: Is there any mail for me?

CURTAIN

FREEDOM FOR CLEMENS

by TANKRED DORST

TRANSLATED BY GEORGE E. WELLWARTH

CHARACTERS

CLEMENS
CLEMENTINE
THE WARDEN

SCENE

A cell

AUTHOR'S NOTE

THE MOVEMENTS of the characters should be pointed, rapid, stylized, almost dance-like—they should in no way resemble the outdated informal attitude of old German regional farces. I suspect that this mode of presentation will create some difficulties for the actors at first. Accustomed to regulating their acting according to spoken lines, they are apt to stumble in the absence of transitional speeches. Here they must be jugglers and acrobats capable of using dialogue the way a tightrope-walker would use a pole to enable him to keep balance on a swaying rope. In order to assist the actors in this method of performance, it might be a good idea to play a Clementi sonatina as overture, or play rapid finger exercises on the piano at appropriate moments.

Tapping on the wall.

In the cell the Warden taps out a message on the wall.

The tapping is answered.

Clementine is bored.

THE WARDEN: No, that's out of the question! I've got no time for it! After all, I am the warden! (*He taps out a message.—To Clementine:*) Just imagine, the gentleman in the next cell there says he wants to dictate his memoirs to me!

CLEMENTINE (*bored*): And he's been in that cell ever since he was a little boy!

(*Tapping on the other wall.*)

THE WARDEN: What's that? Very well, thank you. Always polite, the old gentleman. He's one of the old school. (*More tapping.*) Thank you, thank you! (*He taps back.*) He sends greetings to my beautiful daughter Clementine.

CLEMENTINE (*bored*): But he only knows me through—(*she indicates the action of tapping*)—descriptions.

(*Renewed tapping.*)

THE WARDEN: Slowly! Slowly! That's the new fellow again naturally! Simply no manners at all! Well, he'll learn some all right! We'll teach him (*More tapping.*) A little more respect, you! More respect! (*He taps the code for "more respect." Timid answering taps.*) That's better! After all, this isn't a rest home here. You're a prisoner—understand? A prisoner! (*He taps the code for "prisoner."*)

CLEMENTINE: It's a pity that you're the only one who believes in this nonsense, Papa.

THE WARDEN: What nonsense?

CLEMENTINE: About the messages tapped on the wall.

THE WARDEN: Nonsense? What do you mean? I'm in charge here!

CLEMENTINE: You know perfectly well that I've seen someone going round behind the walls with a hammer and tapping here and there so that you can pretend you've got a prisoner behind every wall and that you're keeping close tabs on them.

(*More tapping.*)

THE WARDEN: This is . . . (*More tapping.*) . . . I'll . . . (*More tapping.*) . . . You can rely on that! (*More tapping. Angered at the interruption by the tapping:*) Quiet!

CLEMENTINE (*to a stagehand in the wings*): You can take a break now. (*Tapping stops.*) Well, what do you say to that?

THE WARDEN (*disconcerted*): Yes, it's true . . . the cells are empty! I am the warden, and I guard empty cells! If the Chief ever finds out about it, I'll be fired.

CLEMENTINE: You don't have to panic right away, Papa. There are always opportunities to stock up on prisoners.

THE WARDEN (*paying attention*): What's that?

CLEMENTINE (*looking out through the bars*): Just a bunch of spectators. I promise you, though . . .

THE WARDEN: It's no good!

CLEMENTINE: . . . just as soon as we have one . . .

THE WARDEN: But we don't have one!

CLEMENTINE: . . . we'll keep him nice and comfy in here, you and I. We'll keep him so nice and comfy, he'll never get away.

THE WARDEN (*deeply moved*): My daughter Clementine! Clementine, my daughter!

CLEMENTINE: I want to take one more look out of the window!

THE WARDEN: I still know my business! I've proved myself! Name? I know all about handling prisoners! Harshly: Name? (*His mechanical mustache snaps ill-temperedly down.*) Or affably: You can call me by my first name! (*His mechanical mustache snaps up.*) And then again . . .

CLEMENTINE (*at the window*): There! There! There's one coming! They're just handing him over!

THE WARDEN: Crime?

CLEMENTINE: Snappy-looking young fellow.

WARDEN: Name?

CLEMENTINE: He's whistling a song. (*She sings:*) "In Toledo we fight the wild, wild bulls. . . ."

THE WARDEN: It won't be long now. (*He taps on all the walls:*) A prisoner's coming! (*Answering taps.*) Thank you! Thank you! They're congratulating me. I'll bring him up. And you promise me, Clementine, my daughter . . .

CLEMENTINE: He'll never get out again, Papa.

(*Warden exits. Clementine looks out of the window again, inspects the audience, and exits rapidly, slamming the door.*)

VOICE OF THE WARDEN (*harsh tone of command*): This way—to the left!

The door of the cell is unlocked with some difficulty. A friendly voice says, "Thank you." Immediately afterward Clemens, a young man with an ordinary, undistinguished face, enters. He is wearing his Sunday suit and holds a battered pasteboard suitcase. The Warden enters after him and awkwardly shuts the door.

CLEMENS (*puts his suitcase down*): Aha. So this is my room.

THE WARDEN (*harshly*): Cell.

CLEMENS: Very nice!

THE WARDEN (*brutally*): Cold!

CLEMENS: Makes sleeping easier.

THE WARDEN: Below zero in winter.

CLEMENS: Oh, by then I'll be far . . .

THE WARDEN: Take your shoes off!

CLEMENS: That's very considerate of you. My feet really do ache from standing around so long waiting for all the formalities to be cleared and so forth and so forth and so forth. (*He takes his shoes off.*)

THE WARDEN: It's because of the shoelaces. (*He rips out the shoelaces.*)

CLEMENS: Do you need them?

THE WARDEN: Shoelaces are not allowed here.

CLEMENS: Oh, I see.

THE WARDEN (*irritated by the prisoner's guilelessness*): Do you know why not?

CLEMENS: I can't imagine.

THE WARDEN: So that you don't hang yourself.

CLEMENS: Oh, I see. (*Mystified:*) Very good of you.

THE WARDEN: I know what I'm doing, believe me. You're not allowed to leave the cell.

CLEMENS (*nods*): Regulations are regulations.

THE WARDEN (*shows Clemens the door*): Triple locks.

CLEMENS (*trying to appear interested*): Nothing like being absolutely sure.

THE WARDEN: The sliding window for the food tray.

CLEMENS: Practical.

THE WARDEN: Three times a day—if you obey the rules.

CLEMENS: Don't worry about it.

THE WARDEN: Attempts to escape are out of the question.

CLEMENS: Why would I want to?

THE WARDEN: No talking to the other prisoners.

CLEMENS: Only to you!

THE WARDEN: Complaints will, of course, be forwarded to the appropriate authorities, but naturally they will tend to mitigate the relationship of trust between prisoners and officials. That would have awkward consequences.

CLEMENS: They're supposed to review my case again.

THE WARDEN: Are you trying to say that you have been treated unjustly? Are you trying to say that your superiors are in error?

CLEMENS: My superiors, never, but . . .

THE WARDEN: You are being treated severely but justly. You have no worries at all. Your stay in this institution is free of charge.

CLEMENS: That takes a weight off my mind.

THE WARDEN: In other words, you have six totally undisturbed months in which to think about your life.

CLEMENS: I'm thinking already.

THE WARDEN: Profitably, I hope.

CLEMENS: What I'm thinking is, if my stay in this room is free, why aren't I allowed to go free?

THE WARDEN: Because you have to be watched.

CLEMENS: But an unassuming person like myself is totally without importance.

THE WARDEN: Every prisoner is important.

CLEMENS: That's just a way of speaking.

THE WARDEN: I'll show you whether it's a way of speaking or not.

CLEMENS: Please don't exert yourself.

THE WARDEN (*angrily*): I'll decide whether to exert myself or not!

CLEMENS: I understand: you are the person on whom everything depends in this matter.

THE WARDEN: You are! (*Furious:*) I am completely without importance in the matter.

CLEMENS (*happily*): Good! In that case I permit you to leave.

THE WARDEN (*fuming*): And you stay! Face to the wall!

Clemens turns to the wall. Warden exits.

Clemens alone. He looks around the cell and notices its dreary emptiness. Then he notices the suitcase he has put down: delighted with it, he puts it on the plank-bed and ceremoniously opens it: it is empty. Clemens disappointed. He tries to take some objects out—a dressing gown, a book, a mirror, a musical instrument—but they seem to dissolve in his hands. He looks around and notices the barred window. He puts the suitcase on the bed in such a way that he can stand on it and look out of the window; but the suitcase collapses under him. He thinks again, jumps down from the bed, tries to break open the door, stops: he hears the tapping sounds. He listens to his heart, puts his ear to one wall, then to the other. He holds his hands over his ears, shakes the door again, and screams:

CLEMENS: Let me out of here! I'm not guilty! Let me out of here!

He turns away. A bouquet is carefully shoved through the sliding window. Amazed, Clemens takes it and begins to smile as he smells the artificial flowers. One of the flowers unfolds and a note drops out. Clemens startled: What should he do with the flowers? Where should he put them? What will happen when the Warden sees them? He looks anxiously at the door. The sliding panel has closed again. Clemens unfolds the note and reads:

"Songbirds want to sing."

He reads it again, shaking his head, mystified. Then he hears steps. Startled, he hides the note, gathers the flowers together, tries to stuff them into his pockets, and finally hides them under his hat. The Warden enters.

THE WARDEN (*severely*): We had baked potatoes and cream cheese.

CLEMENS: Yes, Warden.

THE WARDEN: You have been examined. Result: normal.

CLEMENS: Yes, Warden.

THE WARDEN: Digestive processes in order.

CLEMENS: Yes, Warden.

THE WARDEN: And you *still* want to get out?

CLEMENS: I haven't made any complaints.

THE WARDEN: Ah! In other words, you just went off your rocker a bit just now.

CLEMENS: I really don't know, Warden. I just thought I simply had to do something . . . after all, I can't just stop doing everything. . . .

THE WARDEN: Quite right! You've got to do something! Something sensible!

CLEMENS: But there isn't anything sensible to do in this cell except let people know I'm in it!

THE WARDEN: You could learn how to walk.

CLEMENS: Walk? But—I know how to walk.

THE WARDEN: You don't know how to walk properly.

CLEMENS: Like this: one two three four, one two—you really can't imagine how much walking I used to do. Sometimes, in spring, after it had rained, through the town park and over the narrow little bridge there, or to the office in the morning, or double-time up a little mountain path not more than a few inches wide, or across a fenced-off field, or . . .

THE WARDEN: You've been here a month now and you still haven't got it through your head that your way of "walking"—as you call it—isn't suitable in your present circumstances.

CLEMENS: Of course I can't walk properly in here, but out there, I swear to you, out there it's quite different. Out there you whistle a tune as you walk and you just start out in the morning—listen to this!—you just start out in the morning and the whole street is full of people walking to the right of you and to the left of you and in front of you and behind you—just like a huge procession—and all of them going to their factories or their offices! That's something you should see!

THE WARDEN: You can call yourself lucky you got here in time, before you got trapped in that.

CLEMENS: What do you mean—trapped?

THE WARDEN (jovially): I'll give you an example of something that happened in my own family to show you what I mean: a niece of mine, name of Gertrude—Gertie her parents called her, that is to say, that's what her mother called her, her father had been killed in the war—First World War, that is—twenty-one years old, perfectly responsible young woman, everything in order—walking with her fiancé in the town park one day and who do you think jumped out of the rhododendron bushes? Jack the Ripper, that's who! There—you see!

CLEMENS: But I don't have a fiancée—and I never got ripped up!

THE WARDEN (angrily): Nobody asked you about that!

CLEMENS: In that case there's no need to talk about it.

THE WARDEN (*nonplussed*): All right—I'll give you another example! An uncle of mine, that is to say, I just called him
uncle—my aunt never actually married him, for tax reasons,
you understand—anyway, this uncle went shopping every
morning for my aunt and her six kids. Well, he crosses the
street because the shop that sells gooseberry jam is on the
other side of the street. So what happens? A municipal garbage truck hits the curb so hard that . . .

CLEMENS: But I never eat gooseberry jam!

THE WARDEN (*angrily*): That's purely a matter of taste!

CLEMENS: In that case there's no need to talk about it.

THE WARDEN: All right—I'll give you another example! Twenty-
seven housewives are standing around, waiting for a streetcar.
No streetcar. A colleague of mine on vacation walks by, just
by chance. Because of his uniform the housewives take him
for a streetcar inspector. What happens? They beat him up
and break his nose.

CLEMENS: But I don't wear a uniform! I swear I'm not guilty!

THE WARDEN (*furious*): It's a matter of how you're dressed!

CLEMENS: But I *am* dressed!

THE WARDEN: You're impertinent!

CLEMENS: I'm a student!

THE WARDEN: I'm the head of a family!

CLEMENS: I'm a nature-lover!

THE WARDEN: How old are you?

CLEMENS: Twenty-seven.

THE WARDEN (*triumphantly*): Aha!—I'm fifty-four!

CLEMENS (*amiably*): You don't look it.

THE WARDEN (*furious*): What's that supposed to mean?—All
right, all right, if my experiences don't convince you, take
a look at the newspapers and see the truth about what happens on the outside!

CLEMENS: Truth—there's no such thing.

I

THE WARDEN: The truth is in the newspapers!

CLEMENS: But the newspapers are full of lies!

THE WARDEN: And that's why prisoners aren't allowed to read them.

CLEMENS (*protestingly*): I don't want to be a prisoner!

THE WARDEN (*furious*): That doesn't make any difference—you're still not supposed to read any newspapers!

CLEMENS (*forcefully*): I swear I wouldn't read one even if you gave it to me!

THE WARDEN: I've got strict orders!

CLEMENS: Too bad! I thought you were in charge here. I simply can't imagine anyone keeping an eye on you.

THE WARDEN (*flaring up*): Do you suppose people can trust their underlings? (*He stops, disconcerted by what he has just said; then he pulls a newspaper from his pocket.*) You have no idea of the risks I run for you. (*Clemens tries to take the newspaper.*) Just one moment, young man. You just sit down on that bench and keep your ears wide open. (*Clemens sits down on the plank-bed. Warden unfolds the newspaper, takes out a sandwich, and starts to eat.*) Well now, let's see what's going on out there in your beautiful never-never land where the birds always twitter in the trees.

CLEMENS: Well—go on!

THE WARDEN: I'll just read the headlines that catch my eye right now. "Student Gasses Himself." (*He looks questioningly at Clemens; Clemens remains silent.*) Twenty-four years old, scared of exams, parents divorced. "Man Runs Amok: Kills Nun." An unsuspecting nun! (*He looks at Clemens; Clemens remains silent.*) "Board of Health Orders Stray Dogs Killed." Well? Poor stray dogs—killed! Board of Health decree! That's the way things are out there where you can take your beautiful walks in the morning! (*He looks at Clemens. Clemens sighs but remains silent.*) "Barbaric Mother Murders Child." In her green-tiled bathroom! Its own mother! Her own child! (*He looks at Clemens. Clemens sighs, but remains silent.*) Well—leaves you speechless, doesn't it?

CLEMENS (*impressed*): But nothing like that ever happened to me.

THE WARDEN: Do you suppose a stray dog suspects the Board of Health's murderous intentions? Do you know any particularly pretty small towns?

CLEMENS (*warily*): Smithtown, Lewistown, Boontown . . .

THE WARDEN: Nice people live there?

CLEMENS: Sure!

THE WARDEN: Every year, on the average, the population of just such a town is wiped out in traffic accidents. (*Clemens is shocked.*) "Business Deals in Your Spare Time." Ha! You see, even when you're strolling around out there in the town park, you're really nothing but a dirty old business deal.

CLEMENS: Incredible!

THE WARDEN: Didn't I tell you how lucky you are that you've found a home here?

CLEMENS: If you look at it that way—yes. But if you'll permit me to look at it from another viewpoint, actually people out there aren't free as birds, the way your reports make it seem.

THE WARDEN: Are you trying to tell me I exaggerate?

CLEMENS: No, Warden, absolutely not. I merely wanted to point out that human freedom isn't as great as you make it seem.

THE WARDEN: As a prisoner that's not a point on which you're qualified to speak.

CLEMENS: What I meant, Warden, was that freedom has a few drawbacks, but that we can easily overlook them.

THE WARDEN (*confused and irritated*): Not before someone gives you permission to!

CLEMENS: Every free man has a right to!

THE WARDEN: It all depends on how you behave!

CLEMENS: Whether I'll be released?

THE WARDEN: Whether you'll be permitted to stay!

CLEMENS: Ah—now I understand! It's just that sometimes I get a feeling as if I were—how shall I put it?—well, locked up. . . . Can you understand that?

THE WARDEN (*impressively*): That is a symptom.

CLEMENS: What do you mean by that?

THE WARDEN: Crazy ideas—end up in a strait jacket.

CLEMENS: What can I do to counteract it?

THE WARDEN: How much longer have you got here?

CLEMENS: Another four months.

THE WARDEN: Learn to walk. I'll help you.

CLEMENS: That's really very good of you.

THE WARDEN: I've got my human side too.

CLEMENS: A man-to-man side.

THE WARDEN: You may call me by my first name.

CLEMENS: What is it?

THE WARDEN: Alfons.

CLEMENS (*shaking his hand*): Clemens.

THE WARDEN: I trust our association will be a lengthy and mutually profitable one.

CLEMENS: I'll do my best.

THE WARDEN: All right now, pay attention. Stand like this—there, that way! Now close your eyes—okay? And now forget you're in a cell and pretend you're out there in the town park and it's spring and you're walking—go on, that's the way! (*Clemens walks with his eyes closed.*) Quite calm, not a care in the world, completely relaxed—that's the way!

CLEMENS (*running into the wall of the cell*): Oh!

THE WARDEN: Very good! And now turn around—that's the way —keep your eyes closed! And now go back the way you came —go on, go on—relax, that's right—

CLEMENS (*running into the other wall*): Dammit, that hurts!

THE WARDEN: Can't be helped, can't be helped! You have to develop a feeling for the wall, m'boy. At first it's a bit of a shock and you get a bump on your head. Now, let's do it again—there! Very good! You see! (*Clemens stops in front of the wall with his eyes closed.*) There—now you've got it fixed in your head where the wall is. It used to be just something white and clean and empty. Now it's something that hurts. And all of a sudden you become more careful. A few more times and you won't have to watch at all. You'll be so used to it, it'll seem as if the wall is hot and getting hotter the nearer you get to it. Did you ever notice out there how blind people always seem to know exactly when they're in front of a wall? You can open your eyes now.

CLEMENS: Thank you.

THE WARDEN: And now for the second lesson: how to take long walks.

CLEMENS: That should be particularly difficult in here.

THE WARDEN: The whole trick is in not turning your corners too sharply. Curve around like a watch spring—this way!—and back again! And now to the left and now to the right—

CLEMENS (*walking*): That's nice!

THE WARDEN: And so simple! You just have to get the knack of it, know what I mean? (*Clemens continues to walk in spirals.*) It's also important not to make all your turns in front of the wall—these necessary turns have to be hidden, so to speak, among others. Now make a turn to the left—now one to the right—you can even risk a complete circle now, but not too fast and not too often or you'll end up on the lookout tower! There, that's it—see how many possibilities you can find without any trouble at all? Left—right—you're going great guns already! (*Clemens follows the Warden's instructions with closed eyes.*) There, you see—you feel where the wall is in time all by yourself now! Turn to the left—any direction now—there's a park for you! Not only that—it's an eighteenth-century park. A maze of curves and alleys— over there a nice white bench, right next to the statuette of Cupid, the God of French love! (*Clemens tries to sit down on the "nice white bench."*) Hold it! Wet paint! Walk some

more! Straight ahead! (*Clemens stops and opens his eyes.*)
Fine—and now just the proper way of holding yourself.

CLEMENS: Am I still doing something wrong?

THE WARDEN: You're not going far enough, m'boy! You want to
know why? Because you're not taking enough steps! Take
more steps, but take them very slowly—try that for a change!
You've got to get a feeling for countryside—for hills and
dales—above all you've got to get a feeling for open spaces
again. (*Clemens tries to follow instructions.*) There—that's
better; you're getting it! And don't forget your turns. (*Clemens obeys as if in a trance.*) Terrific—you're doing beautifully!
It's as if you were made to order for it! Bet no one ever told
you that before, eh? A Sunday-morning trip into the country
with the family, that's what it is! And nothing can happen
to you on this one—no unpleasant surprises—make a turn!—
And who can you thank for all this?

CLEMENS (*walking*): You, Alfons.

THE WARDEN: Don't mention it, m'boy. I just want you to be
happy, know what I mean?—Make a turn!—That's it! When
you're released three months from now I'm certain you'll be
able to walk all by yourself.

CLEMENS (*walking as if in a trance*): Do you really think so,
Alfons?

*The Warden exits quietly, shutting the door behind him.
Clemens keeps walking for a while, as if in his trance. He
stops; opening his eyes, he notices that the Warden has gone.
Looks around as if shaking off the spell he has been under.
Makes a move as if to leap at the door, controls himself,
starts to walk quite slowly to the door using the steps he has
just been practicing; suddenly he comes to himself, leaps onto
the plank-bed, and shouts through the window bars:*

CLEMENS: Let me out of here! Goddammit, let me out of here!
This is crazy! I want to take a walk on a real street, do you
hear! On Market Street! On Prospect Street! On North
Street! On Garden Street! (*He sinks down, exhausted.*) Maximilian Square! (*Dreamily:*) Maximilian Square . . . (*Tapping on the wall. Clemens listens, then holds his hands over
his ears. Goes back to the door, automatically dropping into*

the steps the Warden has taught him. He continues to move in this doll-like way to the end of the play. The door opens. Clemens steps back guiltily a couple of paces. Clementine enters carrying an unusually large handbag which has an air of containing all sorts of things and a cloth-covered bird cage. Uncomprehendingly:) Ah—I was just going for a little walk . . .

CLEMENTINE: Pst! I've brought you something.

CLEMENS: How'd you get in here? Do you have a key?

CLEMENTINE: Pst! My father!

CLEMENS: I want to get out of here! I'm innocent!

CLEMENTINE *(offended)*: I'm an innocent girl too.

CLEMENS: Forgive me. *(He takes off his hat, notices the flowers.)*

CLEMENTINE: Charming!

CLEMENS: I picked them in the town park. *(He hands her the bouquet.)*

CLEMENTINE: I've brought you something nice too.

CLEMENS: That's very nice of you.

CLEMENTINE: Guess what! *(She points at the covered cage.)*

CLEMENS: A good-looking necktie?

CLEMENTINE: Shorter.

CLEMENS: Some nice scented soap?

CLEMENTINE: You're getting warmer; but it's something that lasts longer.

CLEMENS: A book on philosophy?

CLEMENTINE: You're getting warmer; but it's something that eats more than that.

CLEMENS: A shoe brush?

CLEMENTINE: You're getting warmer; but it isn't as prickly as that.

CLEMENS: A nice embroidered cushion?

CLEMENTINE: Good guess! But it isn't as patient as that.

CLEMENS: A piano—a real small one, I mean?

CLEMENTINE: You're a marvelous guesser!

CLEMENS: It's just that you hit my taste exactly.

CLEMENTINE: That isn't difficult: you're an extraordinarily congenial young man. Now do you know what it is? (*She takes the cloth off: the cage contains a budgerigar.*)

CLEMENS: A little bird!

CLEMENTINE: A budgerigar!

CLEMENS: Didn't I suspect it right from the beginning?

CLEMENTINE: I knew it would cheer you up a bit.

CLEMENS: But—now that we've got him, what do we do with him?

CLEMENTINE: Talk to him. Dit-dit-dit—where's little Felix gone to?

CLEMENS: Does he understand that?

CLEMENTINE: Of course—he isn't stupid. You're a real sma-sma-smaaart little bird, aren't you, Felix? There's just one thing he can't do yet, I'm afraid.

CLEMENS: You mean there's something he *can't* do?

CLEMENTINE: He can't talk.

CLEMENS: That's a pity. That's exactly what I'd have liked him to do.

CLEMENTINE: We'll teach him.

CLEMENS: I've never taught a bird.

CLEMENTINE: You just have to say the word to him, over and over again, syllable by syllable.

CLEMENS: What could we teach him to say?

CLEMENTINE: Something simple—something that won't confuse him. He's such a sensitive bird.

CLEMENS: And what attentive-looking little eyes he has!

CLEMENTINE: Just as if he wanted to say something!

CLEMENS: And what does little Felix want to say?

CLEMENTINE: Names.

CLEMENS: Your name?

CLEMENTINE: Your name—our names.

CLEMENS: Go ahead—you start.

CLEMENTINE (*shyly*): No, you first—please!

CLEMENS: Or both of us together—you and me?

CLEMENTINE: All right?

CLEMENS: All right?

CLEMENTINE (*puts the cage on the bed, kneels beside it, and whispers persuasively*): Cle-Cle-Cle-

CLEMENS (*in the same way, on the other side of the cage*): Cle-Cle-Cle-

CLEMENTINE: Cle-Clay-red, red clay-

CLEMENS: In a red, red clay-

CLEMENTINE: Clay-Clay-

CLEMENS: Red, red clay-

CLEMENTINE: -two little rabbits hid away!

CLEMENS: Cle-Cle-Cle—in a red, red clay pit-

BOTH: Two little rabbits hid away!

CLEMENTINE: That's sweet!

BOTH (*singing*): In a red, red clay pit two little rabbits hid away. Cle-Cle-Cle-

CLEMENTINE (*puts her finger on her lips*): Pst! He's chirping! (*They strain to hear.*) Do you hear?

CLEMENS: Do you?

CLEMENTINE (*listening and speaking at the same time*): Cle-Cle-

CLEMENS: -mens!

I*

CLEMENTINE: -men-

CLEMENS (*correcting her*): -s! -s!

CLEMENTINE (*persistently*): -men- men-

CLEMENS: -mens! As in mens sana!

CLEMENTINE: In corpore sano! (*Pedagogically:*) How does it go?

CLEMENS (*getting up, in a schoolboy's tone*): Mens sana in corpore sano!

CLEMENTINE (*like a teacher*): Very good. You may sit. -ti.

CLEMENS: -mens!

CLEMENTINE (*stubbornly*): -ti-ti-ti!

CLEMENS (*agreeing*): Cle-

CLEMENTINE: -ti! -ti!

CLEMENS: Cle-

CLEMENTINE: -men-

CLEMENS (*doubtfully*): -ti?

CLEMENTINE: -ti! -ti!

CLEMENS (*happily*): Clementi!

CLEMENTINE: Clementi! Clementi!

CLEMENS (*remembering, pleased*): Page fifty-seven in the *Musical Treasury for Home and Family*, right after the page with grease spots.

CLEMENTINE (*severely*): Clementi, Sonatina in C major!

CLEMENS (*obediently marking the beat*): One two three four one two three four—

CLEMENTINE: (*Hums the beginning of the sonatina and pretends to play it on a piano; she gets stuck at a difficult passage.*)

CLEMENS: Again! (*He tries to do the same but gets stuck at the same difficult passage.*)

CLEMENTINE: The fingering is wrong! You have to play it this way! (*She plays the passage correctly this time. Clemens also plays.*) And now once more from the beginning! (*Both of them "play" the Clementi sonatina. They stop when they come to the "difficult" passage and burst out laughing.*)

CLEMENS: I had on an itchy pullover which Aunt Ella had knitted for me.

CLEMENTINE: I said I felt sick and wanted to go home. Then I went and ate ice cream.

CLEMENS: Clementi!

CLEMENTINE (*energetically*): -ne!

CLEMENS (*looks at her, amazed; then, after thinking about it*): pas!

CLEMENTINE: -ne, -ne, -ne!

CLEMENS: pas! pas! pas!

CLEMENTINE: ne pas! (*Both think, searching their memories. Triumphantly shooting out the words:*) Ne pas se pencher en dehors.

CLEMENS: Right! In the holiday train to the seaside!

CLEMENTINE: In the Trans-Europe Express to Lake Garda! (*To the bird:*) -ne! -ne! (*She listens intently; then explains:*) -ne! He said it!

CLEMENS (*understanding at last*): Ah—so your name is—?

CLEMENTINE: And yours—?

CLEMENS: Clemen-tine?

CLEMENTINE: Cle-mens?

CLEMENS: How beautiful!

CLEMENTINE: How similar! (*They kiss. Worried:*) How long are you staying?

CLEMENS: Another two months.

CLEMENTINE: Listen to little Felix talk! How happy he is there in his own little cage!

CLEMENS: How happy he is and how well he speaks our names!

CLEMENTINE: Cle! (*The speeches accelerate gradually.*)

CLEMENS: -ti!

CLEMENTINE: -mens!

CLEMENS: -ne -Cle-

CLEMENTINE: -ti-Cle-ne-ti-

CLEMENS: -men-Cle-ne-ti-

CLEMENTINE (*breaking off as if startled*): Wait a minute!

CLEMENS (*delighted*): He's talking!

CLEMENTINE (*horrified*): My father's coming!

CLEMENS: Don't worry—we're pals.

CLEMENTINE: You don't know what will happen if he finds me here! You don't know him in his total terrible paternal ferocity!

CLEMENS: But we haven't done anything!

CLEMENTINE: Hide me!

CLEMENS: Behind the door!
Clementine hides behind the door, which is at once noisily opened. The Warden enters.

THE WARDEN (*pretending not to see the cage*): Well? I was just making my rounds and I thought I'd just drop in and see how my boy Clemens was getting on. That's how worried I am about you, m'boy.

CLEMENS (*stammering*): Alfons . . .

THE WARDEN: What's the matter with you, m'boy? Do you think I'm the bogeyman? Haven't I demonstrated paternal concern for your well-being?

CLEMENS: I'm . . . I'm . . . not guilty.

THE WARDEN: Still being stubborn? Let me take your pulse!

CLEMENS (*intensely nervous*): They've got to let me out in a month!

THE WARDEN: Now your tongue! Say aaaah!

CLEMENS: Aaaa—fons!

THE WARDEN: Now your reflexes! (*He pushes Clemens toward the bed, on which the latter seats himself nervously. The Warden crosses Clemens' legs one over the other and hits him on the knee so that the leg jerks up.*) There—you see! (*Same action.*) Just like a Jack-in-the-box! (*Same action repeated.*) I wish I was that healthy!

CLEMENS (*shaking*): Alfons . . .

The Warden pretends to notice the bird cage for the first time. His face darkens and his mustache snaps down: suddenly he is the harsh jail guard again.

THE WARDEN: What's that?

CLEMENS (*stammering*): Just a tiny little bird . . .

THE WARDEN (*with sinister quietness*): Aha!

CLEMENS: . . . in a tiny little cage . . .

THE WARDEN: Aha!

CLEMENS: Alfons . . .

THE WARDEN (*suddenly harsh*): What's this "Alfons"? My title is "Warden," got that?

CLEMENS: Yes, Warden.

THE WARDEN: What have you been doing with the bird?

CLEMENS: Oh, the usual things one does with a bird, Warden!

Clementine clears her throat.

THE WARDEN (*without turning round to look*): Who's that? (*Bellowing:*) Speak up!

CLEMENS (*timidly*): It's Clementine, Warden.

THE WARDEN: As far as you're concerned, it's my daughter, understand? My poor daughter! What have you done to her?

CLEMENS (*timidly*): Oh, the usual things one does with a daughter, Warden . . .

CLEMENTINE: Oh!

THE WARDEN: Libertine! (*To Clementine:*) Has he violated you?

CLEMENTINE (*shrinkingly*): Oh, Papa!

THE WARDEN: My daughter is on your conscience! See what you've done to her! A timid little bird! Silence—not a word! Do you still have the insolence to maintain you are innocent?

CLEMENS: We had the budgerigar between us, Warden.

THE WARDEN (*opens the cage and takes the bird out*): The beast must go!

CLEMENS (*alarmed*): Oh no, please, Warden!

THE WARDEN: Animals are not allowed here. (*He climbs on the bed in order to let the bird out of the window.*)

CLEMENS: Oh, the poor little bird!

THE WARDEN: He'll feel fine outside.

CLEMENS: He can't fly! He can't live out there, Warden!

THE WARDEN: He'll learn. (*He throws the bird out of the window. Clementine utters a short sharp cry.*) Clemens, I trusted you —I thought you were a decent fellow. I taught you how to walk—and not just simple, everyday walking either—and this is my thanks!

CLEMENS: I'm overcome, Warden, I don't know . . .

THE WARDEN: My daughter's honor robbed, myself condemned to suffer the horrible jeers of my colleagues, my reputation gone—for what, for what? Because I put my faith in you!

CLEMENS: Perhaps it isn't all that bad, Warden.

THE WARDEN: Oh, it's all very well for you to say that! You're young, you don't have any worries or responsibilities! I know what you're thinking: that you'll be out of here in a month —and then—and then—the whole affair will be forgotten! But I! Oh, my poor, poor daughter!

CLEMENTINE: Oh!

CLEMENS: But I'd be glad to take the consequences if you think . . .

THE WARDEN: You have brought much mischief from your city here to my peaceful home!

CLEMENS: I never wanted to. I didn't want to come here.

THE WARDEN: Did *I* bring you here?

CLEMENS: But, Warden . . .

THE WARDEN: Or are you trying to say, perhaps, that my daughter seduced you?

CLEMENTINE: Oh!

THE WARDEN: Be silent, my darling innocent child!

CLEMENS: It's all my fault, Warden.

THE WARDEN: Perhaps at bottom there is some decency left in you.

CLEMENS: If there is anything I can do . . .

THE WARDEN: You'll be put on probation.

CLEMENS: Perhaps you'll allow me a few moments alone with Clementine so I can tell her . . .

THE WARDEN: Out of the question!

CLEMENTINE: Oh, Papa!

THE WARDEN: Very well. This is your last chance. After that, everything according to rule—understand?

CLEMENTINE: Oh, Papa!

CLEMENS: Thank you, Warden.

(*The Warden exits, shutting the door.*)

CLEMENS: I'm sorry.

CLEMENTINE: The little bird has gone.

CLEMENS: It talked so nicely.

CLEMENTINE: Cle-mens-

CLEMENS: Cle-men-ti-ne.

CLEMENTINE: You shouldn't have let him do it!

CLEMENS (*looking through the bars*): Perhaps you can still see him.

CLEMENTINE: The sky has swallowed him up.

CLEMENS: The earth has grabbed him up.

CLEMENTINE: The wind has broken him up.

CLEMENS: The cat has eaten him up.

CLEMENTINE (*sobbing by the cage*): Cle-

CLEMENS (*sobbing by the cage*): -men-ti-

CLEMENTINE (*jumping up*): We've got to cover the window! (*She takes the piece of cloth which had covered the bird cage.*) Help me! (*Clemens helps her to drape the cloth over the window. It is now impossible to see out.*) There! No little bird is going to escape now!

CLEMENS: It makes it look cosier in here too. There's nothing to remind you of the misery outside—of the trees and of the streetcar stops.

CLEMENTINE: And of the four-room apartments and of the gooseberry bushes. (*She hangs several pictures on the wall. Both sit on the bed.*) Cle-

CLEMENS: -men-

CLEMENTINE: -mens.

CLEMENS (*tentatively*): I'm due to be let out tomorrow.

CLEMENTINE: Cle-

CLEMENS (*pensively, cheering up gradually*): Do you know where I'll go first? First I'll go see Otto, that's an old friend of mine, and he'll greet me and ask me how it was, and then right away he'll get a bottle out from under the sofa. And then I'll go to the candy store at the corner of Frederick Street and buy myself a pack of cigarettes— Good day, young man, you've been away on a long trip! She calls everyone "young man" as long as he doesn't hobble around on a cane. And Miss Lina, the war widow—she'll be cleaning in the windows upstairs—we call her a war widow because her husband was a fireman and left her— Good morning, Clemens!— Good morning! And the barber in Market Street: High time I got the scissors to work on you again, young man! And the two old aunts I live with— Hello, hello!—and right away they'll run into the kitchen to warm up some coffee—they just can't imagine that I get anything to eat when I'm away from them. Hello there! Hello there!—everyone will be glad to see me again! Hello there!

CLEMENTINE: Oh!

CLEMENS: Yes, indeed!

CLEMENTINE: What'll I do with Felix's bread crumbs?

CLEMENS: Oh, well.

CLEMENTINE: What'll I do with the fish bone on which he sharpened his little beak?

CLEMENS: Come, come.

CLEMENTINE: Tomorrow?

CLEMENS: Hm?

(*A pause. The tapping is heard again.*)

CLEMENTINE: Quiet! Somebody's talking!

CLEMENS: I don't hear anything.

CLEMENTINE: There! It's quite clear! Tak, tak, tak-tak.

CLEMENS (*uncomprehending*): Tak, tak, tak-tak. I thought that was being done by people trying to dig themselves out of here. Do you understand what they're saying?

CLEMENTINE: Yes.—"What is the poor little bird doing?"

CLEMENS: How come you can make that out?

CLEMENTINE: Oh well, it's my mother tongue, after all.

(*Sound of tapping.*)

CLEMENS: What does that say?

CLEMENTINE (*puts her ear to the wall*): "Little birds have to have water." (*She puts her ear to the other wall to hear the tapping there:*) "Little birds need grains of corn."

CLEMENS: And I thought it was people nailing pictures on the wall.

CLEMENTINE: Well, now you know that they're old acquaintances who like to have a word or two with me.

CLEMENS: I'd like to talk to them too. (*He taps on the wall.*)

CLEMENTINE: Don't be silly! That means "I'm not at home."

CLEMENS (*disappointed*): How easy it is to make a mistake! It just isn't as simple as it sounds.

CLEMENTINE: There are people—I actually know such people— who can't speak either Spanish or Italian, and so they don't speak either Spanish or Italian. That's how hard it is.

CLEMENS: I wish you'd help me. I'd like to learn the tapping-on-the-wall language.

CLEMENTINE: The best way to learn a language is to start in early childhood. When one is very young one picks things up easily and retains them longer because, you see, one still has a long life before one.

CLEMENS: I didn't have any opportunity when I was that young.

CLEMENTINE: All right, let's give it a try. What do you want to say? (*She takes a plank out of the bed and lays it across her knee.*)

CLEMENS: Our beloved little bird Felix flew out of the window.

(*Clementine taps the message on the board. Clemens imitates her.*)

CLEMENTINE: Go on.

CLEMENS: —out of the window—over the thick, black wall—over the street—fluttering like a bicycle bell up through telephone wires—and into the wonderful, old-fashioned question-mark shapes of the gardens in the hills behind the houses—

CLEMENTINE: Nonsense! That's no good, that's no good at all. How can you talk such nonsense?

CLEMENS: But those are perfectly simple statements.

CLEMENTINE: But you can't say that here!

CLEMENS: But that's the way it looks out there, where I live!

CLEMENTINE: But there isn't any way to say that in the tapping language.

CLEMENS: All right then, try this: he flew—somewhere, I don't know where.

(*Clementine taps out the sentence. Clemens imitates her.*)

CLEMENTINE: There, you see, you're doing it quite well. You have a gift for languages.

(*Tapping on the wall.*)

CLEMENS: What are they saying?

CLEMENTINE (*listening*): Too bad—how sad—what a pity. You see —they feel for us!

CLEMENS (*tapping on the wall*): It can't even fly!

CLEMENTINE (*tapping on the other wall*): Not far. Not high. Not fast.

(*Answering taps are heard.*)

CLEMENS: What are they saying?

CLEMENTINE (*listening*): How remarkable—how dangerous—

CLEMENS (*listening*): —how careless—

CLEMENTINE: —how thoughtless—See, you're pretty good at the language already—already you can talk to everyone around you!

CLEMENS (*happily*): I'd like to invite them—all of them!

CLEMENTINE: We'll have a party! (*She taps on the wall.*)

CLEMENS: What are you doing?

CLEMENTINE: Inviting them.

(*Answering taps are heard.*)

CLEMENS: They're answering!

CLEMENTINE: We're looking forward to it—We're looking forward to it—We're looking forward to it—

CLEMENS: We're looking forward to it—What pleasant people!

CLEMENTINE: Yes, they're all people that know birds. They know how a bird pecks and when to talk about sex.

CLEMENS: Quiet! (*Tapping sound—this time on the door.*) What's that? It's the door!

CLEMENTINE: It must be Papa.

CLEMENS: Why so timid?

CLEMENTINE: Come in.

THE WARDEN (*entering, self-effacing and timid*): I hope I'm not disturbing.

CLEMENTINE: But, Papa, how can you say such a thing!

THE WARDEN: It's hard to know—an aged father . . .

CLEMENTINE: Oh, don't be silly! We're terribly glad to see you, aren't we, Clemens? (*Clemens nods enthusiastically.*) And we understand each other now, don't we? (*Clemens and Clementine tap signals on the plank.*)

THE WARDEN: Ah yes, I've done my duty—my duty, yes, my duty, and now . . .

CLEMENS: No, no, Warden!

CLEMENTINE (*to Clemens*): You can call him Papa—that always cheers him up.

CLEMENS: Papa.

CLEMENTINE (*formally, to the Warden*): Permit me to introduce us: myself, your daughter; you, my father; him, my fiancé.

THE WARDEN (*severely*): Aha! So I'm your father!

CLEMENTINE (*obliviously*): And this is my fiancé.

THE WARDEN (*severely*): Aha! So you're my daughter!

CLEMENS: I—I'm the fiancé.

THE WARDEN: Aha! So I'm not the father now—I'm the father-in-law!

CLEMENTINE: That's what we were counting on.

CLEMENS: It's a result of family relations.

THE WARDEN: Nonetheless, this occurrence has taken place at a time which does not permit me to speak in my capacity of uncle. It is my duty—yes, my duty, my duty, which even I have to obey, to return your papers to you. From now on you will have to take care of them yourself.

CLEMENS (*indignantly*): I am not authorized to do that!

THE WARDEN (*ceremoniously*): Your time is up!

CLEMENTINE: Stop talking about death, Papa! Once and for all, I will not have unpleasant matters talked about!

THE WARDEN: You are released!

CLEMENS: What do you mean? I simply won't let myself . . .

THE WARDEN: You are free!

CLEMENS: How do you mean?

CLEMENTINE: *Must* you always use your silly official expressions, Papa?

THE WARDEN (*solemnly*): Freedom! A tremendous, beautiful, powerful word!

CLEMENS: Freedom . . .

THE WARDEN: Here is the door—open!

CLEMENTINE: Yes, there's a draft!

THE WARDEN: Permit me to explain freedom to you in a few words. Straight from the horse's mouth, as it were! (*He gets up on the bed and strikes an oratorical pose.*) Freedom is a pepper mill which grinds and grinds until one fine morning it breaks. Then it becomes necessary to declare a National Holiday.

CLEMENS: Very true! But every holiday isn't a National Holiday.

THE WARDEN: Freedom! Freedom is a sock which warms and warms the feet, but suddenly there's a hole in the heel. Then it becomes necessary to throw it away.

CLEMENTINE: Wrong! The thrifty housewife darns the sock!

THE WARDEN: In a word, freedom is a delicate dove, gutted and roasted!

CLEMENTINE (*indignantly*): I don't roast doves!

CLEMENS (*indignantly*): I wouldn't eat it!

THE WARDEN (*confused*): But, children, that's just the way my speech goes!

CLEMENTINE: If you're going to give a speech, give a speech and stop roasting doves!

CLEMENS: They're two entirely different things!

THE WARDEN: It's just that I considered it my duty to explain the matter to you.

CLEMENTINE: Our dear little budgerigar is gone!

CLEMENS: He's gone and will not come again!

THE WARDEN (*getting down from the bed*): The best thing I can do now is leave you two alone. Youth, after all, has its own problems. But if you should need me . . .

CLEMENTINE AND CLEMENS: Thank you, Papa.

THE WARDEN: I'm afraid the door has to stay open, though. That's the regulation for released prisoners. But don't let it disturb you. (*He exits.*)

CLEMENS (*pensively*): Did he really leave the door open?

CLEMENTINE (*hysterically*): Yes—there's a draft! (*A pause. Tapping sounds are heard.*) Here are our guests already!

CLEMENS: What are they saying?

CLEMENTINE: They're worried—it's touching, really, how worried they are! (*Tapping sounds.*) "Songbirds must be protected."

CLEMENS: But our little bird didn't sing at all! (*He taps the message on the wall.*)

CLEMENTINE (*angrily*): How can you tap such a thing!

Tapping sounds are heard.

CLEMENS: But it's true—he couldn't sing!

CLEMENTINE: He could even talk! (*She taps the message on the wall.*) A bird that can talk is like a man that can—fly!

CLEMENS (*listening*): "But the other birds can't understand him."

CLEMENTINE (*listening*): "It's so dangerous for the little bird."

CLEMENS: Yes—but when I think how it flies, how it flies . . . cautiously at first . . . (*He makes a few bird-like movements in the direction of the door.*) . . . to the door, which stands wide open, then the wind catches it under the wings and carries it . . . out there . . . whee! Where to? The wind carries it, the wind blows it along, the wind floats it over the roofs . . . how beautiful it is . . . out there . . . out there . . .

CLEMENTINE: How dangerous! (*Tapping sounds; she listens.*) "Take care!—Careful!—Danger!—Danger!"

CLEMENS (*mechanically, as he walks past the door*): I can't find it any more. (*He has once more dropped into the marionette-like manner of walking that he has learned.*)

(*Tapping sounds are heard.*)

CLEMENTINE (*listening*): The poor little bird! The tiny little bird! The unhappy little bird!

CLEMENS: And no one can protect it! (*He taps this sentence on the wall. Answering taps are heard.*)

CLEMENTINE (*listening*): No one—no one—no one—
(*Clemens taps this message on the plank.*)

(*Clementine answers him by tapping the same message.*)

CLEMENS: From the cat. (*He taps this.*) From the hawk. (*He taps this.*)

CLEMENTINE: It's fantastic how well you understand the tapping speech! (*Tapping sounds are heard; she listens:*) "The poor little bird!"

CLEMENS (*tapping on the plank*): From the birdcatcher. (*He taps.*) From the hunter. (*He taps.*) From the Italian bird-eater. (*He taps.*)

CLEMENTINE: The poor little bird—listen!

Tapping sounds are heard.

CLEMENS (*listening*): No one—no one—no one—

CLEMENTINE (*listening*): What are they saying?

(*Clemens taps the code for "no one" on the plank.*)

(*Clementine nods and answers by tapping the same word three times.*)

CLEMENS: What?

(*Clementine taps the same word.*)

(*Clemens taps the same word.*)

(*The same word is now tapped through the walls on all sides.*)

(*While Clemens and Clementine tap the same word out to each other, the curtain falls.*)

(*The tapping stops.*)

LETS, EAT HAIR!

by CARL LASZLO

TRANSLATED BY GEORGE E. WELLWARTH

Characters

DANIELE
JEAN-CLAUDE
MORTIMER

Jean-Claude and Daniele are discovered seated on a comfortable sofa.

DANIELE: Let's eat hair!

JEAN-CLAUDE: With mustard—but without radishes.

DANIELE: Too bad that we don't have time to eat any clocks.

JEAN-CLAUDE: Too late.

DANIELE: Let's eat candles, flaming candles.

JEAN-CLAUDE: No, fire doesn't belong in the stomach. Let's eat roses, frozen roses.

DANIELE: Ah, ice-cold roses! They'll upset our stomachs. Let's eat foam with roasted memories.

JEAN-CLAUDE: Let's eat dreams, embroidered dreams without meaning.

DANIELE: Let's eat chairs and Louis XVI tables.

JEAN-CLAUDE: And picture frames—lots and lots of picture frames.

DANIELE: And pictures too—oil paintings. Real ones, not reproductions.

JEAN-CLAUDE: Slim lightning rods, door hinges, cigarette boxes.

DANIELE: Neon tubes, spoons, Havana cigars.

JEAN-CLAUDE: Pawn tickets.

DANIELE: Shoes.

JEAN-CLAUDE: Rust and bicycle wheels and automobile tires.

DANIELE: Let's eat love and passion and syllables.

JEAN-CLAUDE: Yes, syllables—words.

DANIELE: Let's eat lies and promises and fairy tales.

JEAN-CLAUDE: Let's eat suspicion and slander and dirty jokes.

DANIELE: Let's eat toothpaste—DENTOGRIND!

JEAN-CLAUDE: Let's gnaw at the icebox!

DANIELE: I can already feel the wonderful sweet taste of slippers in my mouth.

JEAN-CLAUDE: Just once I'd like to lick the second hand on the clock.

DANIELE: I just want to brush the water tower with my mouth.

MORTIMER (*enters*): All I do is sit at my typewriter and write page after page without stopping.

DANIELE: I'll put my arms around the table leg and together we will painstakingly create children.

MORTIMER: I shine my shoes and forget to bring my aunt her tea.

JEAN-CLAUDE: Hair will be transformed in my catalogue.

MORTIMER: The price of milk keeps going up, and the singers sing their songs.

DANIELE: We must swallow the arsenic very carefully, and we must not crawl under the piano when it gets dark.

MORTIMER: The table manufacturer manufactures tables, the shoe-maker makes shoes, and the locksmith smiths locks . . .

JEAN-CLAUDE: The miller makes mills, the tinsmith tin, the lathe-turner lathes. But I want to miss all the windmills and order some rose beer for my beard.

MORTIMER: Spring, summer, fall, and winter are the four seasons. We sit on chairs and eat beans with bacon.

DANIELE: I'll extract wisdom teeth from camels. I'll make rain out of used parasols and I'll smoke Portuguese candles.

MORTIMER: How easily iron rusts! And whenever you forget to wind up the clocks, they stop. Shoes get holes in their soles and wood burns in the stove.

JEAN-CLAUDE: You shouldn't protect bats! Forget your graphs, paragraphs, choreographs! Hide your mercury sticks and tell your suspicions to beware of flags.

MORTIMER: After the flood, the ebb. Two is a factor of six. Marriage always precedes divorce, and clouds turn into rain.

DANIELE: The panic box is full of silver handcuffs. Seated astride a snow-white dolphin, I go further and further east until I come to the blind bishop.

MORTIMER: Steps fade away and bread satisfies hunger. Mirrors might break during an earthquake. It's late—I have to go to bed. (*Exits.*)

(*Daniele and Jean-Claude come slowly closer to each other and look up into the distance.*)

DANIELE: The moon tenderly strokes the clouds.

JEAN-CLAUDE: The eagle flies low, with the night in its claws.

DANIELE: Dim, faraway stars are exploding.

JEAN-CLAUDE: A comet screams, "Good-by!"

DANIELE: The day has celebrated a marriage.

JEAN-CLAUDE: Death has kissed a maiden.

DANIELE: Language is tranquilly disintegrating . . .

JEAN-CLAUDE: The syllables . . .

DANIELE: We're disappearing . . .

JEAN-CLAUDE: Into the soft waves of the alphabet sea. . . .

CURTAIN

THE CHINESE ICE BOX

by CARL LASZLO

TRANSLATED BY GEORGE E. WELLWARTH

CHARACTERS

THE OVERCOAT
THE NEIGHBOR
OLGA
THE BAT
THE QUEEN OF ARAGON

THE OVERCOAT: We've been forgotten!

THE NEIGHBOR: Yes, indeed! We've been forgotten, callously forgotten.

OLGA: We've been betrayed!

THE BAT: We've been sold out!

THE QUEEN OF ARAGON: It's always so peculiar when a man gets together with a woman, or a man with a man, or a woman with a woman . . .

THE OVERCOAT: We've been cleaned!

THE NEIGHBOR: We've been beaned!

THE QUEEN: It just puzzles me, that's all—no, actually, it doesn't puzzle me at all.

OLGA: There simply has to be a solution, after all!

THE BAT: Bats in the belfry!

THE QUEEN: Ever since I became a corresponding member of the Society for Up and Coming Arts I've been using the telephone ever so much more.

OLGA: Ever so much more than before?

THE QUEEN: Do you intend that to be a personal question?

OLGA: No, I intended it to be an indirect question.

THE NEIGHBOR: How poetic.

THE BAT: And pornographic.

THE OVERCOAT: And pernicious.

OLGA: Yes, indeed, you've guessed it: it's me. There's no point in pretending anything else any longer. It's me, all right.

THE OVERCOAT: And we're supposed to put up with that, I suppose?

THE NEIGHBOR: Yes, we're supposed to put up with that, are we?

THE QUEEN: I wish everyone could become happy. On one condition—that everyone does it at a different time of day.

OLGA: Night after night I wrestled with myself, trying to decide

K

whether I should reveal myself or not. Now I'm revealing my-self. I'm it.

THE BAT: When you look into a mirror you see things! And you always act as if it were yourself you were seeing in the mirror. But it isn't you. You just think it is. Maybe we ought to de-stroy all mirrors before anyone notices it?!

THE OVERCOAT: We've been forgotten. We've been cleaned. We've been beaned.

THE NEIGHBOR: Yes, indeed! We've been forgotten. Yes, we've been cleaned. It's quite true: we've been beaned.

THE QUEEN: I wish everyone could become happy!

OLGA: Yes. It's me. It's me, all right.

THE BAT: The question is, should all mirrors be destroyed or not?

THE OVERCOAT: We've been forgotten!

THE NEIGHBOR: Yes, we've been forgotten.

THE QUEEN: I wish everyone could become very happy!

OLGA: Yes, it's me. It's me, all right.

THE BAT: The question is, should all mirrors be destroyed or not?

THE OVERCOAT: We've been forgotten!

THE QUEEN: I wish everyone could become very happy!

OLGA: Yes, it's me. It's me, all right.

THE BAT: The question is, should all mirrors be destroyed or not?

THE OVERCOAT: We've been forgotten!

THE BAT: Yes, we've been forgotten.

ALL: Aaaaaaahhhh (*they all yawn together*).

CURTAIN

ROCKING BACK AND FORTH

A Curtain-Raiser

by GÜNTER GRASS

TRANSLATED BY MICHAEL BENEDIKT AND JOSEPH CORADZA

Characters

CONELLI
THE DIRECTOR
THE ACTOR
THE PLAYWRIGHT
DOROTHY
KARL-HEINZ

In the center of the empty stage the clown, Conelli, rocks back and forth on a rocking horse.

CONELLI: Isn't that nice! Everybody says I'm dead. The circus wants to kick me out. "You're not funny anymore," they yelled and yelled until I couldn't keep from laughing. And then they noticed that yelling itself is funny. Now they do the act all by themselves, but I'm the one who gave them their ideas. (*To the rocking horse:*) Ingeborg, do you think they could use us on TV, or maybe even in the theater? Now let's rock back and forth another thousand times and then ride off into the distance!

(*He rocks back and forth. From the left, behind his back, enter a Director, a Playwright, and an Actor.*)

DIRECTOR: Now, now kiddies, that just cannot be done, it just *can not*. What would we have if we brought the circus to the stage?

ACTOR: Cabaret, that's what!

PLAYWRIGHT: Don't be so inflexible! Dress things up differently! Leather jacket, crash helmet—instead of a rocking horse, a motorcycle!

DIRECTOR: We've already seen that kind of stuff in Cocteau.

PLAYWRIGHT: Look—I'm willing to listen to reason. New suggestion: a Vespa!

ACTOR: Right! or a rocket! A sputnik!

PLAYWRIGHT: I absolutely refuse to take any part whatsoever in this topicality mania of yours. The clown stands, isolated, outside ordinary human society. He is the single hole in the universe, creation's exception. He is the truly tragic figure.

DIRECTOR: And what about that Vespa business? That wasn't funny?

PLAYWRIGHT: Just another way to underline his inner tragedy.

ACTOR: I consider Sputnik much more tragic.

PLAYWRIGHT: To strike precisely the right balance between tragic Sputnik and comic Vespa, I sought at the outset the proper, appropriate, tragicomical motorcycle.

DIRECTOR: Which brings us back to Cocteau. Let's just drop that whole business: rocking horse, Sputnik, motorcycle, Vespa. The problem's still this clown here. They won't allow him to appear in the circus anymore and before TV picks him up for advertising purposes it's up to us to grab him.

PLAYWRIGHT: You mean without the rocking horse?

DIRECTOR: *With* the rocking horse is out of the question.

ACTOR: Mr. Conelli, dismount from your thoroughbred stallion.

DIRECTOR: Thoroughbred! That's a good one! Did you hear that, Conelli? Swing out of the saddle now, your thoroughbred is tired.

CONELLI (*to the rocking horse*): Ingeborg, we have to go faster. There's somebody just behind us saying something about a stallion.

PLAYWRIGHT (*standing next to Conelli now*): That's all right, Conelli—nothing to worry about; no harm meant. Pretty horsie!

CONELLI: Ingeborg!

DIRECTOR: And an even prettier name. Why don't you get off now, you Sunday Driver you. Hey, Angelman, there's our title: The Sunday Driver!

PLAYWRIGHT: I think the rocking horse should be cut out right now.

CONELLI: Ingeborg?

DIRECTOR: Oh hell, Conelli, don't listen to Angelman. Ingeborg stays. (*All three, aside:*) It can be disguised, that's all. Do it amorphously, fragmentarily! And now you tell us how to do it, Angelman, you're the writer around here.

PLAYWRIGHT: How about a horse skeleton—a framework of bare bones?

DIRECTOR: Brilliant! Realistic—and at the same time abstract. It will speak to the man of today, if not actually stir him to his innermost depths!

PLAYWRIGHT: You see, now *you* want a tragedy, too.

DIRECTOR: Nonsense, Angelman. That business with the bare bones is a real scream! And after all, people want to laugh in the theater; our times are sad enough as it is.

ACTOR: Perhaps we might decorate the nag a little? A tail, a few tufts of hair, a little flesh here and there?

DIRECTOR: Magnificent! On the one hand it's surrealistic, recalling the French, Beckett and so on—on the other hand something like this will deeply appeal to us, the typical German public. Think back a little and what do you find: Grünewald, Hofmannsthal, Everyman, Death and the Maiden, Death the Grim Reaper. Only now he doesn't have the conventional, clichéd equipment of scythe and hourglass anymore, but a big fat nose, and a ridiculous comic hat instead!

(*Conelli cowers in fear.*)

ACTOR: The whole thing could be converted into a little junior Olympic racing contest: "Riding for Germany will be . . . !"

(*Actor and Director laugh. Conelli looks on hopelessly, then laughs—louder and louder, without stopping.*)

DIRECTOR: What's his problem?

PLAYWRIGHT: You've intimidated him.

CONELLI (*softly, to his rocking horse*): Ingeborg, now our lives are at stake. Those men are meat inspectors, come from the slaughter house. I'm going to try and distract them. (*He turns around backwards on his horse and addresses the Actor:*) Farm production has fallen off this year—too many rabbits around these days.

PLAYWRIGHT: Answer him, Perkatsch, improvise. His instinct for play is aroused!

ACTOR: But most people believe that we've just been having an exceptionally dry year.

CONELLI: No, we just have far too many rabbits.

ACTOR: Yes, but it's been a very dry year, too.

CONELLI: The rabbits lie around quietly, all pretending to be dead. The people run after the bunnies as fast as they can, but they never catch them because the bunnies always pretend to be dead.

ACTOR: But I'm not running after rabbits at all—in fact, look!—I'm lying here in bed.

PLAYWRIGHT: Excellent—bring in a bed! (A *bed is pushed onto the stage, and the Actor lies down in it.*)

ACTOR: I ask you now, am I running? I am lying down quite calmly here, and it's so cozy and snug. . . .

CONELLI: That's because you're tired now. Later, after you've rested awhile, you'll start running again.

ACTOR: As a matter of fact, I'm actually *afraid* of rabbits.

DIRECTOR (*in a low voice*): Not bad at all.

CONELLI: Everybody's afraid of rabbits—that's why they go running around after them.

PLAYWRIGHT: Introduce a fresh concept, Perkatsch. He's tying you up in knots.

ACTOR: I'm running around for another reason entirely, Conelli. I'm a married man.

CONELLI: How nice.

ACTOR: My wife is married to me.

CONELLI: That must be very nice!

PLAYWRIGHT: Still he resists, but the conflict is inevitable.

ACTOR: My wife is lying here with me now—in bed.

CONELLI: How nice.

ACTOR: And do you know what my wife is doing here, right now?

CONELLI: Surely something very nice.

ACTOR: She is pretending to be dead just like those bunnies of yours.

CONELLI: Busy busy, always busy.

ACTOR: You exaggerate.

CONELLI (*rhythmically, rocking*): Busily the seamstresses sew and sew and sew.

ACTOR: You're overdoing it again.

CONELLI: Still—a hundred strokes per minute!

PLAYWRIGHT: Watch it, Perkatsch.

ACTOR: You see, Conelli, no woman is perfect—and that includes mine.

CONELLI: Then she can't really be a bunny. Your wife is either a mouse or a terrible sleepyhead. However—

ACTOR: What should I say now, Angelman?

CONELLI: —most likely she's a mouse.

PLAYWRIGHT: I'd avoid letting myself get involved any further in this. A mouse always means a mousetrap. Any other animal— okay. As a matter of fact, this scene could use a little extra color right about here.

ACTOR (*to Conelli again*): But my wife keeps on dreaming that she's a zebra.

CONELLI: You mean she can play the piano?

PLAYWRIGHT: Well! there we are, now. A grand, if you please! (*A grand piano is pushed onto the stage.*)

ACTOR: She is still a very small zebra. First of all she'll have to learn the notes of the scale—also, she has a tendency to use the pedal far too much. Would it satisfy you if my wife just played a few snatches from Strauss with one finger? . . .

CONELLI: It's an outright swindle! I'm riding away right now! Even at birth zebras know how to play four hands. (*He starts rocking back and forth.*)

ACTOR: Stay, stay—for heaven's sake, stay! My wife just happens to be an exception.

CONELLI: Zebras are never exceptions.

ACTOR (*to Playwright*): Quick—give me your pistol. (*The Playwright hands him the pistol.*) Stay where you are, Conelli, or I'll shoot.

K*

CONELLI: Go ahead and shoot. That's the kind of thing people like to laugh at most! (*The Actor puts away the pistol.*)

ACTOR: All right, Conelli, we'll postpone the shooting—we'll play the piano instead. I'll ask my wife to play a little something for us.

CONELLI (*no longer rocking*): How nice.

ACTOR (*beneath the bedclothes*): Mouse, mouse, listen to me. Mr. Conelli is here. Stop pretending to be dead. You are no longer a sweet little rabbit, nor even one of those cute little moles; you're a zebra now. Do you hear? A zebra! (*He withdraws his head from under the bedclothes.*) She's still pretending to be dead.

CONELLI: Then she's certainly no zebra, either. Zebras never pretend to be dead, zebras play piano all the time, even while they sleep. And now I'm riding away. (*He rocks.*)

ACTOR: Damn it, what kind of dialogue do you call this?

DIRECTOR: A director keeps outside of the action—but he listens attentively to everything.

PLAYWRIGHT: Keep talking! More, more—otherwise we'll lose him for sure.

ACTOR: Listen, Mr. Conelli, my wife is only dreaming that she's a zebra. In reality she is only an ordinary, everyday rabbit.

CONELLI: If she isn't a zebra, I'm riding away. I can always come back when she finally becomes one. (*He rocks.*)

DIRECTOR: Perkatsch, you have to try and get him off that ridiculous rocking horse, or he'll never stop this zebra nonsense.

PLAYWRIGHT: Coax him into the bed.

DIRECTOR: The conflict is long overdue!

ACTOR: As if anything to do with beds mattered to him.

DIRECTOR: It will be hard to get around that, all right.

ACTOR: How about slipping into bed for a bit, Mr. Conelli?

CONELLI: How nice.

ACTOR: Perhaps, if you were to come to bed, perhaps, my wife might turn into a zebra and stop pretending to be dead and play the piano as nimbly as a mouse.

PLAYWRIGHT: Watch out, Perkatsch!

ACTOR: Or even more nimbly than that, since—ummmm—since only a zebra can play the piano truly nimbly. Just imagine it, my dear Conelli: you're lying in your little beddy-by with your legs drawn up or stretched out just the way you do every night, and my wife plays—what am I saying, "plays"?—she *intones*. Are you coming now?

CONELLI: I'm on my way! (*He turns the rocking horse around and rides toward the bed.*) Hurry, Ingeborg, hurry. We can lie right down in bed. It will be just like in the zoo. That's where they have zebras, bunnies, mice, and zebras. (*He rocks.*)

DIRECTOR: This guy just can't be pried off that nag.

PLAYWRIGHT: Tell him to hitch Ingeborg to the bedpost.

ACTOR: So, Conelli, at long last we have safely arrived. Come on now, tie Ingeborg carefully to the bedpost so she doesn't go running off. And then into the nice fluffy feathers with you!

CONELLI: Without Ingeborg?!

ACTOR: The bed's too small.

CONELLI: But the smaller the bed the nicer it is.

ACTOR: You'd just keep bumping into one another and in the end you wouldn't know whose leg was whose.

CONELLI: O how nice that would be!

ACTOR: But your Ingeborg would probably react rather vigorously to all this in certain sensitive spots.

CONELLI: Nothing delights her more and I don't know anything more delightful either than such a real nice old higgledy-piggledy pudding as that would be.

ACTOR: There he goes again with his stupid "how nice that would be." Look—I simply can't go and stick the two of them in bed like that.

DIRECTOR: Under no circumstances.

PLAYWRIGHT: But why not, actually?

DIRECTOR: Think of the reactions on Broadway and at the ASPCA!

PLAYWRIGHT: How would it be if right about here we introduced a bit of excitement: "The Rape of the Clown." A pleasant pantomime with prostitutes, buffoons, harlequin as the villain, Columbine in bed naturally, and so on and so forth. Style: "Children of Paradise." It's sure-fire.

DIRECTOR: There's just about nothing else left for us to do, anyway.

PLAYWRIGHT: We might try running through it again this way. We could save the buffoons and such for later.

ACTOR: But what's left for me to say now?—Listen, Mr. Conelli, what will my wife think if you let her wait around so long? What choice has she got but to pretend to be dead all the time like a poor little rabbit?

CONELLI: Surely she must be feeling a little lonely now.

ACTOR: It's dead certain.

CONELLI: I've got an idea! Let's keep her company. I'll pretend to be dead. You'll pretend to be dead too, since your wife is already pretending to be dead. Then we'll all three of us pretend to be dead rabbits and we'll all dream together of zebras until we actually *are* zebras. Then we'll get up and play six-handed piano, only Ingeborg can't play along with us because she is so unmusical and always hits so many wrong notes. (*He clasps the neck of the horse and pretends to be dead.*)

ACTOR: Conelli!

DIRECTOR: Now you've done it.

ACTOR: Mr. Conelli! Now what? Am I supposed to play dead too?

DIRECTOR: End of the performance after barely ten minutes! Everyone pretends to be dead because he's a little bunny rabbit—then, curtain! Get out of that bed, Perkatsch! You can go home now.

ACTOR: That's just great. My wife has probably gone to bed hours ago having decided to pretend to be dead—dead as a possum. (*He storms off.*)

DIRECTOR (*calling after him*): If that's really the case I'd pretend to be dead too, if I were you. Do you hear, Perkatsch, simply play dead!

PLAYWRIGHT: I didn't find it all that bad. Considerably shortened and streamlined it might do as a warm-up, a curtain-raising scene. It doesn't really have to be the last act.

DIRECTOR: A few fair sequences in there—but that's about it. I wouldn't have said a word if the scene with the bed had been a success. That would have resulted in action—tension! The reaction of the wife, the behavior of the husband and so on and so forth.

PLAYWRIGHT: The age-old triangle. You see the clown in an improper light. He is completely nonerotic—in fact, let's face it, he's impotent. We can't possibly grasp him from the perspective of the bed.

DIRECTOR: I would certainly agree with that theory if I hadn't previously researched the subject thoroughly. Mr. Conelli is more or less happily married, although we won't concern ourselves with his wife here, but rather with his eighteen-year-old daughter, Dorothy.—Come here, my child. (*A young lady steps forward.*) This is Mr. Angelman, one of our most promising dramatists. He's already written several successful radio plays. (*The gentlemen bow.*)

DIRECTOR: I believe I can speak frankly with you. Your father is pretending to be dead.

DOROTHY: Oh, don't pay any attention to *that*. He always does that when somebody wants him to get off his rocking horse.

DIRECTOR: Well, every madness has its method. I believe you've just been engaged?

DOROTHY: My boyfriend is a film-splicer, but my father is opposed to our union.

DIRECTOR: Do you observe, my dear Angelman? "Reach deeply into the heart of human life. . . ." On the one hand a clown, occasionally pretending to be dead, perpetually on the rocking horse Ingeborg—on the other hand a strict, if not actually narrowminded, father.

CONELLI (*sits up on his horse and yells at Dorothy*): That film splicer! That splicer of film! Just what is a film splicer anyway, I'd like to know! Either filmer or splicer, either spliced or filmed! But that isn't enough for you! You have to splice and film simultaneously! Aside from that the creep parts his hair to the left and he's got smelly feet! (*He goes back to pretending to be dead.*)

DOROTHY: There—that's exactly the way he always treats us! Listen to this: up until two weeks ago I still used to appear with him in Bauman's Circus. My fiancé came to every performance until my father noticed something.

DIRECTOR: You are an equestrian, are you not?

DOROTHY: My father forced me to become one.

PLAYWRIGHT: What are you driving at, anyway? This is the simplest kind of big top local color. It's been done a thousand times. It's good for the movies—but on stage?

DIRECTOR: Hold it, Angelman, hold it.—And what did your father do when he noticed your friend and fiancé hanging around the circus?

DOROTHY: He treated him very shabbily.—Isn't that so, Karl-Heinz?

(*Enter a young man.*)

KARL-HEINZ: Karl-Heinz Brenner, film splicer, at your service. (*He bows.*) I can testify that Mr. Conelli—with all due respect for his capabilities as a clown—hasn't exactly acted fairly where I'm concerned.

DOROTHY: He got him into the ring and he ridiculed him in front of the whole circus audience.

PLAYWRIGHT: But after all, that's part of his profession.

DOROTHY: Every joke has to have its limits.

KARL-HEINZ: When Conelli motioned me into the ring, naturally I didn't want to be a spoilsport, because of Dorothy. I stood next to him and he said in his characteristic manner that I was a rabbit and that I ought to pretend to be dead since that's what all rabbits do. I went along with him, acting as though I were pretending to be dead, and then with lightning speed he took off my shoes and socks and threw them into the audience.

CONELLI (*straightens up and shouts*): Ladies and gentlemen, our bunnyrabbit has such smelly feet because our bunnyrabbit is not a bunnyrabbit at all but a baby pig. (*He squeals like a piglet and goes back to pretending to be dead.*)

DOROTHY: You can just imagine how we felt then. His silly rabbit story, well, why not; that's okay, nobody laughs at *that* kind of thing anymore. But what he did was definitely going too far.

KARL-HEINZ: Among the members of the audience were my parents and several co-workers and top executives of the Excelsior Film Company.

DIRECTOR: What do you say now, Angelman?

PLAYWRIGHT: As a supplementary plot, not bad. You could make a lion tamer out of the film splicer and underline the old conflict between the witty spirit of the clown and pure, brute strength. But as the main plot? It would be like presenting Romeo and Juliet as a circus act. That would hardly be your esteemed intention, I trust?

DIRECTOR: Where is the *plot*, Angelman? Up to now we've only had a series of more or less funny episodes.

PLAYWRIGHT: Yes, the grand design is missing. But observe! Soon the tragedy will take its inevitable course.

DIRECTOR: Comedy, you mean.

PLAYWRIGHT: The first act of the tragedy, colon:—!

DIRECTOR: Just a moment, please. (*To Dorothy and Karl-Heinz:*) Would you both be so kind as to leave behind your names and addresses in the outer office. It's been a pleasure. Your story was extraordinarily gripping and timely. At last, a genuine problem for us to deal with again! We'll be in touch with you shortly. (*Dorothy and Karl-Heinz exit.*) Well, Angelman?

PLAYWRIGHT: Conelli the clown is sitting on his rocking horse. Let's leave it that way for the moment.

DIRECTOR: I'd almost be in favor of a motorcycle myself now.

PLAYWRIGHT: A rich gentleman chances to pass—then drops his bankbook. Conelli scoops it up and what does he do? He learns by heart all the numbers in it, from first to final digit, forward and backward, all by heart—the ins and outs of a dazzling bank account including all the accumulated interest.

DIRECTOR: And what happened to the tragic element?

PLAYWRIGHT: Isn't the air absolutely charged with it?

DIRECTOR: I can't even consider this comical.

PLAYWRIGHT: After Conelli has memorized the entire account he throws away the bankbook. Children jump onto the stage, hear him mumbling, listen, learn the text of the savings account book also, run off again, recite it to their mothers; the mothers tell it to the fathers, the fathers to their co-workers, the co-workers to their higher-ups, and the higher-ups to the president, the president to the board of directors, and so what happens?—

DIRECTOR: The board of directors begins to play the horses with the advantage of all those secret figures and wins an even million.

PLAYWRIGHT: That would be comedy. However, in my particular treatment that sudden avalanche of numbers causes a run on the banks, the market fluctuates, drops, and finally hits rock bottom. Within a few hours the currency of the entire world collapses. Even the fiscal structuring of the German mark creaks and groans. Inflation, unemployment, revolution! And all because Conelli the clown found a bankbook.

DIRECTOR: And what happens in the second act?

PLAYWRIGHT: In the second act Conelli finds a telephone directory. He memorizes this completely too, then summons onto the scene the secret service organizations of both the East and the West. You can just imagine all the things that begin to happen now. Suspicion, the breaking of diplomatic relations. . . .

DIRECTOR: And the third act?

PLAYWRIGHT: Catastrophe strikes. Conelli, still on his rocking horse, finds a Federal German Railroad timetable. And now we come to the climactic dramatic clash! War, atom bomb, H-bomb. End of the world.

DIRECTOR: And Conelli?

PLAYWRIGHT: The last representatives of mankind, among them his own daughter, Dorothy, and the film splicer, see Conelli as the culprit in all this. He is lynched in a crowd scene. The fourth and last act presents his funeral.

CONELLI (*sitting up*): Ingeborg, we're dead. We must hurry up now. Otherwise we will be late for our funeral, and if we miss the funeral we'll miss the children's performance which begins punctually at five o'clock in the afternoon and to which we cordially invite kiddies and grownups alike. Bunnies get in free; zebras half-price. Giddy-up Ingeborg, giddy-up. Otherwise the beautiful ironwork door of the cemetery will be closed. The people will take their wreathes back home again and won't know what to do with them.—Besides, we're also invited for coffee and cake. (*He rocks.*)

DIRECTOR: And what if he arrives too late for the funeral?

PLAYWRIGHT: Under those circumstances this play could become a comedy.

DIRECTOR: . . . because it looks for certain as if he's going to arrive too late. Too late for the funeral, too late for the coffee and cake. Perhaps he might make it by five o'clock and appear just on time for the children's performance— children don't like to be kept waiting, you know.

(*Both look anxiously at their watches, synchronize them, and then go off. Conelli rocks vigorously back and forth while the curtain falls.*)

NIGHTPIECE

by WOLFGANG HILDESHEIMER

TRANSLATED BY WOLFGANG HILDESHEIMER

CHARACTERS

A MAN WHO WANTS TO SLEEP
THE BURGLAR

A *large dark old-fashioned bedroom. It might be in a castle or in a manor house. There are two doors, one leading into the bathroom, the other to the landing. Dark, patterned wallpaper. A high window with heavy red velvet curtains. In the center of the stage a wide four-poster bed. At its left a night table. On the night table a telephone, a pitcher of water, a glass, a pair of spectacles, a gold pocket watch. Other furniture: a heavy two-door wardrobe, a tall mirror, a dresser, two Gothic chairs with very high backs. Around one of these chairs a rope is loosely wound, as if somebody were to be tied up there. A clothes stand at the foot of the bed. On the wall a large gold Louis XVI clock and four or five very dominating portraits of male ancestors, life-sized, but very much darkened by time: a general, a statesman, a judge, etc. The atmosphere of the room is oppressive.*

It is night. The room is lit.

The Man Who Wants to Sleep comes out of the bathroom. He limps a little. He is wearing a nightgown and slippers. He carries his clothes—jacket, vest, trousers, shirt, tie, undershirt, shorts, etc. —over his arm, puts them on the bed, goes back to the door, switches the bathroom lights off, shuts the bathroom door, goes back to the bed, picks up his clothes again and distributes them silently and with great care over the clothes stand. Then he takes one step toward the bed, but a thought strikes him: Have I switched off the bathroom light? He goes back to the bathroom door, opens it, looks into the bathroom: the light is off. He shuts the door, goes back to the bed, sits down on it, looks around the room, rests his forearms on his thighs and puts his palms together. He remains sitting this way for a moment. The clock strikes ten.

MAN (*looks at the clock*): Ten o'clock. My hour. The hour of preparation. (*Takes the pocket watch from the bedside table, looks at it.*) No. Not yet. Another two minutes. (*Puts the watch back.*) Two minutes more. Don't start too early! Best to postpone things a little. Otherwise you'll have to pay for it in the morning. (*Pause.*) In the morning. (*Savoring the word.*) "Morning." (*Pause, sigh.*) No—there's no hurry. (*He puts his palms together again. Pause, then suddenly:*) Have I . . . ? (*Turning to one of the portraits:*) Have I switched off the bathroom light? (*He gets up, goes to the bathroom door, opens it. The light is off.*) Of course I've switched it off. (*Shuts the door.*) I always switch it off. (*Goes toward the bed, stops in front of the mirror. To the mirror:*) Why? (*Stops, turns away, talks to one of the portraits.*) Why must I always think that I haven't switched it off? (*Pause, to himself:*) Am I the only one who always thinks that? (*Sitting down on the bed.*) If not (*pause; softly*)—where are all my brothers? (*Pause.*) And if so—why me? Of all people—me? (*He looks around the room; loud:*) Why always me? On top of everything else! (*Softly:*) But I suppose it's only a part of everything else. (*Pause.*) What can I do about it? (*Pause, shakes his head.*) Nothing. (*Turning to one of the portraits:*) No. I can't do anything about it. It's too late for experiments. (*Pause, then to another portrait:*) Of course: while switching off the light, I ought to say to myself: now I am switching off the light. And then, later, when I ask myself whether I have switched off the light or not, I should remember that I've switched it off. (*To another portrait:*) But this is just what I always forget (*Into the room, including the audience*), while I *never* forget to switch off the light. (*Pause; to another portrait:*) I always think . . . (*Interrupts himself, then to another portrait:*) I always think: Sometime there will come a night when I *know* that I've switched off the light. (*To another portrait:*) But when? Time is running out. (*To another portrait:*) And who knows: that night might be just the night when I *have* forgotten to switch it off. (*Pause; then to himself:*) And then there's the front door. (*To a portrait:*) Yes, take the front door, for instance. I know and I have known for some time that I've locked it; I don't go down anymore to make sure. (*To another portrait:*) But the question remains: is it really locked? (*Turns around, facing the audience.*) What has my knowledge of the front door to do with the front door? (*Pause. He gets up.*) Perhaps (*undecided*)—I should—today—just for one—? (*Makes up his mind.*) Yes: today I am going to look . . . (*to a portrait*) . . . just once more . . . (*to another portrait*) . . . the last time . . . (*to another portrait*). And then never again. . . . (*Goes toward the door, stops in front of the mirror, looks at himself.*) No. (*To the mirror, shakes his head:*) No. It's ridiculous. (*To a portrait:*) The front door *is* locked. (*To a portrait:*) I needn't go down to make sure. (*Looks at the clock, then at his watch on the night table.*) It's after ten. My hour has begun. (*Opens the night-table drawer, takes out a list, takes the spectacles from the night table, puts them on and reads:)* "Number one: switch off the light in the bathroom." *(Lowers the list, reflects.)* I *have* switched it off. I *am* certain. *(Pause, wavering.)* Almost certain. *(Banishing his doubt.)* Certain enough. *(Reading from the list:)* "Number two: close the shutters." *(Puts spectacles and list on the table, gets up.)* Close the shutters! *(On his way to the window.)* I wonder why I always open them again. *(At the window, opening it.)* How cool the night air is. *(Looks out of the window. The moon is shining.)* Moon. Of course! There she is again, God's suspended slingshot stone. *(Pause.)* But whom did he want to hit? *(Pause.)* Who knows! *(Turns around again.)* Ah, if we knew that, it would be a great step ahead! *(Unlatches the shutters.)* But the mystery would not yet be solved. *(Looking at the moon.)* There she is. Looks like nothing else in the world—an old inedible piece of cheese maybe. *(Closing the shutters.)* And yet *(latches the shutters)*—she penetrates, forces her way through the walls. *(Shutting the window.)* You can't keep her out, not her. *(To a portrait:)* She sucks the sleep out of your very brains. Oh yes, I know her—the bitch—she's one of the worst. *(Turning back toward the room.)* Doesn't even have to shine *(to a portrait)*—just think of her *(to another portrait)* just touch her with a point of your thought, and there she is, rumbling, droning *(pointing between his eyes)* here, between your eyes or in the back of your head. *(Going back to the bed.)* Ah yes—I should like to sleep *(sitting down on the bed)*—I should like to rest—to lie, without my senses spreading out their tentacles in all directions *(pause)*—trembling tentacles, antennae vibrating. *(To a portrait:)* They feel their way through the night, receiving her noises, drawing them into me through my ears *(turning around; loudly)*—I am everywhere *(softly)*—and nowhere. *(Gets up, restless.)* Often I have asked myself— *(Interrupts himself, then to a portrait:)* It was only yesterday that I asked myself: just what do I need ears for? *(Stopping in front of the mirror.)* But questions which you ask yourself are not answered. *(To the mirror:)* Or are they? *(Turning around; very loudly:)* Or are they, I'd like to know! *(Shrugging his shoulders, sitting down on the bed, to himself:)* And yet: these are the only important questions *(picking up list and spectacles)*, *if* there is any such thing as an important question. (*Puts on his glasses, reads:*) "Number three: draw the curtains!" (*Puts spectacles and list on the table.*) Yes. That's important. (*Gets up.*) Draw the curtains tightly. (*Goes to the window.*) Darkness is not dark enough for me, when I want to sleep. (*Drawing the curtains.*) And indeed: when do I *not* want to sleep! (*In front of the curtains:*) I want darkness, blackness, a room packed full of black, caught, imprisoned time. (*Goes back to the bed.*) Masses of it. (*Sitting down on the bed.*) I shall make my bed in it and lie down, softly, snugly, when the moon goes down. (*Picking up the list, putting on the spectacles, reads:*) "Number five: lock the door." (*Is about to put list and spectacles on the table, stops, reflecting.*) Lock the door? But surely that comes last. I've left out something. (*Reading, softly:*) "Number two: close the shutters. Number three: draw the curtains—" (*Loud again:*) "Number four: look under the bed." (*Puts down list and spectacles.*) I knew there was something else (*opening the drawer*). But it always catches up with me again. (*To a portrait:*) Again and again I've tried— (*Hesitates, then to another portrait:*) Sometimes I've tried to do without it. (*Unlocks the safety catch of the revolver.*) But I can't. It doesn't work. Somewhere in my head there remains a tiny pocket of disquiet. (*Goes down on his knees beside the bed.*) Sometimes it comes over me very much later (*lies down on the floor*) and robs me of my precious sleep. And yet: there isn't anybody under the bed. (*Lifts the hanging part of the bedspread.*) My God, if I were so sure of everything as I am of that! And yet (*looks under the bed*), there might be someone under the bed (*drops the bedspread*) just at the very moment when I give up looking under it. (*Gets up, arrests action.*) No. (*Lies down again, lifts the bedspread.*) Nobody! (*Looking under the bed again.*) How *could* there be anybody under the bed? (*Gets up.*) How could he have come in? (*To a portrait, laughing:*) Through the locked front door perhaps? (*To another portrait:*) What? (*Laughs, turns around.*) I'm asking: through the locked front door? Well? (*Puts the revolver back into the drawer.*) No. (*Reassuring himself.*) No. (*Shakes his head.*) No. (*Sits down on the bed.*) Or—? (*Looks around, stares at the chair with the ropes.*) Or—perhaps it isn't locked? (*To the chair:*) Perhaps I should go and make sure? (*Pause, then to a portrait:*) Well? (*Pause; to another portrait:*) Should I? (*An-

other portrait:) For the last time? (*Another portrait:*)
And then never again? (*Gets up, hesitates, makes one
step toward the door, stops in front of the mirror. Pause.*)
No. Don't go and make sure! It's ridiculous. After all (*to a
portrait:*), I locked it myself. (*Loud, tries to convince himself:* Yes, the front door is locked. (*To the portraits:*) Right?
(*Pause.*) Of course. (*The telephone rings.*) Damn telephone!
(*Goes to the bed.*) Ruining the best part of my day! (*Puts
his pillow over the telephone.*) Always. (*Telephone ringing
muffled.*) The only bearable hour of my waking day. Grudges
me my hour of quiet. (*More muffled ringing.*) Not even the
precious moments of preparation. As if they knew at the
other end (*to a portrait:*)—wherever that other end may be
—that I am preparing for sleep. For peace and quiet. (*Ringing muffled.*) Peace—a horizontal landscape. I am moving
toward it, slowly, gradually, carefully— (*Telephone rings
mutedly, then stops.*) I am floating nearer and nearer— no: I
am creeping toward it (*turns around*) in humility and ex-
pectation, waiting for it to accept me, to draw me in (*getting
up, moving toward the wardrobe*), so that I might dive into
it, go under, submerge in its depths (*opens both doors of the
wardrobe. Its shelves are filled up with sleeping pills and
tablets in large bottles*), face forward and down into the
earth (*going back one step so as to have a better view*)—
there it is, spreading, expanding itself before me! (*Looking
at the shelves:*) A magnificent view! (*To a portrait:*) I say
to myself (*to another portrait:*), what could happen to me
now? (*Pause, then to himself:*) Nothing. (*Turns around.*)
Almost nothing. (*Goes to the bedside table, picks up his
spectacles, is about to put them on, sees the list, checks himself.*) Wait! Not yet! (*Picks up list, puts on spectacles.*)
There's something missing. (*To a portrait:*) I know what it
is, too. (*Looks at the list.*) But it is advisable to look it up.
(*Reads:*) "Number five: lock the door." (*Puts list and spectacles on the bedside table.*) I knew it. (*Takes a key from the
drawer.*) Lock the door! All right, why not? (*Goes to the
door.*) A matter of habit, no more. (*Puts the key into the
lock.*) It isn't really necessary. (*Locks the door.*) Because the
front door is locked. (*Moves toward the bed, stops in front of
the mirror.*) Or (*in doubt*)—is the front door not locked?
(*Makes up his mind.*) This time I shall go and . . . (*Goes
back to the door, tries to open it, but it is locked. He turns*

the key, opens the door and listens.) No—all the doors are locked. Everything's locked. (*Locks the door; about to withdraw the key, stops.*) Once more. (*Turns the key again.*) Safer. (*Withdraws the key.*) After all, there might be someone in the house. (*Goes back to the bed.*) He would be locked in. (*Puts the key back into the drawer.*) Caught between the locked front door and the locked bedroom door. (*To a portrait:*) Not a bad hunting ground. Might do worse. (*Takes up the spectacles; very loud:*) But there *isn't* anyone in the house. (*To a portrait:*) Who could there be? (*Another portrait:*) Right? (*To the chair:*) Nobody's there. (*Low, to himself:*) Nobody. (*Puts on spectacles, goes to the wardrobe.*) My landscape. (*Looks inside wardrobe.*) Designed over many long years, I my own god, who—behold!—saw that it was good. (*Pause.*) A good sight. Unalterable. (*Takes out a bottle, looks at it, reads label, shakes his head.*) No. (*Puts the bottle on the dresser.*) There isn't the right one yet. Too weak for the night. (*Takes out another bottle.*) Not this either. This just scurries across the brain pan, it merely tickles the skull— (*Puts the bottle on the dresser.*) Good enough for a little nap in the afternoon (*examines a few more, puts them on the dresser*)—and not even that anymore. No little naps in the afternoon for me. (*Another few bottles, puts them on the dresser.*) I'm saving—saving up for the night. (*Looks at the bottle.*) Not that either, that used to work (*puts it on the dresser*) when the weak was strong enough. (*To a portrait:*) Why do I keep all this? (*Pauses.*) Well (*pause*)—I suppose (*pause*)—for the sake of completeness. I collect—collect— (*To himself:*) I am a collector who collects the sand under his feet as he goes. (*Pause.*) Goes? (*Low:*) Goes where? (*Takes out another bottle.*) That wouldn't go far either, not now. (*Puts it on the dresser, which is almost full.*) It just oozes away in the blood. (*Hesitating.*) And yet (*picks up the bottle again*)—I should begin with something weak. It prepares the organism. (*Shakes his head, smiling.*) Organism! (*Looks at the label, reads:*) "Diethyl-dioxo-" (*He sits down on the bed, bottle in hand, and reads:*) "Diethyl-dioxo-tetra-hydropyridine." (*Pause. He lifts his spectacles onto his forehead and repeats the word, staring in front of him, trying to remember something.*) Diethyl-dioxo-tetra-hydropyridine . . . (*Reflecting.*) Yes—it is fairly weak, if I remember rightly—and yet, a good solid

drug, not for heavy sleep—to be sure—but it prepares the dis-
position toward sleep—it prepares the ground for the next one,
the stronger one, as it were. (*To a portrait, holding up the
bottle:*) It was good enough for several years, this one (*to
another portrait*)—before the generals' widows (*to himself*)—
it was before the cardinals, too (*shakes his head as if to get
rid of unpleasant memories*)—but when was it? When? (*Puts
spectacles on again.*) And where did I buy it? (*Holds the
bottle up to the light.*) Half empty. Perhaps I take it still—
sometimes? Perhaps to prepare myself for the stronger ones?
(*Opens the bottle, smells it.*) Now—where did I . . . (*Trying to remember.*) Was it London? Or Montevideo? (*Thinking.*) No, it wasn't Montevideo. I've never been to Montevideo, as far as I remember. (*Pause.*) My memory fails me.
(*Pause. To himself:*) But I'm almost sure that I've never
been there. (*To a portrait:*) And if I *have* been there, it must
have been a long time ago. A time when I could still sleep.
(*To a portrait:*) Or at least (*to another portrait*) when this
drug was strong enough to put me to sleep. (*To another portrait:*) I don't remember much about those times. But (*to
himself*) come to think of it—I don't remember much about
other times either—in fact: very little (*low*) almost nothing
(*almost voiceless*)—nothing—except the horrible. That remains. (*Pause. He looks at the bottle.*) However—it wasn't
Rome. (*Tormented by memories.*) No, God knows, it wasn't
there. (*Takes a handkerchief from the drawer.*) In Rome
(*wipes his forehead*) there were the cardinals. (*To a portrait:*) There I needed something stronger than this. (*Another portrait:*) This wouldn't have been strong enough. Not
in Rome. (*Shuts his eyes in remembrance of horror.*)
Rome! Dimethyl-amino-propylidene-dibenzo-cycloheptadiene
—yes, that's what it was. (*To a portrait:*) And even that isn't
the strongest of all. Of course, it's a good solid tablet and (*to
another portrait*) comparatively harmless—of course, only
comparatively. (*To another portrait:*) There is no danger of
addiction (*another portrait*); at least: no imminent danger.
(*Turns around.*) Danger of addiction is in everything, to a
certain extent, of course. (*To another portrait:*) Taken in
sensible doses, it has no aftereffect. (*To the chair:*) Of
course: the question is: what is a sensible dose? (*Turns
around.*) A good question! A question with a catch to it.
(*Looking at the bottle in his hand.*) But this one here is

much weaker. A gentle wave beating against the coast of the skull. (*Trying to remember.*) But where *was* it that I . . . (*Gets up, walks a few steps, stops.*) I think I know. (*To the chair:*) It was somewhere in the country, some provincial town (*to a portrait*), perhaps in Heidelberg or some such place. Or in Cambridge. (*To another portrait:*) Or Strassburg? (*Turns around.*) It's all the same, really (*pause*), or isn't it? (*Pause; low:*) Yes, it's all the same. (*Pause.*) But in those days I didn't know that. (*Turning to the chair:*) A young girl— (*Interrupts himself, turns to a portrait:*) Was it my niece? (*Another portrait:*) Yes, it may have been my niece— (*To the chair:*) Her name must have been Hildegard or Irmgard or something like that, that's what they're called as a rule—but I'm not certain (*pause*)—it's long ago, I still had nieces in those days—or, at least, one niece (*turns around*)—anyway—this girl had asked me to attend a concert (*pause; to himself*) "attend a concert" yes, that's what she called it—what they used to call it. (*Low, reflecting.*) A concert! (*Loud, turns around, to the audience:*) A concert, I thought, can do no harm, or, at least, not much harm. There can be no terrible conclusion to a concert, so I thought. (*To a portrait:*) But too late I discovered that it was a concert of choirboys (*another painting*), these terrible little infants whom they drill in falsetto—they turn out lots of them— (*Sits down on the bed, reflecting a moment, shakes his head at the unpleasant memory, then to himself:*) There they stood, in a half-circle, with their greasy little partings over their pimply foreheads, and their little faces white and pink, their rosy little lips (*to a portrait*) so wide open that you could see the gold of their voices in their throats. (*Another portrait:*) Especially when they went up to the high G-sharp which they all reached without the slightest difficulty. (*Takes out the handkerchief.*) And their clean white little collars and their dirty black little thoughts. (*Wiping his forehead.*) No. It wasn't beautiful. Indeed not. (*Turning to the chair:*) There they stood, all of them model pupils, little grinds, all gamekeepers' sons and farmers' sons and in between, here and there a little eunuch, usually son of a count and a stable maid. (*To the audience:*) There they stood twittering and chirping an Ave Verum or an Ave Maria (*to himself*), if, indeed, they aren't the same thing. (*Pause.*) Anyway the effect is the same. (*Into the room:*) There they stood singing with a terrible ringing, resounding ardor; so angelically pure, so completely without overtones. (*To the audience:*) And all their eyes were directed heavenward, as if they saw their savior in the shape of an angel on a Christmas tree. (*Shakes his head violently, takes a tablet from the bottle.*) But what they were really looking at was their conductor. (*Closing the bottle.*) He was called Father Emmeran (*opening the bottle again*), they're all the same (*takes out another tablet*) if it comes to that. (*Into the room:*) He was a kind gray educator, a mild gentle friend of the Religious Muse. (*Closing the bottle.*) He was arrested soon after (*swallowing the tablets*) because he had (*takes a mouthful of water*) violated three of his little singers (*another mouthful*), two sopranos (*another mouthful*) and one contralto (*puts the tumbler down*), if I remember rightly. (*Puts the bottle on the floor, since there is no more room on the dresser.*) But there I may be wrong. (*Takes spectacles from the night table.*) Perhaps it was one soprano (*puts spectacles on*) and two contraltos. (*He goes toward the cupboard, stops in front of the mirror.*) My memory is beginning to fail me. (*Looking at himself in the mirror.*) Thank God! (*Takes another bottle from the wardrobe; absentmindedly:*) Singing boys— (*Looks for room for the bottle on the dresser and finally puts it on the floor.*) Open mouths (*looks at another bottle, puts it on the floor*)— a Father all in black with a gentle face and gentle hands (*takes bottles out and puts them on the floor absentmindedly*) —that makes for a sleepless night. (*Another bottle.*) I remember (*stops taking out bottles*) hurrying through dead moonlit streets in search of a pharmacy with night service. (*Another bottle.*) Well, that was long ago (*puts the bottle on the floor*), very long ago. (*Sitting down on the bed, takes off spectacles, wipes his eyes, tired.*) Diethyl-dioxo-tetra-hydropyridine. (*Shakes his head.*) Today that wouldn't put me to sleep anymore. (*To a portrait:*) But then—I slept (*to himself*), as far as I remember. (*Pause.*) And yet: every now and then—at this time of the night—those terrible boys are after me (*tormented*)—an Ave Verum lurks around a corner—a high soprano echoes— (*Pause; shaking it off:*) Well—even worse was to come—later. My God, there are other things after me— (*Pause; then suddenly:*) Have I switched off the light in the bathroom? (*Gets up, goes to the bathroom door, opens it. The light is on.*) No. Of course I haven't switched it off. (*He switches it off.*) I never switch it off (*shuts the door*), I always forget. (*Goes toward the bed, stops, goes back, opens the door once more to convince himself that the light is off. It is off. Shuts the door, goes toward the bed, stops.*) Have I closed the shutters? (*Goes to the window, opens the curtains.*) Yes, I've closed them, of course; I remember, there was the moon. *That* thing is after me, too. (*Goes to the bed; softly:*) But even that isn't the worst. It drones in my head, yes, but at least it doesn't touch me with its hands. (*Pause; he sighs, tired.*) What next? (*Looks around, notices that the curtains are open.*) Number three: draw the curtains! (*Gets up.*) That is important. (*Goes to the window.*) Black time, dense masses of black time, that's what I want in here. (*Draws the curtains.*) Never let darkness escape once you've caught it. (*Goes to the bed, turns around.*) To sleep, in the midst of accumulated time. (*He sits down on the bed, picks up the list.*) But there was still more. (*Puts on spectacles.*) Or wasn't there? (*Reads:*) "Number four: look under the bed." (*Takes revolver from the drawer.*) But surely I've done this before . . . (*Releases safety catch, a cartridge jumps out.*) Yes, I *have* done it before! (*Looks questioningly from one portrait to the next.*) But with what result? (*Goes down on his knees.*) I am beginning to forget the most important things. (*On his knees, looking around.*) Important? What is important? (*He lies down on the floor, lifts the foot of the bedspread. At this moment the Burglar crawls from under the bed and atop it, opposite. He tries to jump over the bed and leap on the Man from above. But the Man jumps up—developing an unexpected fitness and efficiency—and, still lying on the floor, seizes the Burglar by the throat, holding him down on the bed and threatening him with the revolver.*) Stop! Don't move! (*He gets up, holding the Burglar down tight on the bed.*) Now do what I tell you! (*Pressing the revolver against him.*) Otherwise I'm going to shoot. (*He moves back a step, constantly aiming at the Burglar.*) What happens now I have rehearsed more than once. (*Aiming at the Burglar.*) Now get up! (*The Burglar gets up slowly, looking at the Man.*) Put your hands over your head. (*Burglar does so.*) Fold them! (*Burglar does so.*) Now stay there! Don't move! (*The Man moves around the bed, constantly aiming at the Burglar.*) I am quite capable of shooting you! (*He stands in front of the Burglar, puts his hand into the Burglar's right trouser pocket, pulls out a black-jack and throws it on the foot of the bed.*) I've seen action in a few world wars. (*Puts his hand into the Burglar's left trouser pocket, pulls out a crowbar, tosses it on the foot of the bed.*) Not voluntarily, naturally. Don't think that! (*Puts his hand into the Burglar's back pocket and produces a pair of gloves, puts them on the foot of the bed.*) But I made the best of it. I was young then. (*Puts his hand into the right hip pocket, pulls out a tin sandwich box, puts it on the foot of the bed.*) Now I am old and don't make the best of anything (*left hip pocket: a flashlight. On the foot*)—and yet, you know: eventually you get used to everything. (*Vest pocket: a pair of pliers. Foot.*) I could tell you a lot about that, I suppose. (*Right breast pocket: a Thermos bottle: Foot.*) In fact: I *shall* tell you a lot about that. (*Left breast pocket: a bunch of keys and picklocks. Foot.*) After all, I've been expecting you for a long time. (*Searches his pockets again.*) Since my childhood, to be exact (*frisks him one last time*), although, I must confess that I imagined you a little bigger—broader and more distinguished in a sinister sort of way. But come to think of it: everything that happens is at least one dimension smaller than you've imagined it to be. (*He goes back one step, still pointing the revolver at the Burglar.*) At *least* one dimension. Often much more. Now sit down on that chair! (*The Burglar sits down on the chair with the ropes.*) Put your hands on your thighs. Press tight! (*Burglar does so.*) As you see (*he begins to tie him up, first with one hand, with the other pointing the revolver at the burglar*)—everything is prepared (*puts down the revolver*) very carefully (*tying him up with both hands*) for the long-awaited guest who has put off his arrival again and again. (*He begins to knot the rope.*) Developed them myself, these knots. I've worked on them many winter months (*making a number of artful knots*) —wasn't easy inventing them, but it was much more difficult not to forget them again. (*He has finished the tying up.*) Now try and free yourself! (*Burglar does so but cannot move.*) You see? Doesn't work, does it?—Well, I have not spent my years in vain. (*Picks up the revolver and moves away, stops, turns to the Burglar again.*) Of course: I can't be certain of that until they're over. (*Reflects a moment.*) What's next? (*He goes to the bed, sits down, puts the revolver back into the drawer, looks around, sees the list, reads:*) "Number four:

look under the bed." (*Pause.*) I *have* looked. This time I'm certain. (*Reads:*) "Number five: lock the bedroom door." (*Puts down spectacles and list.*) Lock the door, yes. (*Gets up, goes to the door, opens it, it is not locked, listens. Pause.*) As long as I'm here—perhaps I should go and see whether the front door . . . (*Interrupts himself, looks at the Burglar, locks the door with the key, withdraws the key, goes to the bed, puts the key into the drawer, goes slowly toward the Burglar.*) How did you get into the house?

BURGLAR: Me? I never enter any house except through the front door. Never!

MAN: Through the front door. . . . I see. You broke it open, then.

BURGLAR: Not this time. Wasn't necessary. It wasn't locked.

MAN (*turning away from the burglar; after a pause*): . . . wasn't locked. So the door was open. I knew it.

BURGLAR: If you knew it—why didn't you lock it?

MAN (*not listening*): I always wanted to lock it. But I never got down to it. There was always something else to think of. (*To a portrait:*) Isn't that true? (*Nods; to himself:*) Yes. There was always . . . (*Interrupts himself. To the Burglar:*) Under the circumstances it surprises me that you didn't come earlier.

BURGLAR: I've been in the house for some time.

MAN: And where have you been up to now?

BURGLAR: In the rooms downstairs. They were beautiful rooms.

MAN: Beautiful rooms—

BURGLAR: They *were* beautiful. But I more or less took them apart.

MAN (*not listening*): So—I left the front door open. (*Pause; then, turning to the Burglar:*) Did you lock it?

BURGLAR: I? Why should I?

MAN: Yes, why should you. . . . (*Decisive.*) I *am* going to lock it. Right now! (*He moves toward the door, stops in front of the mirror.*) But why? Why now? Now it's too late. (*Turning away.*) There's no reason to lock the front door anymore.

BURGLAR: No reason whatsoever, as far as I can see.

MAN (*not listening*): Too late. After all: you're here now.

BURGLAR: You've got a point there.

MAN: That's right—he's here. Nothing else can happen now.

BURGLAR: I wouldn't say that.

MAN (*not listening. Turning to a portrait*): There won't be two burglars in one night, will there?

BURGLAR: It's at least most unlikely, I should say.

MAN (*not listening*): Not very probable. (*Sitting down on the bed.*) It would be against the law of probability.

BURGLAR: There is no law of probability.

MAN (*not listening*): To think that I once expected as many as four—

BURGLAR: I know that from long experience—

MAN: One has expected much—

BURGLAR: Probability—

MAN: But whatever happened—

BURGLAR: —defies all laws—despises them—

MAN: —was always the most improbable thing.

BURGLAR: . . . just as I do.

MAN: —until it was the improbable that one expected. So the improbable became the probable. (*From here on the Burglar begins to try to free himself by straining against the rope with one arm or one leg at a time.*) And when there were two possibilities, it was always the more unlikely one that occurred. (*To a portrait:*) I admit (*another portrait*) in retrospect, this seems actually to have been the more likely one. (*Turning to the Burglar, who, whenever the Man turns to him, interrupts his efforts and suddenly sits still:*) But you— I've been expecting you. Otherwise I would have locked the front door. (*To a portrait:*) Wouldn't I? (*To another portrait:*) Most certainly. (*Pause.*) Otherwise I would have— (*Loses his thought.*) But what for? (*Pause. He gets up and*

L

goes to the wardrobe.) Tomorrow I shall hand you over to the police. (*Savoring the word.*) Tomorrow! (*Takes out a bottle, looks at it, puts it on the floor, takes another bottle, without concentrating.*) Mercilessly. (*Pause.*) Do you hear?

BURGLAR (*has not listened*): What was that? (*Perfunctorily:*) Oh, mercilessly, yes, of course.

MAN (*looking at a bottle, softly*): Mercy? (*Turns around; loudly:*) Has anyone mercy on me? (*Puts the bottle on the floor.*) No. No one. (*Looking inside the wardrobe.*) Except my landscape. I am drawing nearer now. (*Looking at a bottle.*) Former days. (*Puts it down. Holds another bottle to the light.*) Empty. (*Throws it into a corner, takes out another bottle, looks at it.*) That's it. (*To the Burglar:*) My favorite drug. (*Qualifying:*) Or shall we say: my favorite drug of moderate strength. (*Reads:*) "Dimethyl-amino-propylidene-dibenzo-cycloheptadiene." Yes, that's it. (*He sits down on the bed, bottle in hand, pushes his spectacles up onto his forehead.*) I took this for the first time in Rome. (*Holds the bottle to the light.*) I shall have to order a new bottle soon. It's almost empty. (*Opens it.*) Only one tablet of this. (*He shakes one tablet out.*) So that it doesn't spoil my appetite for the others. (*To the Burglar:*) You have to know the proper dosages. (*Closes the bottle.*) But I'm an expert at that (*is about to put the bottle on the floor, stops*), if only at that. (*Opens the bottle again.*) Perhaps I should take two. (*He shakes another tablet from the bottle.*) I shall. And then take less of the next one, the stronger one. (*Closes the bottle.*) You have to be economical with your system. (*Puts the bottle on the floor, remains in this position for a moment.*) Be "economical"? Yes (*nods*), that's what I was taught. But what for? (*Gets up.*) That's what I wasn't taught. (*He pours himself a glass of water.*) Yes, in those days, in Rome, I wasn't resigned yet, I was (*swallows a tablet*) young then, I was (*takes a mouthful of water*) full of hope (*second tablet*), I was still in my prime (*mouthful of water*), I felt alive (*interrupts himself*)—no, not that. (*Mouthful of water.*) No. (*Changes subject.*) Anyhow, it's a good solid tablet of medium strength. (*To the Burglar, who has meanwhile managed to loosen the ropes considerably, but who always interrupts his efforts when the Man turns to him:*) Naturally, today it isn't strong enough anymore. Even two wouldn't work, not even three. But it augments the next, it prepares the palate, as it were. It complements the effect of the tablet to come, you see? (*Puts his spectacles down and goes to the wardrobe.*) And now for the stronger one. I'm nearing the peaks of my landscape now, the highlights. (*Takes out a bottle, looks at it, shakes his head.*) Naturally (*puts the bottle on the floor*), it will have its aftereffects. (*Another bottle.*) But when you want to sleep (*puts the bottle down*), you have to put up with aftereffects. After all (*looking at another bottle closely*), waking has its aftereffects, too, hasn't it? (*Puts the bottle down.*) Everything has its aftereffects, if it comes to that—not to mention its side effects. (*Turns around.*) Or hasn't it? (*Pause.*) Yes, it has. (*Takes out a bottle, stops suddenly.*) Yes, in Rome, that's where it was. There was a parade (*trying to remember*)—a kind of procession— (*To the Burglar:*) Would that have been Candlemas?

BURGLAR (*matter-of-fact*): No. Assumption of the Blessed Virgin Mary.

MAN: Yes. (*Nods.*) Perhaps it was that. Something like that, in any case. Something terrible, frightening.

BURGLAR: Immaculate Conception.

MAN: Perhaps that, too. Yes, that's what it was, I think. (*Remembering.*) The cardinals were carried through the streets. All 715 cardinals of the world. The black ones, too, and the yellow ones.

BURGLAR (*nods confirmingly*): Yes. Immaculate Conception.

MAN (*as if remembering a bad dream*): They sat upright in their litter chairs. The litter chairs were carried by bishops. By all the bishops of the world. (*Taking out his handkerchief.*) All the bishops of the world carried all the cardinals of the world through the streets of Rome. (*He wipes his forehead.*) And the cardinals were all in red, blood red, like at the Inquisition. Some of them were tall and thin, others were short and fat, still others—perhaps the majority—were tall and fat—there were some short and thin ones, too, but not many—they don't make them cardinals very often. (*Pause. He puts his hand over his eyes for a moment.*) The short fat ones—those were the most dangerous. They had small, shifty eyes. Eyes which penetrate the skirt of every penitent, tearing it to

pieces and grabbing the sin underneath by its tail— (*Nods.*)
Oh yes, they always manage to get hold of that— (*Pause.*)
They had long painted fingernails; I could see that because
they held large gold-plated crucifixes in their hands—made in
the mission jails of Peru—and each one (*interrupts himself,
tries to shake off the horror of this memory*)—and each one
had a huge cauldron with holy water in front of his belly.
They dipped their crucifixes into the holy water and sprinkled
it right and left and again right and left until it sizzled and
steamed. (*Wiping the sweat from his face. The Burglar has
abandoned his efforts and listens spellbound.*) All in strict
rhythm—because in front (*interrupts himself*)—yes—in front
there was, striding—no, he wasn't striding—he was riding: in
front rode on a dapple-gray horse a priest of the papal house-
hold with a kettledrum. He was beating the drum and giving
the rhythm. (*He acts the scene.*) Bang! Right!—Bang! Left!
—Bang! Right!—Bang! Left!—(*Shuts his eyes for a moment,
then opens them again.*) The streets emptied themselves as if
it were suddenly hailing from a sunny sky. The people fled
in panic, fear, in terror and anguish, they made the sign of
the cross, some of them were crawling on their knees, everybody was squirming and writhing in sin and guilt (*softly*)—
only I—I have no sins—or, at least: I can find none. I stood
there, horror-struck, until the parade was over and gone.
(*Wiping his face; then, more quietly:*) I heard the terrible
beating of the kettledrum in my ear for a long time after
that—the holy water was burning in my eyes—

BURGLAR: Why didn't you run away—or shoot?

MAN: . . . until the droning had died away and everything became calm again.

BURGLAR: In these situations you have to shoot!

MAN: A deadly quiet. Suddenly—I felt—as if I'd lost my ears. . . .

BURGLAR: Why didn't you shoot?

MAN (*to the Burglar*): I was unarmed.

BURGLAR: One machine gun would have been enough to wipe
out the whole lot. . . .

MAN: Would you have shot?

BURGLAR: I? I have nothing against cardinals.

MAN: I was in the minority. (*The telephone rings.*)

BURGLAR: You've got to take a risk sometimes.

MAN: I was told that, too. But it's not true.

BURGLAR: I always take risks. (*The telephone rings.*)

MAN: You do, yes—and you'll be sorry, this time.

BURGLAR: We'll see.

MAN (*shaking his head*): I had nobody on my side. (*The telephone rings.*)

BURGLAR: How do you know? You can never tell.

MAN: You can feel it. I was alone.

BURGLAR: Sometimes that's best. (*The telephone rings.*) Don't you answer your telephone?

MAN: I was lonely. As lonely as I am now. More lonely. You're here now.

BURGLAR: I am, yes. And not only that, but there's somebody on the phone. (*The telephone rings.*) Go on! Answer the phone. This is unbearable.

MAN: How should *you* know what's unbearable! (*He goes to the bed and covers the telephone with the pillow again.*) It's not for me. (*Muffled ringing.*) It's never for me. (*Sitting down on the bed, wearily.*) Yes, that was a frightful experience— but it wasn't the most frightful one. (*The telephone rings once more, then stops.*) When I looked into the mirror that night, I discovered the first gray hair on my head. (*The burglar has turned away and yawns.*) And a slight trembling of my hands. (*Looks at his hands.*) I've never got rid of it. (*Gets up and goes to the wardrobe.*) Yes, that was in Rome. (*Puts spectacles on.*) In the Via di—Via di—(*Takes a bottle from the wardrobe.*) I've forgotten. (*Looks at the bottle but his mind is obviously elsewhere. The Burglar yawns and shuts his eyes.*) Yes—that was dimethyl-amino-propylidene-dibenzo-cycloheptadiene. In those days you could still get it without a prescription. (*Puts the bottle on the floor.*) Those were the good old days. (*Takes spectacles off, rubs his eyes.*) Well—

for all I know, you can still get it without a prescription. I haven't tried lately. (*Pause. He takes another bottle from the wardrobe.*) After all—it isn't strong—it's only medium strength. (*Puts spectacles on again, looks at the bottle.*) But you can't get the strong ones without a prescription anymore. (*Puts the bottle down. The Burglar is falling asleep.*) But I doubt that you could get the stronger ones without a prescription even then. (*Turns around.*) Perhaps times haven't changed that much, after all. (*Takes spectacles off, puts them on the night table, goes to the mirror.*) And it's only I (*looking at himself in the mirror*) who've changed. Have the drugs changed me? (*Pause.*) Or do I take them because I've changed? (*Leaves the mirror.*) No. (*Looking around.*) Everything has changed, the drugs have changed (*looking at the paintings*), and the times (*in front of the mirror again*) and I. (*Is about to turn away from the mirror but notices in the mirror that the Burglar has fallen asleep. He speaks to him in the mirror.*) Hey! You! (*Turns to the Burglar.*) You! (*Goes to him.*) Stop sleeping! (*Shakes him.*) Stop sleeping! Have I lured you into my house for *that*? (*Shouting at him:*) I haven't left the front door open for years to have someone come and sleep here!

BURGLAR (*waking up*): Why don't you let me sleep!

MAN: I want someone to listen to me. To rid myself of all the terror so that I'll be absolutely empty when sleep finally comes.

BURGLAR: I won't listen.

MAN (*not listening—emphatically*): Have you ever been alone in a room with someone who is asleep? (*Shouting:*) Horror flaps its wings and flutters through the room and bumps against the walls.

BURGLAR: I'm not dangerous when I'm asleep.

MAN: What do *you* know of sleep! And what do you know of danger! A man who is dangerous is also dangerous in his sleep, more dangerous even than when he's awake. But you, you're not dangerous, neither asleep nor awake. Not you. There are other things I could tell you about. I've been through terrible things. (*Turns away from him.*) You'll stay

awake as long as I stay awake. (*Goes to the night table.*) And
longer! You'll be awake when I've fallen asleep. (*Takes his
spectacles from the night table.*) You'll stay awake whether
you like it or not—and watch me sleep! (*Puts on spectacles,
goes to the wardrobe. The Burglar proceeds with his attempts
to free himself.*) Now the time has come. Time for heavier
fare. (*Searching in the wardrobe.*) The barbiturate. (*Takes
out a bottle, looks at it, shakes his head.*) No, not this one
yet. (*Tries to put the bottle on the floor, but the floor's
crowded.*) That isn't the right one yet. (*Looks for a place to
put the bottle down, stops.*) But that one, too (*holds up
bottle*) has served me well on more than one occasion. (*He
takes the pillow from the telephone and puts the bottle on
the night table.*) It contains a good quantity of phenyl—that
takes the edge off many a terror. (*At the wardrobe again.*)
That, of course, you couldn't get without a prescription
(*searching in the wardrobe*), but I have prescriptions (*pulling out a bottle*), a whole collection of autographs by famous
physicians (*burglar takes notice of this*); it should have a
certain value by now. (*He looks at the bottle in his hand.*)
This still isn't it. (*Is about to put the bottle away, stops.*)
Although (*reflects*) this one isn't bad either. I seem to remember— (*The Burglar has turned away again and proceeds
with his attempts. His neck is free by now.*) Perhaps I should
take a tablet or two of this (*setting down bottle in hand on
the bed*)—before I take the barbiturate. And then the most
powerful of all, at the very end. (*Pushes spectacles up on
forehead.*) Of course—there is the aftereffect (*pause*)—but
that comes later—after my sleep. (*Opens the bottle.*) We are
not that far yet, thank God. (*Looking into the bottle.*) You
have to take things as they come—wait calmly (*smelling the
bottle*), have them come over you while you sleep (*pause;
then, weakly*), and then they fall upon you when you wake
up. (*Pause; he pulls himself together, lowers spectacles, reads
the label:*) "Dimethyl-benzol-amino-propylidene-cyclo-quinu-
clidinium—bromide—" (*Takes off spectacles, closes his eyes,
repeats by heart:*) Dimethyl-benzol-amino-propylidene-cyclo-
quinuclidinium-bromide? (*Reflecting.*) Well, it isn't really
much more than an intensified dimethyl-amino-propylidene-
dibenzo-cycloheptadiene. Yet: it *is* intensified, it's stronger.
(*Puts his spectacles on the night table, pours himself a glass
of water.*) One of these will do. (*He takes out one tablet.*)

Or perhaps two. Just to be on the safe side. (*He takes two more out.*) It can't do me much harm, not anymore. (*Takes one tablet with a mouthful of water and looks at the bottle again.*) I haven't taken any of these for a long time. (*Meanwhile the burglar has freed his hands. He begins to untie the rope.*) I've forgotten, where (*smells the bottle*)—would that have been—? (*Puts the bottle on the night table, takes another tablet, savoring its taste.*) It was (*tasting it, shutting his eyes*)—it was Paris! (*Takes the third tablet, savoring its taste.*) Yes—it was Paris. (*Drinks the whole glass of water, pours himself another.*) Paris! (*His face darkens at unpleasant memories.*) Yes— (*He empties the glass.*) That's where it was. The generals' widows! (*Burglar interrupts his attempts, listens.*) They came from seven different European countries. (*Gets up, puts his hand to his forehead.*) They—they were reinforced by a regiment of Daughters of the American Revolution! (*He takes a few steps, very much disturbed.*) They were all over seventy and thin as rakes—they were like great big black spiders. (*Interrupts himself and shuts his eyes.*)

BURGLAR (*bored*): Skip it.

MAN (*pays no attention to him*): Yes—they were all in black. They marched down the Champs Élysées to the Tomb of the Unknown Soldier, goose-stepping— (*softly:*) There were three thousand of them—

BURGLAR: Just skip it!

MAN: Imagine! Three thousand of them. It was a silent protest march. (*Pause.*) But what were they protesting against? (*Walks up and down, trying to remember.*) I don't remember. (*Stands still.*) Yes, I do. They were protesting against Peace. (*Reflecting.*) But—was it peacetime then? (*Pause.*) I don't remember. My memory fails me. I'm getting tired, too. (*Sitting down on the bed.*) But not tired enough yet. I haven't all the ingredients of sleep in me yet. (*Tormented.*) The images have to disappear! (*He takes out his handkerchief and wipes his face.*) Yes—there they were, marching past me —and with every step they threw up their skirts (*shakes his head as if trying to shake off this unpleasant memory*) so that you could see their stockings and their bloomers, all black. Their bloomers went down to their knees, the knees were bare, the hollows of their knees, too (*terror in his voice*), and around their legs there was a ring of thin, shrunk, shriveled grayish-yellowish-white skin! (*Hides his face in his hands.*)

BURGLAR (*nervously*): Stop it! Shut up!

MAN (*not listening to him*): It was a frightful sight! I'll never forget it. Three thousand . . . !

BURGLAR (*shouting*): Stop! (*He tries to untie the knots at his legs.*)

MAN (*faltering*): And each one—each one carried a wreath of laurel made of plastic in her right hand on which it said in gilt letters: Liberté, Egalité, Fraternité. Their lips were stiff, there wasn't any red, there was nothing but a straight color-less slit where we have a mouth. And in their left hands—in their left hands they were carrying crumpled white lace hand-kerchiefs. They had narrow lace collars on, yellowed with age, and no hats. Their hair was stringy and gray. (*Sits down on the bed and shuts his eyes to dispel the image.*) And—and the crowns of their skulls were getting bald, the naked skin was shining through—yellow-white.

BURGLAR (*trying to rise, but still unable to*): Won't you shut up?

MAN (*paying no attention*): And—in front—in front there was marching a band—a female band. All daughters. Generals' daughters in the uniforms of their dead fathers, with drums and trumpets and cymbals and tubas and bassoons. But they were not playing, it was a silent march, you heard nothing but footsteps and dreadful silence.

BURGLAR (*furious, tries in vain to reach the blackjack on the bed*): Are you finished now?

MAN (*paying no attention*): That silence! It was streaming ahead, miles ahead, it expanded, penetrated everything, it came down on everything like a thick, sticky, disgusting layer (*working himself up*)—it was floating up in all directions over the streets and squares with frightful wings. (*Wipes his face, picks up the bottle again, opens it, takes out another tablet, pours himself some water and swallows the tablet with the water. Then silent and exhausted, sits on his bed, bowed down. The telephone rings.*) It was one of the most

L*

frightening silences I have ever heard. (*Pause. The telephone rings.*)

BURGLAR (*also exhausted, from his own struggling*): Why don't you at least answer the telephone?

MAN: I shall never forget it. That night when I looked into the mirror, I saw that I had gone gray, and (*touching his eyes*) my eye sockets had deepened. (*The telephone rings.*)

BURGLAR: Answer the telephone!

MAN (*gradually recovering, taking his spectacles from the night table*): It isn't for me.

BURGLAR: How do you know?

MAN (*puts on spectacles, goes to the wardrobe, takes out a bottle*): I know. I'm certain. (*The telephone rings. He looks at the bottle and puts it down on the night table.*) Nobody ever calls me. I don't know anybody. (*Takes out other bottles, looks at them, shakes his head, puts them down.*)

BURGLAR: Perhaps somebody wants to meet you.

MAN (*looks at the bottle, tries to put it on the night table. There is no room, so he puts it on the bed*): Me? Who'd want to meet me? (*Telephone rings.*) Who is still aware of my existence? Of the few who ever were aware of it? Of the few I permitted to become aware of it?

BURGLAR: Maybe *you'd* like to meet somebody—for a change?

MAN (*by the wardrobe*): I don't want to meet anyone. It's too late for that now. I want to sleep.

BURGLAR (*has meanwhile managed to extricate one leg*): Perhaps there are relatives worrying about you somewhere? (*Telephone rings.*)

MAN (*taking out a bottle, looking at it*): About me?

BURGLAR: Perhaps you have some nephews—or even nieces?

MAN (*startled*): Nieces!! (*Puts the bottle down.*) Yes—maybe. (*He goes slowly to the phone, but it has stopped ringing.*) Perhaps I have nieces or—or one niece. (*Reflecting.*) I remember that . . . (*Picks up the receiver, listens.*) No one.

It was nobody. (*Going back to the wardrobe.*) And if it was somebody, he certainly didn't want to speak to me. (*Takes out a bottle.*) He dialed the wrong number. (*Looking at the bottle.*) Do you understand? (*Suddenly loud and wild:*) The wrong number!! (*He throws the bottle into a corner so that it breaks. He crosses slowly to the Burglar and speaks the following with increasing speed, working himself up into a hectic state. The Burglar sits motionless, as if still tied to the chair.*) Do you understand? My number is 6068. When my telephone rings, it's always a wrong number. Always. (*Loud and wild:*) Always! Always! (*Low and fast again:*) Either they want 6067 or 6069. The first number, 6067, belongs to the firm of Emil Christoph Verkade and Son, a world-famous firm of organ builders. It was established in 1706, when Friedemann Gottlieb Verkade built his first organ for Christian Dietrich Buxtehude. Calls for that firm generally come in the daytime, of course, but sometimes they come at night, too; oh yes, they come at night quite often now, any hour will do to get me up from my sleep. From America they ring me at night—it's daytime then in America. They are mostly Presbyterians or Mormons or . . .

BURGLAR: Mormons don't use organs.

MAN: Well then they're Adventists.

BURGLAR: Adventists prefer the harmonium.

MAN: All right, Presbyterians then or any sect that uses the organ —there are still plenty of them. And then there's the other number, 6069 . . . (*Pause; then, abruptly:*) I don't know about them. (*Pause.*) No, that one I don't know about. (*Goes back to the wardrobe.*) I've never been able to find out. (*Takes out a bottle, looks at it absentmindedly.*) Perhaps some kind of statistical office. (*Puts the bottle on the bed.*) Or something similar. (*Another bottle.*) Perhaps something else—anyhow, I don't know. (*Suddenly wild, throws the bottle into a corner, yells:*) I just don't know!!! (*Takes his spectacles off, puts them on the night table. During the following he is coming ever nearer the Burglar, speaking softly and quickly again, with increasing urgency.*) There's a voice on the phone, not always the same one, but mostly the same one, mostly male, but sometimes also female, but that's less frequent. They ask me whether this is number 6069. I say no, it's not, no (*yells*)—no—no. (*Quiet again:*) But they are not listening to me at the other end. They just say: please take this down. And then—they begin to dictate. They dictate numbers with one letter in between. Like this: 3227-B-4, 8539-M-2, 9582-S-7, and so on. There are always five numbers, and then—then they hang up. At the beginning I didn't wait for the numbers; I shouted, "Wrong number!" and hung up. (*Softly:*) Wrong number. (*Suddenly yelling:*) Wrong number! (*Quiet again:*) But then—later—I began to listen to the numbers, first only to one or two—and then—gradually to more and then to all five of them. I always hoped that something more would come at the end—the solution to the mystery—or perhaps a kind of statement that it had all been a joke. But nothing came. After the last number they always put down the receiver at the other end, always, without another word. And then—still later—I began to take down the numbers; I thought that I might—perhaps—make out a certain sense in them—some kind of connection might come to light, by subtraction or addition or multiplication. I sat over the numbers, trying to decipher something. I sat here, in this room, multiplying, adding, subtracting. The room filled up with figures, white figures and red figures—here and there a tiny hint seemed to be appearing; but no, it was all wrong, I was being led astray, there was nothing. Nothing. My brain became all fuzzy, and the mystery remained. And finally—lately—I—I don't know why—I have begun to call others, in the middle of the night. I dial a number, any number, and I say: Please take this down. And then I pass on the figures. (*Breathless:*) And do you know what happens? Every one I ring is prepared, as ready as if he'd been waiting for my call. Everyone says: I'm ready—and takes down the figures. In the dead of night. I hear, at the other end, the pencil going over the paper; I hear the scribbling. Each one writes down and repeats the figure I say, as if it were quite natural, without surprise, and always awake, whatever hour it may be. (*Whispering:*) It is—it is as if they all knew a secret from which I am excluded. I alone am the sole exception; I alone know nothing at all. I only transmit, I am the go-between, I pass it along from one to the next, completely ignorant, like a fool, a messenger whom nobody bothers about—without the least notion (*in great agitation*)—and perhaps even a tool in terrible hands—who knows! (*Pause. Softly:*) But whom do they

want to destroy if not me? (*Pause.*) Sometimes—sometimes—
I've tried to pass on figures I've made up myself, but then
they hang up immediately at the other end. They aren't
taken in by that. (*Pause.*) Yes—once they were. Once I gave
them an invented number which they seemed to listen to.
I thought then that I'd made progress; I thought: Now I
might develop a secret system myself which would help me
to solve the greater mystery gradually—but no: they hung
up at the second figure. And when I looked at my writing
pad later on—there was the first figure. I had, quite by accident, repeated a figure which I had been given. That gave
me the idea to pass on the figures of the previous night—but
when I did, they hung up immediately. Each night has its
own figures, its five figures, made up by unknown people.
They only ring once a night, and not even every night. Lately
I've started getting worried when they didn't ring. (*Exhausted.*) There's nothing I can do; it remains a mystery.
They all know it, only I—I don't know it. (*Pause; he fixes
his eyes on the Burglar, suddenly suspicious.*) Perhaps *you*
know it?

BURGLAR: Me? (*Ignoring the question.*) Why don't you get rid
of your telephone?

MAN: I've asked myself that, often. I did want to get rid of it,
then, when the calls first began. But when I began to pass
on the figures myself, I didn't want to get rid of it anymore.
I may not know what it is that's happening around me—but
I do want to know whether it's happening or not—or if perhaps some night it stops happening. Perhaps some night the
figures will be exhausted and the mystery will dissolve into
nothing—who knows? (*Pause; then, with emphasis:*) I am
asking you whether you . . . ?

BURGLAR (*interrupting*): And why haven't you tried to locate the
owner of number 6069?

MAN: I have tried. And I have located the owner. I went combing
through all the telephone directories; it took me many nights.
And finally I found the number. (*Pacing up and down the
room.*) But it didn't solve the mystery—on the contrary (*goes
to the bed*)—it made everything more mysterious. (*Sits down
on the bed, sighs in exhaustion.*) Söderbaum. Dr. Alfred G.

Söderbaum, that's his name. He's an orthopedist. His real number is 3111. And under that number it says in very small letters: if no answer, please ring number 6069. I've dialed this number many times—what am I saying: many times? For weeks I've tried to get him on the phone, day and night, every half hour. No one ever answered. Only, once, the phone was busy. Now—I thought—now I've hit upon it, now I've made a great step forward. I stayed on the phone, I kept dialing and dialing so as not to let it escape me, four hours I sat here, picking up the receiver, dialing, putting it down again, picking it up again, until finally the phone wasn't busy. But no one answered. Since that night it has never been busy again, and no one has ever answered. Then, one day, I rang number 3111. The phone was answered by a girl, probably a receptionist; it was during consultation hours. I didn't want to ask *her* my question. I rang again in the evening, there was a woman on the phone, probably Söderbaum's wife, and I hung up again. But finally, after several more attempts with the other number, I rang 3111 again, and this time I got Dr. Söderbaum himself. (*Pause.*) A pleasant, agreeable voice. I asked him point-blank what his other number, 6069, stood for. He said that if he could not be reached at 3111, he could be reached at 6069! I said I realized that, it said so in the directory, but what I wanted to know was: when! *When* could he be reached at 6069? He seemed a little surprised. He said, mostly he could be reached at 3111, but if not, there would always be his receptionist. I wanted to go on questioning him, I didn't want the thread to be broken, but I didn't know how or what to ask, as, in a way, his answer had been quite sufficient. Anyway, before I could think of something to say, he'd hung up, and there I was, alone. I could do nothing. (*Exhausted.*) Nothing. And I've done nothing since. (*Gets up, goes to the night table, picks up his spectacles.*) I wouldn't know what to do. And now I won't be able to find out anything else again. (*Goes to the wardrobe. The telephone rings, he runs to the phone, lifts the receiver.*) Six—O—No! This is *not* six—O—six—nine! Yes, I'm taking it down! (*He writes on a pad.*) 3188-B-6 (*pause*), 0242-C-7 (*pause*), 9854-N-1 (*pause*), 2653-H-8— (*Pause; then he puts the receiver down, astonished.*) Hung up! (*Lifts the receiver to his ear again, listens, then:*) Nothing! (*He jiggles the bar of the telephone a few times, shouting:*) Hello! Hello! (*Slowly puts down the*

receiver.) Strange! (*Disturbed*.) There were only four numbers, this time. (*Sits down on the bed, troubled*.) Now *that*,
on top of everything! (*Exhausted*.) I might have got used
to the fact that I couldn't get to the bottom of the mystery.
But now the mystery itself is changing. It's assuming another
shape. (*Softly*:) What's happening here? (*Louder*:) How is
it possible? They all know something I don't know, I, the
sole exception. (*To himself*:) How is that possible? (*To the
Burglar, louder and violently*:) How is it possible? Tell me:
how is it possible! (*Yelling*:) Tell me!!

BURGLAR (*who has meanwhile managed to free himself completely, sardonically*): Anything is possible.

MAN (*not yet noticing that the Burglar is free, calm again, turns
away from him, with contempt*): Yes. I expected that answer. (*Goes back to the wardrobe*.) "Anything is possible."
(*Burglar shakes and massages his ankles and knuckles*.) It is
the answer to everything and to nothing. (*Takes out a bottle,
looks at it, quoting*:) "Anything is possible." Of course. (*Puts
the bottle on the bed*.) Infinitely foolish is he who expects
a better answer. (*Taking out a bottle*.) Foolish enough is he
who puts the question. (*He puts the bottle down, stops,
looks at it again*.) That's it. (*Setting down bottle in hand
on the bed*.) The reliable drug, the most reliable of them all.
Good and strong. (*He reads*:) "Sodium-ethyl-phenyl-butyl-
barbiturate." That's it. (*To the Burglar who stretches and
walks toward the bed*:) I know—it doesn't sound like much
—it reads like a very modest combination. So short, so simple,
as if it had been concocted by an amateur. As if you could
give it to sleepless children. But believe me, that is not the
case; children would die of it. In its very simplicity lies its
effect. It is, in fact, a wonderful drug. (*Looks at the bottle*.)
Very strong because of all the phenyl—that's its most active
agent. For centuries the emperors of China used to poison
their enemies with it. And then, of course, there's the barbiturate, that, too— (*Puts his spectacles on the night table*.)
With a few tablets of that in me, I shall sleep, and no moon
will disturb me, no cardinal frighten me, not even a general's
widow will do me any harm. (*Yawns*.) I seem to feel Sleep
as he crawls out of this bottle toward me like a ghost. Where
(*yawns*), where did I buy that? (*Pause*.) When did I take it
for the first time? (*Trying to remember*.) It must have been

in a provincial town, too (*yawns*), some small place (*pause; suddenly disturbed*)—yes—it was somewhere by the banks of the Rhine—or in the Neckar Valley—or is that the same? (*Disturbed by unpleasant memories.*) Yes—that's where I got it—I remember—it was in the only pharmacy of that particular place, an old pharmacy in practically idyllic surroundings . . .

BURGLAR (*stands by the foot of the bed; has taken up his Thermos bottle, unscrewed it, and now pours some liquid into its cup*): You can skip it.

MAN (*not minding him*): . . . in the market square, under an ancient oak tree. There was moonlight.

BURGLAR: I said: You can skip it!! (*Drinks from the cup.*)

MAN: Or was it a statue? Or a monument?

BURGLAR (*puts the cup down*): Enough! Shut up! (*Another mouthful, then screws the cup back on the bottle.*)

MAN (*takes his handkerchief from the table*): The occasion was terrible enough (*mops his brow*)—it all comes back to me now.

BURGLAR (*throws the Thermos on the bed, picks up his blackjack*): Shut up, I say!

MAN (*gets up, spellbound by terrible memories*): Yes—it all comes back to me—there it was, the little town, the moon, the mountain, and on it the castle. (*Shakes his head as if to shake off the memory, takes a tablet from the bottle.*) No—one is not enough. (*Takes out another tablet.*) The castle was on the mountain above the town, a kind of citadel. (*He puts his hand over his face. The Burglar is leaning against one of the bedposts, the blackjack dangling from his hand.*) There were—what were they?—yes—they were state representatives—or even state secretaries—yes, they were state representatives *and* state secretaries—a great many of them. (*He takes a third tablet from the bottle.*) Four thousand of them—four thousand and twenty-two, to be exact (*pours himself a glass of water*)—I counted as many as that before I could escape (*he takes a tablet with a mouthful of water*)—but that was much, much later. (*Takes the second tablet with water.*) Yes, finally I did manage to escape— (*Takes the third tablet with water, pours himself another glass; breathlessly:*) Water! (*He drinks the whole glass in one gulp; breathlessly:*) By the skin of my teeth. Before they got hold of the beer and started boozing. (*Sits down on the bed, breathing heavily.*) I was up in the citadel to have a look at the thing—eleventh century—loopholes early twelfth—I had already even then begun to sleep badly—castles always helped a little—especially early castles with loopholes (*wipes the sweat from his face*)—there I was and there they all came up from the town—marching in rows of four (*working himself up*)—there was no escape. (*Gets up again and turns to the Burglar who is standing before him, legs apart, grinning, blackjack in hand.*) I was pushed back uphill again, backward—by the police—they were in full state uniform and had small sprigs of edelweiss on their helmets—I couldn't get past them—not I. Somebody else might have been able to— *you* might have been able to (*Burglar laughs*)—finally I jumped into the moat. Out of the window. I hurt myself. Since that day I limp. But that wasn't the worst thing—indeed, that was negligible, relatively. (*Breathing heavily, in great agitation.*) They held a meeting there. Whether they were petitioning for something or were celebrating something —that I don't remember—probably both. (*With the corresponding gestures.*) There were fat ones and thin ones, but otherwise they all looked alike—you couldn't have said (*pointing*): this one is better than that one. I admit: I don't know my way around with that sort of person—perhaps someone else might have known better—you, for instance. (*Burglar laughs.*) They were all bald. They wore black striped suits, snow-white waistcoats, with gold buttons, gray silk ties, white silk handkerchiefs, pink carnations in their buttonholes; all the same, you could only tell them apart by small brass plates which they wore (*pointing to his breast*) here, above their hearts—and on them there were words like Justice, Education, Culture, Development, Fishery, Religion, Agriculture. That was the only difference. (*The Burglar leans against the bedpost, legs crossed, blackjack swinging in his hand, watching and listening. He is amused.*) The fat ones had fleshy necks with deep horizontal flesh folds, and the thin ones had long white sinewy stringy necks (*interrupts himself, then very fast and breathless*), and all had the Order

of Merit on their lapels, the older ones First Class in gold,
the younger ones Second Class in silver, and all the older
ones had the Maltese Cross with diamonds and the "Stamp
of Diligence and Industry" on their right forehead. The
younger ones had the "Golden Star of the Republic of
Nicaragua," and half of them had the "Medal for Good
Conduct in Face of the Enemy," conferred upon them by
the Ministry of Public Decoration—that was represented, too,
by nine state secretaries and one ministerial councilor Third
Class—there were also two women, both state secretaries of
the Ministry of Morals, one Roman Catholic, the other
Protestant—she was the smaller one—they both wore black
tailored suits and white lace blouses and had nosegays of
white lilies in their arms. (*He wipes the sweat from his face,
opens the bottle again and takes another tablet. He pours
himself a glass of water, gulps down the water. Then, almost
in a whisper:*) They entered the castle hall (*closes his eyes
and puts his hand to his forehead*), stood up in a semicircle
and (*whispering now*) began to sing. (*Burglar laughs
loudly.*) They sang—they sang the last movement of Bee-
thoven's *Ninth Symphony!*

BURGLAR (*sings, conducting with the blackjack*):

"Praise to Joy, the God descended
Daughter of Elysium . . ."

MAN (*in despair, joining in*):

"Ray of mirth and rapture-blended,
Goddess, to thy shrine we come. . . ."

(*Mops his brow.*) At the right, there stood the old state secretaries First Class. They sang bass.

BURGLAR (*singing bass*):

"By thy magic is united . . ."

MAN: And at the left, there stood the younger ones, Second Class.
They sang mezzo-soprano.

BURGLAR (*mezzo-soprano, falsetto*):

". . . what stern custom parted wide . . ."

MAN: And in the center, there stood the two women and sang tenor.

BURGLAR (*singing tenor, raising the blackjack over the Man*):

"All mankind are brother plighted . . ."

MAN (*getting giddy, staggers, thus evading the blow, joining in the Ode*):

" . . . where thy gentle wings abide."

(*He staggers through the room; breathlessly:*) And in front, there stood someone—and conducted—that was the President. (*Pause; he shakes his head.*) No—he wasn't the President— he was all in yellow—it must have been the Postmaster General—no—no (*he staggers through the room; the Burglar has put down the blackjack and watches him*)—no—he was the Superintendent General of Forestry—he was wearing green (*nodding*)—yes, he was the Minister of Forestry—he had a hunting cap on his head—and he had a pack of dangerous hounds with him—I think they were Alsatians—or worse— they were snapping at the onlookers (*leaning against the wardrobe, exhausted*)—especially at the pigtails of the little girls—they had garlands of daisies and forget-me-nots in their hair—there were also— (*He loses the thread. The Burglar has thrown the blackjack onto the bed and has picked up the crowbar.*) No—yes—there were children—they were throwing flowers and medals (*he staggers to the bed*) and wreaths of laurel (*trying to support himself by the bedpost*)— and the widows cheered and threw lace handkerchiefs into the air (*the Burglar has pushed a few bottles aside with his foot and begins to break open the wooden floor with the crowbar*)—and they marched along with the cardinals. (*Staggers to the window singing:*)

" . . . where thy gentle wings abide."

(*Standing by the window, holding himself up by the curtain. The Burglar has taken his flashlight from the bed, switched it on, and is examining the holes in the floor.*) And then came the chaplains (*staggers and rips down the curtain*)— and the bishops (*wraps himself up in the red curtain*)—and (*makes the sign of the cross*)—blessed the crowd with holy water and incense. (*Wrapped in the red curtain, he walks through the room, blessing the working Burglar, making the sign of the cross.*) Amen!—Amen!— (*Suddenly yelling:*) Amen! (*Burglar has arisen. He looks at the Man for a moment indifferently, then picks up the crowbar again and goes into the bathroom. The Man leans against the bedpost, exhausted.*) Amen! (*He lets the curtain drop and clasps the bedposts.*) So they sang—loudly—in front the kettledrums—and then the President—and then the widows with their daughters—all in uniform—in the uniform of choirboys (*low, very tired*) no (*shakes his head*)—I don't remember—or—perhaps I do (*nods*)—yes—it was in the woods (*calmer*) the choirboys had become little angels—they played the shawm and the recorder (*noises from the bathroom—breaking glass, etc.*), flying and floating along, flapping their little wings—they were following the old white-haired priest—he was flying in front—that was God—yes, God—he knows no sin (*yawning*)—he knows only forgiveness. (*Pause; he yawns.*) Amen! He forgives me, too (*yawns*), although I haven't done anything. (*In a low voice as he looks at his hands:*) I have nothing—not even a good sin—as others have. (*Looking around the room; to the portraits:*) I haven't done anything wrong—although I might have been able to (*yawns*)—I haven't said much—I haven't asked much either. There are no answers—or at least (*crash in the bathroom*) I don't know any. Often—often this or that person has asked me what language I spoke. Language? I said to them: "Language? What do you mean by that?" (*He pulls off his slippers with his feet.*) "I speak no language," I said. (*He pulls off the bedspread; the bottles on the bed fall on the floor; some of them break. The Burglar's things at the foot of the bed remain there.*) No language, I said. I speak no language —except the language of the lizards. (*Yawns.*) The language of lizards, yes, that's the only language I speak. (*Long-drawn-out yawn.*) But (*turns around*) who speaks that language except me (*lying down slowly on the bed*)—me—and the lizards—of course. (*Lying in bed, pulling up the blankets.*) Nobody. (*Sitting up again.*) No, literally nobody. (*Picks up the pocket watch, winds it and puts it down again.*) No— (*Lies back, closes his eyes.*) No (*softly*) no— (*He lies motionless. The telephone rings.*)

BURGLAR (*comes from the bathroom, with some loot: a silver hand mirror, a silver brush, etc. Pushing aside the bottles in his way with his foot, he goes in leisurely fashion to the ringing telephone. He lifts the receiver, while, with his other hand, he pushes the Man on the bed aside a little and sits down on the bed beside him*): Six-six-O-four— Who? (*Looks around in the room.*) Presbyterian Association where? (*Opens the drawer.*) Oh, Wellington, I see— (*Takes out the revolver and examines it.*) Wellington, New Jersey, or Wellington, Pennsylvania? (*Pockets the revolver.*) Oh, I see, Wellington, New Hampshire. (*Looks into the drawer.*) Yes, quite right (*shuts the drawer*)—quite right (*looks around on the night table*), this is Emil Christoph Verkade and Son, organ builders since 1706. (*Picks up the gold pocket watch.*) I said: since 1706. (*Examines the watch.*) Oh yes, very old! (*He weighs the watch in his hand.*) But I shall have to ask you —it's one of our regulations—to confirm your order in writing. (*Pockets the watch.*) Yes, I understand (*looks around on the night table but finds nothing*)—well now—that's a big project, isn't it? (*Looks around the room; then, severely:*) No! We do not build colored organs—we serve tradition, not fashion—we only build the old worship type— (*Draws the clothes stand toward him with his foot.*) Of course we'll install it ourselves; we are not in the habit of leaving that to others. (*Pulls the shorts from the clothes stand and throws them on the floor.*) I suggest most emphatically a tin-copper alloy. We have had the best results with that (*pulls the tie from the clothes stand, looks at it*) since the time of Buxtehude. (*Throws the tie on the floor.*) Oh—a famous composer. Yes—I understand, I understand— (*Grabs hold of the shirt.*) Well—I recommend the following (*searches the sleeves of the shirt for cuff links*): four manuals of five-and-a-half octaves and a swell box. (*Finds the cuff links, examines them.*) And a hundred and twenty stops, Roosevelt Chest with exhaust system. (*Takes the cuff links out of the sleeves.*) Well—I suggest our tubular pneumatic crescendo-decrescendo-stop-control pedal—and, of course, swell-shutters. (*Examines the cuff links in his hand.*) Beg pardon? Oh yes, we made one for St. Paul's and for St. Michael's—they were a great success. (*Weighs the cuff links in his hands.*) Yes— pneumatic Poppet Pedals—Hope-Jones Stop Keys. (*Puts the cuff links in his pocket.*) Now, the Principals: Mixtures,

Trumpets and Quintation Stops (*throws the shirt on the floor*), Open Diapason, Lieblich Gedecht, Salicional (*puts his hand into the pocket of the Man's jacket*), Tibia Plena, Tromba, Trombone (*other pocket*) about twenty-two inches across the mouth (*pulls out a wallet*) up to the flageolet. Yes, that's something for children's services; it fascinates our young people (*opens the wallet with one hand, examines its contents*), even babes-in-arms remain quiet. (*Puts the wallet in his pocket.*) And as a suitable accompaniment for serious prayer, I recommend our heavenly Vox Celesta (*throws the jacket on the floor, picks up the trousers*), Clarabella, and Bassetto. (*Other trouser pocket.*) Sound quite wonderful, especially all together. (*Takes some coins from the trouser pocket.*) And then of course Bourdon and Dulciana. (*Examines the coins.*) That's really a little something for the ladies. Keeps them happy. (*Pockets the coins.*) Yes, it sounds sad—melancholy, I should call it. (*Throws down the trousers.*) I always say—"the sweetness of melancholy." (*Pushes away the clothes stand.*) And of course you mustn't forget the Vox Humana. (*Turns to the Man.*) That's our great hit, the Vox Humana. (*Bends down to the Man and listens to his chest to hear whether he is still breathing.*) It's quite unsurpassable. (*Sitting up again.*) We put a new one into the Organ of Oberbiederneustadt Abbey last year. (*Lifts up the Man's left hand.*) And since then the number of worshipers has doubled. (*Pulls a ring from the Man's hand, lets the hand drop.*) The console will be gilded, of course. (*Examines the ring.*) The cabinet of African rosewood. (*Pockets the ring.*) Oh yes, much better than Caucasian. (*Lifts up the Man's right hand.*) Much stronger, much more durable. It'll last for centuries. (*Lets the Man's hand drop on finding that he wears no ring.*) And after all: we build for the future. (*Looks around the room.*) If not, indeed, for eternity! (*Seizes the frame of the nearest portrait, tears it from the wall and lets it drop to the floor with a crash.*) An estimate? But of course! I shall start working on it right away. (*He examines the wall behind the picture by tapping it with his knuckles.*) Yes—thank you—I'm quite certain that you'll be satisfied. (*He tears off a large strip of wallpaper. The room gradually gets a demolished look.*) Yes—thank you— right way. (*He puts the receiver down, examines the walls, finds nothing, looks around the room. A loud, long yawn.*

Yawning, he turns to the Man, watches him for a moment,
then he takes Thermos bottle and sandwich box from the
foot of the bed, sits down on the bed, unscrews cup, opens
box, sits down with them on the bed. He takes a sandwich
from the box, pours himself a cupful. The clock strikes
eleven.) Eleven! (*Casually he puts the sandwich and cup*
down, picks up receiver and dials a number—any number—
takes the writing pad from the night table. After a pause:)
Please take this down: 3188-B-6. (*Pause.*) 0242-C-7. (*Pause.*)
9854-N-1. (*Pause.*) 2653-H-8. (*Pause.*) Yes—there are only
four now. Perhaps there'll even be fewer before long. (*Pause;*
he laughs.) No cause for alarm, no. Good night. (*He puts*
the receiver down. Pause.) No cause for alarm. (*Takes a*
bite out of his sandwich.) Everything's all right, everything
flows on (*drinks from the cup*), everything functions and
moves forward, everything turns (*chewing*)—interlocks, re-
volves, meshes (*swallows*)—and falls into its proper place
(*grinning broadly*)—nothing to worry about. (*Breakfasts*
leisurely.)

THE END

THE TOWER

by PETER WEISS

TRANSLATED BY MICHAEL BENEDIKT AND MICHEL HEINE

Characters

PABLO
DIRECTOR
TOWER MANAGERESS
MAGICIAN
DWARF
CARLO
LION TAMER
VARIOUS OTHER PERFORMERS

Confused humming of street sounds. Steps coming closer and closer. The steps become very loud, and stop.

PABLO (*lost in thought*): The lion's head . . . with the ring in its muzzle. . . . (*Knocks three times with the iron ring on the door.*) All that echoing going on in there . . . they're all still in there . . . all the others . . . but I'm coming from the outside now . . . I have to get inside again though . . . back in to them. . . .

(*He knocks again, three times. Repetition of the sounds in an echo chamber.*)

MANAGERESS (*in a whisper*): There's somebody outside. . . .

DIRECTOR: Just some drunk probably . . . somebody wandering around lost. . . .

MANAGERESS: That might be important, though. . . .

DIRECTOR: But so late at night—? (*Pause.*)

PABLO: I can see the door from outside . . . I come from outside . . . I'm not locked up anymore . . . I know how it is outside now. . . . (*Shuffling of feet. Rattling of keys.*) I hear her . . . as she comes shuffling down the stairs. . . . It's still possible to get away. . . . (*The key clanks in the lock. The heavy door squeaks and groans open. Pause.*)

MANAGERESS: Well, say something. What do you want here? (*Pause.*) Well, what do you want here?

PABLO: I'm looking for work. . . .

MANAGERESS: At this hour?

PABLO: I almost came later than this. . . .

MANAGERESS: Well, we can always use new blood here. But we insist on quality. We maintain the highest standards in our performances!

PABLO: Yes, I know. . . . I've heard about this tower of yours before. . . .

MANAGERESS: Everything depends on what your specialty is . . . (*Sighing.*) Really skilled labor is so rare these days.

317

PABLO (*in a matter-of-fact way*): Escape artist. Lock picker. Chain-breaking act.

MANAGERESS: Escape artist? It's been a long time since we had an escape artist around here. Well, we can always give you a tryout. Do you live in the hotel?

PABLO: No, I don't. Can I spend the night here?

MANAGERESS (*suspiciously*): Don't you have even *one* piece of luggage?

PABLO: I don't need any luggage. I suppose you have a rope. And somebody to tie me up?

MANAGERESS: And that's all you'll need?

PABLO: That's right . . . that's all.

MANAGERESS (*still a little uncertain*): Well, come in. (*She locks the door behind them.*) You can lie down here in the hall. You can sleep on the bench over there. I'll go and get you a blanket.

DIRECTOR (*calling from overhead somewhere*): Who's down there anyway?

MANAGERESS (*calling back*): It's a performer! Don't you want to welcome him yourself?

DIRECTOR: Why did he have to come so late at night?

MANAGERESS: He had no place to stay. . . .

DIRECTOR: Well, this isn't exactly a roadside inn. . . .

PABLO (*to himself*): I've got to stay here . . . I've got to stay here. . . .

DIRECTOR (*his steps approaching*): But to come so late at night . . .

PABLO (*in a matter-of-fact way*): My name is Niente, Sir. I'm an escape artist.

DIRECTOR: How long have you been in our profession?

PABLO: Since my earliest childhood. Started out in a balancing act. Switched to a one-man hanging act. (*Very agitated sud-*

denly:) Hanging there in a noose that tightens up on you at the slightest motion . . . I've had enough of that. . . . (*With sudden aggressiveness:*) Maybe you can understand how fed up you can get with an act all of a sudden when you've been at it for a long time—you just can't take it any more. You have to renew yourself. . . . I knew that if I did it even once more it would be all over for me. Those perpetual death leaps. That feeling of being throttled. (*Lost in thought.*) I began to think only of liberation. Now and then I let them tie me up just so I could enjoy the feeling of liberation. While they were tying me up I was practically bursting with the sensations of freedom. The truth is, you have to be free even beforehand, before you even start. The actual breaking loose becomes a mere matter of confirmation then. . . .

DIRECTOR (*who has not heard a word; to himself*): An escape artist . . . we *did* have an escape artist once. . . .

CARLO (*his voice coming from far, far off*): Well, who's there? What does he want, anyway? Isn't this place filled up enough as it is? Isn't our program already booked up solid?

DIRECTOR: Carlo! Aren't you asleep yet? . . . Get back in bed! You'll be in bad form again tomorrow.

CARLO (*coming nearer*): Who is that, anyway?

MANAGERESS (*in a kindly way*): Better get back up there now.

CARLO (*withdrawing again*): But just who is it, anyway?

MANAGERESS: We've leaving you now, too. Here's your blanket.

DIRECTOR: Right; come on.

MANAGERESS: Good night.

DIRECTOR (*already at a great distance*): Good night.

PABLO (*mechanically*): Good night. (*Pause. At a great distance a piercing whistling; it echoes through the tower interior.*)

MAGICIAN (*still at some distance*): Is it really you? Why are you jumping back like that? Probably still afraid of me . . . and you've become so big and strong now, too. . . . No, I

can see, this is no longer our dear little Pablo who ran away
that time with the lion.

PABLO (*violently*): Be quiet!

MAGICIAN: You're telling me to be quiet? Wasn't I the one who
helped you get out of this place? Wasn't I the one who unlocked the cage for you? What would you have done without me?

PABLO: And why did you sound the alarm when we were hardly
out the gate?

MAGICIAN: I had to in order to divert their suspicion. What do
you want, anyway—you got away, didn't you! But that lion
—that poor lion! Bang! There he lay. I'll never forget how
they dragged him away by the tail.

PABLO: I know why you opened the gate. You wanted me to kill
myself trying to get out. You knew I had that noose around
my neck.

MAGICIAN: But Pablo—we were always such good friends!

PABLO: *You* were the one who had me captured. I didn't know
anything then. . . . I'd never been outside. Yes . . . you
were kind to me. Overcome with love, you handed me a
knife so I could cut up my wrist a little. You said I ought
to throw myself down the stairs. You said I ought to lie
perfectly still and hold my breath . . . and I did lie perfectly still until something in me seemed to burst!

MAGICIAN: But Pablo!

PABLO: You were everywhere with your whisperings. In the dressing room I suddenly saw your face in the mirror. At night
I suddenly felt that you were seated beside me on the edge
of the bed.

MAGICIAN: But Pablo—you used to trust me so much!

PABLO: I only "trusted" you because I was so frightened of you.
I was terrorized by your staring, stark white face!

MAGICIAN: Pablo!

PABLO: Magician, you called yourself. Clairvoyant. But you never
seemed to perform. Parasite! What are you doing here any-

way? What did you do with me? And with Nelly? What
have you done with Nelly?

MAGICIAN (*threateningly*): Did you come back here just to accuse
me? You seem to have forgotten about the way you carried
on with the lion tamer. You seem to have completely forgotten just why they locked you in that cage with the
lion . . . there you both lay like two animals behind those
bars . . . with the rats squeaking all around you. You con-
fessed everything to me then . . . begged me for help. . . .

PABLO: I still haven't told you everything. . . .

MAGICIAN: I suppose she was the one who seduced you, right?
Who tore the clothes off you, right? Rolled you around on
the floor? And I suppose when she screamed that way she
was screaming out of pleasure, right?

PABLO: She screamed at me because I refused to touch her. Because I moved away from her. It was as if I were paralyzed
suddenly. I could see only Nelly before me. Could only see
that she was lying there in that ring. . . . What did you
do with Nelly?

MAGICIAN: Poor little Pablo. Pablo who never got out of the
tower. Pablo . . . the great acrobat on the big red ball.
(*These last words echo resoundingly, then die away. He continues in a tantalizing, hypnotizing voice:*) Come on . . .
come on . . . give me your hand . . . just like that . . .
that's a good boy . . . balance nice and firmly right on that
ball . . . what a bright boy . . . just like that . . . right
on your tiptoes . . . slipping forward . . . forward . . . forward . . . going right around the ring . . . just like that
. . . shoulders back . . . standing straight up . . . legs
straight . . . absolutely straight . . . stiff as a poker . . .
toes alone moving . . . faster . . . faster . . . that's good,
Pablo . . . very good . . . soon you'll be able to have your
debut . . . ah . . . and outside they'll carry your name all
through the streets . . . in huge letters: PABLO, THE
GREAT BALANCING ACT . . . slip right forward . . .
accomplish everything with those toes . . . standing perfectly straight . . . don't shift those shoulders around! . . .

PABLO (*furiously*): I'm not Pablo anymore! I come from the
outside now. I know how the tower looks from out there.

I know how the streets look out there . . . the city . . . the harbor . . . the sea . . . I know about the other cities too . . . I was in the mountains . . . in the forests . . . on the roads . . . on ships . . .

MAGICIAN: You were never outside. You are inside the tower. (*With great emphasis:*) You are here now because you were never, ever, outside.

PABLO (*crushed*): It's true. All the cities and the forests and oceans were really here in this tower. My real bonds were everywhere. Everything I touched—bondage. Every word, every feeling is still sealed up tight, here in this tower. Yes —you're right. I never escaped. (*More firmly:*) But I'm not Pablo any more! I'm not going to balance on that ball any more! I'm not going to hang myself any more! I'm only here now in order to break out!

MAGICIAN (*in a sepulchral voice*): Nothing has changed. Everything still affects you, just as it used to.

PABLO: No! Everything's changed! I'll break open that door myself!

MAGICIAN: Only if you get the key!

PABLO: But to go *slowly*, carefully out. Not just to rush out blindly. (*In sudden agony.*) How it hurts me to see myself running wildly through the street. As if actually something were pressing me in again . . . everything gets so out of focus. Just to go out quietly. . . .

MAGICIAN: Nothing's changed here.

PABLO: No! Everything's different now. I'm not afraid of you anymore. And the Manageress . . . how gray and tired she is! She used to come running over to me . . . her hair like black tentacles. She won't hit me any more . . . and the Director himself . . . when I saw him there in the stairwell . . . with his wrinkled old pants . . . I was almost sorry for him. I keep asking myself: did I come back here for their sake? For these two old people . . . what do I have to do with them any more? . . . Perhaps they'd still want to capture me with their weaknesses . . . with their lonelinesses . . . but they can't touch me any more with their power. . . .

MAGICIAN: Everything is the same as always. Listen to the clock.

Listen to the sounds of breathing. Everything is as it was. Listen . . .

(*His last words again echo loudly, then die away. The muffled ticking of a clock can be heard. The clock rasps, straining toward striking. A broken, feeble chiming. Then the ticking returns. The Director snores. The Manageress groans in her sleep. The mattress springs squeak. Everything muffled as during the surge and fall of a huge wave. Then, again, silence.*)

PABLO: Yes, I hear it. At night . . . I used to sneak out to Nelly. Nelly . . . wake up! What have you done with Nelly?!

MAGICIAN: That's enough of that!

PABLO: She lay there in the center of the ring. The horse was gone. You told me that she had been thrown. But there were no hoofprints anywhere near her. You were standing beside her. Her face unrecognizable. And that terrible silence there in those rows upon rows of empty seats. . . . (*Silence.*)

CARLO (*voice soaring down with an enormously echoing sound*): I . . . Carlo . . . I loved her most of all!

PABLO: I crept into her room when everyone else was asleep. . . .

CARLO: I . . . Carlo . . . was awake. . . .

PABLO: I waited until I heard them all snoring upstairs. Nelly had left her door ajar . . . she was sitting up in bed . . . waiting just for me. . . .

CARLO (*his voice all but hissing as he approaches*): She was waiting for *me*. Once when we were pressed together . . . she told me that she loved me most of all. You want to take everything away from me! You're always standing in my way! But she loved *me* the most!

PABLO: You! You couldn't have been tied more tightly to that old lady s apron strings!

MANAGERESS (*rushing in*): Is he being insolent again . . . that Pablo? Is he attacking you again? How dare you! Wait— I'm going to tell this to Uncle right now!

DIRECTOR (*rushing in*): What's going on again in here?

M

MANAGERESS: It's Pablo again!

PABLO: Yes, I! It's me! You haven't been able to conquer me yet!

MANAGERESS: What's that? You can say that to me? I, who was like a mother to you!

PABLO: But you aren't my mother. None of us here has a mother. None of us was born here. We were all brought in here from outside somewhere. You were left on the threshold, just like a dirty bundle—you too. There aren't any blood bonds around here. Just the tower. Only the tower holds us together.

MANAGERESS: How can you be so heartless, so cruel! You should be punished! Yes, severely punished!

PABLO: Yes, severely punished. I've severely punished myself. I was so overwhelmed by your power that every single thought I hurled at you came bouncing back at me, twice as hard.

MAGICIAN: Look—what's all the fuss about anyway? You got a few hard knocks, you learned a little discipline . . . sometimes we did tighten up the reins on you a little, but it was only so you'd be a good performer. What did you want from us, anyway?

PABLO: Yes . . . what did actually happen then? Sometimes I feel as if my thoughts have to be extracted from some kind of deep, dark pit before I can examine them, before I can seize on something solid, something certain. Something unfathomable lies behind every thought . . . something for which there aren't any words. And it was there, in that darkness, that I was created. By the time I first became conscious of the ball on which I stood, I was already something signed, sealed, and delivered.

DIRECTOR: We were too lenient with you. You never learned any discipline!

MAGICIAN (*again intoning in a hollowly echoing voice*): Chest out . . . stomach in . . . shoulders back . . . that's right . . . arms all the way out . . . stand straight on the ball . . . just like that . . . now faster . . . faster . . . let your toes slip out from under you . . . right around the ring . . . always in a circle . . .

PABLO (*hynotized and shaken*): Those faces in the rows of seats
. . . that buzzing and murmuring . . . (*noises of voices,
volleys of applause*) those terrible hands. . . .

MAGICIAN: And then you bowed, so, so politely. You were always
the audience's favorite. Beautiful in your white knitted tights
with your powdered face and your long black hair. You threw
kisses at them.

PABLO: Out of fear! I was afraid of them. I thought they were
wild animals. When I finally saw they were just like we were,
I thought I was seeing things. You said to me that they would
tear me up if I ever dared go out to them. Why did you keep
everything secret from me? Why wasn't I allowed to know
anything about the outside? When I asked, you simply put
your finger to your lips!

DIRECTOR (*severely, and in a mechanical way*): This is where our
work is; this is where we must stay. First you have to prove
that you can do something. That you can master your as-
signed task. First fulfil your obligations!

PABLO: Yes . . . that's the voice of the tower speaking now. Only
now I'm answering it. I'm not silent anymore. But even then
I had some strange feeling of rebellion. I always knew there
was a world outside!

MAGICIAN (*severely, and in a mechanical way*): For us only the
tower exists. Except for it everything is uncertain. Only the
walls of the tower are solid. Outside everything melts, everything flows. We submit ourselves gladly to the discipline of
the tower. (*Contemptuously:*) And why do they come here
anyway—all these people? In order to gather strength from
us. From us! *We're* really the source of *their* strength!

PABLO (*as if possessed*): But I've seen the world outside! I discovered the opening in the attic . . . like a square of white
fire! It was right after that I slashed my wrist with your knife
. . . and while I was going around with those heavy bandages
I didn't have to work on the ball for a while . . . you were
the ones who taught me that a man had to kill himself if he
wanted to free himself . . . but there was another voice
deep in me somewhere . . . a voice which I still couldn't
quite hear . . . and it's to answer you with that strangled
voice . . . it's for *that* that I had to come back here just once

more! It was this whispering which ruled my life. And it was this same soundless voice which drove me to the attic where I found the window! It took just a second. I was blinded . . . I screamed . . . I felt a huge strength in front of that light! Then suddenly you stood behind me . . . you dragged me back . . . down the stairs . . . and the attic was locked up . . . the key thrown away!

DIRECTOR (*very mechanically*): To work now! Enough of this idling!

PABLO: Yes—you returned me to my place on that ball. But I had already seen it all! I had seen it all there outside. It's true that upstairs, in that moment, I had seen only a single, fused, incandescent abyss. But now little details appeared through the glimmering light. I kept picking things out . . . new things appeared to me constantly . . . I saw a sea of roofs . . . I saw tall columns . . . animals . . . smoke . . . colored cloths fluttering . . . I saw windows . . . behind the windows, rooms . . . in the rooms, figures . . . someone was carrying a glass sphere . . . someone was undressing . . . someone was painting a wall with a big brush . . . a giant was riding on a green horse . . . a sword in his outstretched hand . . . children were playing in the street . . . one vanished suddenly in a hole . . . people were everywhere . . . alone or in groups . . . I saw a gigantic picture and looked for the sense of that picture . . . I found fresh meanings again and again . . . a terrible restlessness came over me . . . I wanted to get out . . . but I didn't dare yet . . . you held me so tightly in your grasp. . . .

MAGICIAN: You wouldn't dare. . . .

PABLO: You don't understand what I'm saying. You'll never understand me. And you'll never be able to say anything but what you've been trying to hammer into me since the very beginning. When you speak I hear only the echo of your words! Where are you, anyway . . . just where are you?

VOICES (*replying in an echoing chorus*): Everywhere! Everywhere!

PABLO: I'll catch you yet! I'll rip you out of me!

VOICES: Just what do you want from us, anyway? We have our own life here. You're the one who sees only distortions! You've misunderstood everything! You can't criticize us!

PABLO: You invaded me. I was at your mercy. Even now I'm permeated by you. I never struck back! I never stood up for myself!

DIRECTOR: Well! That's the last straw!

PABLO: When you paddled me across your knees I screamed in hopes of making you forgive me. And once you praised me, I completely forgot the way my face burned from your slaps and blows.

MANAGERESS: How can you be so cruel to us? To us—who gave you food and work! I used to cook you a special broth because you were so sickly and feeble—an invigorating, stimulating broth. Have you forgotten how much you used to like it?

PABLO: It would end up rotting in the garbage every night. Or I vomited it right back up again. And late at night I'd creep out to the pantry to steal what I wanted. . . . All those nocturnal trips! (*A muffled rumbling fills the tower. The clock ticks. Snoring, together with the breathing of the sleepers can be heard. Then a kind of rustling, rushing sound.*) It's like being in a sinking ship . . . the water rushes in . . . Uncle and Aunt upstairs . . . like hydraulic pumps. And I go gliding through the house on that big ball. I fly—whee!—down the stairs . . . through the hallways . . . through the halls . . . how noisy all those sounds upstairs seem now, how big this house is—whee—to the cellar . . . to the lion . . . the lion! Lion? . . . Are you there? . . . Lion! . . . his eyes shine . . . how quietly he lies there . . . (*Mysteriously.*) He's bewitched, that's what. Lion, I'm going to free you— we'll run together through the world outside . . . we'll run —run—run! . . . and no one will stop us. . . .

MAGICIAN: Bang! And there he lies! A well-aimed shot. Straight through the brain. I never miss!

PABLO: Lion: the strong; the wild; and the imprisoned. The beaten-to-death. . . . Lion! I'll wake you up again! Lion! Arise and come out of there!

(*A kind of giggling growling is heard, and a jingling of bells.*)

DWARF: Yes, yes—I'm here!

MAGICIAN: Come here now. Come to your master. Give me your paw . . . that's right . . .

DWARF (*growling and giggling*): It's my true, true Pablo, finally come back . . . and he wants to save me? Me, just a poor old hunchbacked dwarf. . . .

MAGICIAN: Yes—the great rescuer has come!

DWARF (*cheering*): Free! Free!

MAGICIAN: There's your new lion for you! A twisted dwarf decorated with bells! And Nelly—how would you like to see Nelly again?

PABLO: Nelly. . . .

MAGICIAN: Come on, lion—dance with Nelly! (A *giggling, tramping, and jingling of bells is heard.*)

PABLO: Nelly's dress . . . her white dress . . .

MAGICIAN: The last shreds of her dress . . .

PABLO (*to himself*): Is this really all that's left of her now? . . .

MAGICIAN (*icily*): That's all there ever was!

PABLO: But what about those nights . . . when I was with her . . . (*Suddenly stricken with doubt.*) when I was with her? . . .

MAGICIAN (*very aggressively*): Yes—what then?

PABLO: Actually I was only with her that once . . . but it was as if I had always been with her . . . she showed me her breasts . . .

MAGICIAN: Well—and then?

PABLO: Yes, and then . . .

MAGICIAN: She asked you a question . . .

PABLO (*whispering*): Yes . . .

MAGICIAN (*brutally*): She asked: Can you do what Carlo can do?

PABLO: Yes . . . I can hear those words even now. I went away after that. I never went back to you again, Nelly. But after your death you became mine alone. I was with you every night.

CARLO (*his voice drifting in from the distance*): She loved me most of all . . . me, Carlo . . . I was with her every night.

PABLO: And just what did you create with your love? What's become of you now? (*Again the giggling and the jingling approach.*) Give it to me—give me that dress! (*Silence. Rustling of material.*) Nelly . . . it's your smell . . . (*Whispering.*) Nelly . . . Nelly. . . .

(*Slowly the muffled echoing roar rises again within the tower. The clock ticks. Heavy muffled breathing. Then, a moment later, the Director and the Manageress awaken. They stretch themselves, groan a little, yawn.*)

DIRECTOR (*very drowsily*): Ah yes . . . it's time. . . .

MANAGERESS: Ah yes . . .

DIRECTOR: Another day. (*The mattress springs squeak. Yawns and clearings of throats.*)

MANAGERESS: Ah me . . . let's put the coffee on. (*Shuffling of her slippers as she goes down the tower stairs. She yawns very loudly.*) Look at that. Lying there right on the floor—he didn't even use our blanket. What's that over his face? What kind of a rag is *that*? Would you mind standing up now? I have to set the breakfast table here. (*Much clattering of crockery.*)

DIRECTOR (*yawning and coming down the stairs*): Ah me. Here we are. I've brought along a rope—think it'll do? What's wrong with him anyway? What's he still asleep for? What kind of behavior is this anyway? (*To the Manageress.*) Is the coffee ready?

·MAGICIAN (*from far off*): Good morning, sir!

DIRECTOR: Ah—early as usual, I see! But what's going on with him over there? Why isn't he up yet? It would be a good idea to get another look at him before we start our rehearsal.

MAGICIAN: Not really necessary, sir, not really necessary. He's a famous name already. Niente. Escape artist. We can put him right in the program.

DIRECTOR: Him—famous? Never heard of him myself.

MAGICIAN: Believe me, he's absolutely big time.

DIRECTOR (*still somewhat uncertain*): So . . . he is, eh? All right then . . . if you really think so.

(*Manageress pours the coffee. Clattering of cups and rattling of stirring spoons. Many confused voices approach. The performers come down the stairs.*)

PERFORMERS: Good morning, sir. Good morning. 'Morning, Ma'am. (*Chairs are pulled out and drawn in. Sound of cups and spoons. Noisy sipping.*)

DIRECTOR (*taps his cup with his spoon*): Today we shall be augmenting our program with a brand new number. Let's see . . . what's first on the list now. . . . (*Leafs through papers.*) "Deep Feelings" . . . "Fine Points of The Duel" . . . "A Lesson in Animal Training" . . . hmmm . . . well, I think we'll put him in right at the beginning, hit them with something fresh right off. (*Turns to Magician.*) Listen—are you absolutely one hundred per cent certain . . . I mean . . .

MAGICIAN: Absolutely certain, sir, absolutely.

DWARF (*approaches, giggling and jingling*): Absolutely . . . absolutely!

PABLO (*very loudly, to himself, above the confusion of voices*): It's beginning now.

DWARF (*also loudly, but in a hoarse whisper*): Where am I. . . . Where am I?

(*During the following interchange, crockery sounds, slurping, murmuring, all continue in the background.*)

DIRECTOR: Who starts our rehearsal today?

STRONG MAN: The Strong Man!

DIRECTOR: Heaviest weights first.

STRONG MAN: Heaviest weights first!

DIRECTOR: And then?

SHADOW DUELIST: Shadow Duelist.

DIRECTOR: New routines for the big fight?

SHADOW DUELIST: New routines—right!

DIRECTOR: Next?

LION TAMER: The Lion Tamer.

DIRECTOR: A workout with the big whips.

LION TAMER: With the biggest whips, sir!

DWARF (*very loudly, whispering*): What's happening here? . . . What's going on?

DIRECTOR: Carlo's next.

CARLO: Yes, Uncle.

PABLO: I'm inside the tower now. . . .

DIRECTOR: And remember: more vigor! More enthusiasm!

MANAGERESS (*in the background*): A little more coffee?

PABLO (*whispering*): Now I have to get out of that rope. . . .

DWARF (*whisperings echoing*): Get out of that rope . . . get out . . .

DIRECTOR: More feeling! You've been letting up lately! We must never forget the traditions of the tower!

DWARF (*imitating him*): Tradition . . . tradition.

MANAGERESS (*coming near*): Well now . . . did you sleep well? My, but you're a late sleeper. A little coffee?

DIRECTOR: Well, how are you . . . Mr. Escape Artist?

CARLO: Escape Artist . . . is he an escape artist?

LION TAMER (*in a highly suggestive way*): It's been quite a while since we had an escape artist. . . .

CARLO: You mean Pablo?

LION TAMER: He even looks a little like Pablo. . . .

CARLO: And he's taking Pablo's old place, too!

(*Pablo jumps nervously to his feet*)

M*

MAGICIAN: Please remain seated, Mr. Niente!

DIRECTOR: What's all this talk about Pablo—we can do without any of that!

PABLO: Who is this Pablo, anyway?

DWARF (*imitating him*): Who am I?

MAGICIAN: An absolutely marvelous performer—the best we had. But he's gone now.

DIRECTOR: Now that's all we're going to hear about Pablo!

MAGICIAN: How pretty he was, too . . . powdered white . . . just charming . . .

DWARF: The favorite of all the ladies . . .

LION TAMER (*dreamily*): Yes . . . he was a very pretty boy . . . Pablo . . . have you ever heard of Pablo, the great balancing act? Haven't you ever met him out there anywhere?

PABLO: I really don't know . . . no . . . I don't believe so. . . .

MANAGERESS: What could have happened to him? I never understood him too well, myself. He was such a quiet boy. You couldn't get a word out of him.

PABLO: Why did he run off like that?

DIRECTOR: He didn't "run off"—he was dismissed!

PABLO: But why?

DIRECTOR: Why, why? He was lazy, that's why. He was arrogant! I tried to make a proper performer out of him but he didn't have a disciplined bone in his body!

MANAGERESS: He always seemed to be dissatisfied. Nothing was good enough for him.

DIRECTOR: He simply didn't fit in. He lacked the proper respect. And now I don't want to hear another word about Pablo! We have to concentrate on our performance!

MANAGERESS: More coffee?

PABLO: What did he do here?

LION TAMER (*coyly yet dreamily*): He balanced on the ball. . . .

MANAGERESS: By the way—didn't you say you used to do a balancing act too?—do you suppose you could do a balancing act for us? His old ball is still around here somewhere. I really don't know whether people are in the right mood to see an escape artist these days anyway. It might turn out to be a little too daring for them. You have to take into consideration the kind of people you find here in our city.

PABLO: I'm an escape artist.

MANAGERESS: Think it over anyway.

PABLO: I'm through with balancing now.

STRONG MAN: Time for me to start working out with my weights. . . .

(*Shifting of chairs. Everyone rises. Plates rattle.*)

DIRECTOR: Wait! Where do you think you're going?

PABLO: Can't I watch the practice session?

DIRECTOR: That's not the way we do things here. Everyone works on his act in private.

PABLO (*asking among the performers*): Does each of you work alone? . . . What do you do? You—what do you do? Why don't you answer me? Don't you ever talk about your work? . . .

(*The performers disperse. It is quiet.*)

LION TAMER (*very near*): My dear . . . you just can't disturb things like that here. It's easy to see you come from outside. (*With sudden longing.*) Have you traveled around very much? Tell me about the outside. . . .

PABLO (*lost in his own thoughts*): I don't even know any more whether I really *was* outside . . . perhaps I only wanted to go very badly . . . where was I . . . there was a pier . . . a beach . . . a sail . . . but me . . . my real self . . . where am I really? . . .

MAGICIAN (*whispering, very near*): An entire tower surrounds you. . . .

(*Again the upsurge of sound rises in the tower, like a wave. Indistinct voices. The clock ticks. Shouts of the performers:*)

*allez-oop, allez-oop; one, two—one two! Then again the sound
dies away.*)

PABLO (*lost in his own thoughts*): I remember the day you first
came here . . . I was standing here on the stairs . . . they
shut the great door behind you . . . you went past me with
your suitcase . . . I took the suitcase from you . . . I carried it upstairs . . . I was thinking of what might be in it
. . . I followed you into the room . . . I stood near the
door as you unpacked . . . I was frightened when I saw that
everything in your trunk was either leather or metal. Then
you came up to me . . . asked me what my name was . . .
held me by the arm . . . by my hair. . . .

LION TAMER: You were trembling from head to foot. . . .

PABLO: I was thinking of Nelly . . . I couldn't get away from
Nelly . . .

LION TAMER: You were completely beside yourself when you came
to me that night . . . oh . . . (*They embrace.*) don't be so
violent . . . don't get so excited. . . .

PABLO: Your armor . . . you're armored . . . your whole body is
armored. . . .

MAGICIAN (*quickly, like a fight announcer*): Now she kisses him
. . . she rips his shirt open . . . she bites him . . . she digs
her claws into him . . . he embraces her . . . she steps back
. . . he goes after her . . . she hits the floor . . . he throws
himself onto her . . . this is it . . . (*Calling out.*) this is
it . . . Pablo!

(*The cry of "Pablo" becomes a powerful echo throughout
the tower. From all sides the hollow, resounding cry: Pablo,
Pablo, Pablo!*

PABLO: Here I am! I'm here, I'm here!

(*The word "here" echoes back from all directions. Then
silence.*)

PABLO: Isn't it my turn yet?

DIRECTOR: Turn to do what?

PABLO: Rehearse.

DIRECTOR: That won't be necessary.

PABLO: Won't be necessary?

DIRECTOR: No. We have absolute confidence in you.

PABLO: Absolute confidence . . .

DIRECTOR: The rope—is it satisfactory?

PABLO: The rope?

DIRECTOR: Yes. This rope here—didn't you ask for a rope?

PABLO: A rope . . . yes, of course . . . a rope.

DIRECTOR: Is it strong enough for you? Long enough?

PABLO: Absolute confidence . . . you trust me because I'm a total stranger to you. I come from the outside. But if you knew who I was. . . .

MANAGERESS (*in a kindly way—suddenly coming very close*): But don't you understand that we only want the best for you? What are we doing wrong? If you'd just think for a moment about how much time and effort we spent on you . . .

PABLO: What was I to you anyway—or Nelly?—or Carlo?

MANAGERESS: But we did everything we could for you. You were all entrusted to us. We brought you all up like our very own children. And for what? Not a single word of gratitude! Oh how meaningless it all turned out to be! I used to lie awake nights, just thinking about what I could do for you. And not even a thank-you out of you! Just reproaches and criticism! What did I do wrong?

PABLO: It's the tower. It's all because of the tower. You yourselves grew up in the tower. And you all wanted to get out too—yes, of course you wanted to get out too. But a longing like that—you didn't even want to admit it to yourselves. Didn't you beat me because really, deep down, you knew just how much I wanted to get out? We're all so close together here it's as if we had become fused. I was a part of you—a rebellious part which had to be suppressed—for the good of the tower. . . .

MANAGERESS (*startled*): Did you say something?

PABLO (*still deep in his own thoughts*): What. . . . Did I say something?

MANAGERESS: Where was I now. . . . Where is that Dwarf, anyway? The signs have to be set up out there.

DWARF (*his bells jingling*): Yes Ma'am. I'm ready to paint them now. (*Pronouncing the words very slowly:*) THE FEATURE ATTRACTION—ONE AND ONLY APPEARANCE OF THE GREAT ESCAPE ARTIST!

PABLO: One and only?

DWARF (*in a sing-song voice*): One and on-ly, one and on-ly . . .

PABLO (*suddenly hysterical*): How can I get out of here—the door! Open the door! (*He beats on the great door. His blows echo loudly.*) I want to get out of here now! I want to get out of here!

DWARF (*imitates him, squealing and crying*): I want to get out of here now! I want to get out of here! Poor pathetic thing that I am, that I am—everybody holds me back—drags me down. Look how crippled and crooked I am already—oh poor, poor me—won't somebody come to my aid? HELP! (*With sudden matter-of-factness:*) So—our sign's finished now. ONE AND ONLY APPEARANCE OF THE GREAT ESCAPE ART-IST! (*Rattle of key in lock.*) So—unlock the gate and out we go!

PABLO (*runs after him*): Me too—I'm going with you!

MAGICIAN (*sharply*) Stop right where you are!

(*Sound of a quick scuffle; heavy breathing.*)

Yes, that's the way you'd like it, wouldn't you—just to run out on us now!

(*The door slams shut. It is immediately locked from outside. Very faintly, moving off, the voice of the dwarf is heard.*)

DWARF: Greatest of all escape artists! One and only performance tonight! See for yourself! See for yourself the world's greatest escape artist! One and only performance! Come and see for yourself! Come and see for yourself! Before your very own eyes . . . (*His voice fades away.*)

PABLO (*Breathlessly*): Oh . . . this tower . . . this tower . . .
(*Again the surging sound rises inside the tower. Voices.
Shouts. Clock ticks. Distant voice of the Director.*)

DIRECTOR: Carlo—to the rehearsal!

CARLO (*from afar*): Yes—I'm coming!

(*A door closes. Muffled directorial commands.*)

DIRECTOR: Head up high . . . corners of your mouth down . . .
twist those shoulders around . . . dance . . . like that . . .
just like that . . . legs higher . . . arms higher . . . like
that . . . now, is that really so hard . . .

(*Pablo runs up to the closed door, opens it. Voice of the
Director.*)

DIRECTOR: What's this?—How dare you!

PABLO: I want to watch.

DIRECTOR: What are you thinking of! Haven't I expressly forbidden—

PABLO: Yes, yes—but I have my terms and conditions too! I want
to be able to move around in here freely—otherwise I won't
be able to perform properly!

DIRECTOR: You're dismissed. Get out of here! Immediately!

MAGICIAN (*interrupting suddenly*): But sir—he's already been an-
nounced!

DIRECTOR (*beside himself*): Sir. You have to make yourself fit in
here! Here *I* make the rules!

PABLO: Then I can't perform.

DIRECTOR (*very loud*): Damn the whole lot of you! You all stand
around here and gape. Well you can go on gaping without
me! Without me! (*The Director stamps off.*)

CARLO: Do you really dare to just—

PABLO: Come on—we feel like getting a breath of air, right?

CARLO: You mean outside? But that's impossible!

PABLO: Who's got the right to deny us that? We're not prisoners here—we'll simply ask for the key. (*Shouting:*) Sir! We want the key! We want to go out! The key!

(*The enormous echo returns: Key! Key! Key!*)

DIRECTOR (*voice coming from a distance*): What is it? What's going on now?

(*Other cries from within the tower merge with the key-cry.*)

VOICES: What is it? . . . What's happening? . . . What's going on here? . . . Are we on fire? . . . Yes, the tower's on fire! . . . The tower's on fire! . . . Fire! . . . The tower's burning down! Help! Help!

(*Amid the screamings—in which are mingled those of "key," "fire," "help," etc.—steps are heard coming down the stairs at top speed.*)

DIRECTOR (*plunging past*): Who has the key?

PERFORMERS (*in complete panic*): Fire! Fire! Open the door! We're locked in!

DIRECTOR: Where is the key?

MAGICIAN (*with sadistic pleasure*): The key is outside!

PABLO: You mean there's only one key?

(*Performers in panic at the doorway. Screams. Poundings at the door.*)

PABLO: But where's the fire supposed to be?

PERFORMERS: Yes . . . where's it burning . . . where's it burning?

DIRECTOR: Is it going upstairs somewhere?

PERFORMERS: No. . . . Nothing upstairs. . . . We thought it was downstairs. . . . Where is this fire anyway?

MAGICIAN: There isn't any fire. It was just a little joke. The gentleman escape artist had to have his little joke. You can all go back upstairs now. Nothing's wrong. Just a little fire drill.

(*The performers leave, grumbling and muttering, while from outside the voice of the dwarf is heard returning.*)

DWARF: One and only performance tonight. Gala performance in the tower!

(*Sound of key in lock. With a gradual creaking, the door slowly opens. Immediately it slams shut again. The bells of the dwarf are heard. The door is locked once more. Pause.*)

DIRECTOR (*near—menacing sinisterly*): What were you trying to do!

CARLO: He just wanted the key—he just wanted to step outside with me for a bit. . . .

DIRECTOR: What's that! Don't interfere here! What are you still doing down here anyway. March! Upstairs! (*To Pablo, threateningly, very near:*) I'll teach you to do that again!

DWARF (*giggling*): He's just not quite right, that Pablo!

MAGICIAN: He was never quite right. He always wanted to leave.

PABLO: Yes. . . . I always wanted to leave. . . .

DWARF: He hasn't been quite right since that time he got a widdle bumpy-do on his widdle head. . . .

PABLO (*startled*): What—what was that?

MAGICIAN: Nothing—absolutely nothing.

PABLO: Yes—you said something. What was it?

DWARF: I said bump—a widdle bumpy-do on the head!

MAGICIAN: Go away now!

(*The Dwarf giggles.*)

PABLO (*gradually remembering something*): Yes . . .

MAGICIAN: It was absolutely nothing—you fell down once. . . .

PABLO: That's right. . . . It was outside, too. . . . Outside on the street. . . . I was outside. . . .

MAGICIAN: Now just where did you get that idea!

PABLO: Yes. . . . I *have* been outside. . . . Once before. . . . Down there in the street. . . .

MAGICIAN: Really now!

PABLO: Yes . . . I ran . . . I ran and I came out . . . down in the street . . . but I wasn't quite fast enough . . . you came after me . . . Yes . . . I *was* outside . . . Yes . . . I am outside . . . it wasn't that time when I tried to escape with the lion . . . it was even before that . . . long before that . . . yes . . . I know now . . . I escaped once before. . . .

MAGICIAN: You're imagining things! . . .

PABLO: No . . . I've always seemed to know . . . just how it was outside . . . yes . . . it was at night . . . the wet streets . . . the large windows right and left . . . those gigantic vehicles . . . those big masts . . . I run incredibly fast . . . but not fast enough . . . You come after me and chase me . . . you catch up with me . . . yes . . . and then the blow. . . ,

DWARF: A widdle bumpy-do!

MAGICIAN: He doesn't have the remotest idea of what he's talking about. . . .

PABLO: Yes—now I understand it. Now, finally, I see everything perfectly clearly. Now I can see this tower. And I *was* outside. I know how it is outside now. In here everything is unchangeable. Coming in here was like falling down a well. This foul, sealed-up air in here! No window! Even the trapdoors in the attic locked tight. Now I can see this tower from within. Now I recognize it for what it is—and now I know that I can escape.

MAGICIAN: You're not outside yet!

PABLO: I'll get outside!

MAGICIAN: You'll have to prove it first. We haven't tied you up yet. And we *are* going to tie you up, my boy. Tonight we're going to tie you up as you've never been tied up before!

DWARF (*keeping the rhythm with his bells*): Yes, we're going to tie you up, we're going to tie you up!

MAGICIAN: Rest. Collect your strength. You'll need it tonight. Rest just as much as you can.

(*The surging sound returns within the tower. The clock ticks.*)

MAGICIAN (*monotonously, hypnotically*): Listen to the way the clock ticks . . . how time flows away from you . . . and you sit here weakly and wearily . . . listening to endless time . . . hours . . . days . . . months . . . years . . . this is where you've always sat and waited . . . and you wanted so badly to get out . . . and you never got out . . . and there you sit with your rope now . . . time rushing away under your feet . . . you'll never succeed . . . soon we're going to tie you up . . . we'll wrap you up in the rope . . . we'll lace in your chest . . . you'll never get out . . . and we're going to throw the rope over you to begin with right now . . . please pull your shirt up so its easier to tie you up . . . that's right . . . and now let's begin . . . listen. . . . (*A great buzzing of voices is heard, the sound of feet shuffling.*) Look! The arena's full—we're sold out tonight. All those faces and hands. . . .

DIRECTOR (*excitedly*): Are you ready? We're starting now! (*The voices grow louder. A drumroll begins. Applause. Then a trumpet joins the drum for a fanfare. The drum continues to roll mutedly, behind the words of the Director:*) Ladies and gentlemen!

(*A trumpet-like voice echoes with his words:*)

TRUMPET: Ladies and gentlemen!

DIRECTOR: Allow me to present!

TRUMPET: Allow—present!

DIRECTOR: Niente the Escape Artist!

TRUMPET: Niente—Escape Artist!

(*Applause. Whistling. Stamping of feet.*)

DIRECTOR: You are about to see him tightly bound!

TRUMPET: Bound!

DIRECTOR: From head to foot!

TRUMPET: Head—foot!

DIRECTOR: With this very rope!

TRUMPET: Rope!

DIRECTOR: From which he will free himself!

TRUMPET: Free himself!

DIRECTOR: Without any outside help whatsoever!

TRUMPET: Help whatsoever!

DIRECTOR: The Magician and the Dwarf!

TRUMPET: Magician—Dwarf!

DIRECTOR: Our trusty assistants!

TRUMPET: Assistants!

DIRECTOR: Will now begin the binding!

TRUMPET: Binding!

    (*Applause.*)

DIRECTOR: Please, ladies and gentlemen, absolute silence!

TRUMPET: Silence!

    (*Loud drumroll. Groaning sounds. A dull thud. Moanings, gruntings. Pause. The restrained drumroll continues.*)

MANAGERESS (*anxiously*): That's completely impossible. He'll never get out of that.

DIRECTOR: That rope's going right through his skin.

MANAGERESS: It's getting tighter around his neck!

DIRECTOR: Tsk tsk—what a shame!

MANAGERESS: He should have balanced on the ball, after all.

PABLO (*straining violently*): I need more time!

DIRECTOR (*stepping forward*): Please—ladies and gentlemen!

TRUMPET: Ladies and gentlemen!

DIRECTOR: A moment's patience!

TRUMPET: Patience!

    (*Loud drumroll.*)

PABLO (*whispering*): I need more time!

DIRECTOR (*whispering*): Remember our reputations!

MANAGERESS (*whispering*): Spare us from shame!

PABLO: I'm going to need more time. . . .

DIRECTOR (*stepping forward*): Ladies and gentlemen!

TRUMPET: Ladies and gentlemen!

DIRECTOR: Rest assured!

TRUMPET: Assured!

DIRECTOR: That this gentleman is doing his very best!

TRUMPET: Very best!

> (*Loud drumroll. Murmuring of voices. Laughter. Scattered whistling.*)

PABLO: More time!

MAGICIAN (*very near—whispering*): You *have* time . . . unlimited time! The entire tower is full of time just for you!

PABLO: Let me lie here a moment. Announce the next number!

DIRECTOR (*nervously*): Ladies and gentlemen!

TRUMPET: Ladies and gentlemen!

DIRECTOR: Please—may I humbly beg your indulgence!

TRUMPET: Indulgence!

DIRECTOR: And meanwhile we present—the extraordinary Carlo!

TRUMPET: Carlo!

> (*Drum and trumpet fanfare. Applause. Whistling.*)

DIRECTOR: In a pantomime!

TRUMPET: Pantomime!

DIRECTOR: His dance expresses the most genuine, deeply experienced feelings!

TRUMPET: Feelings!

DIRECTOR: First: Love!

TRUMPET: Love!

(Drum, trumpet, xylophone and gong intone a trembling, wavering music.)

MAGICIAN *(near—whispering)*: See how he quakes, he faints with love . . . how he clasps the air and dreams of his dear Nelly . . . how he twists and turns . . . how he distorts his face . . . how desperately he looks for his love . . . but here there is no love . . . now he wriggles like a worm on a fish-hook . . . he wriggles just like you wriggle, Pablo . . . and he'll never get free. . . .

(The music dies away.)

DIRECTOR: And next! Fear!

TRUMPET: Fear!

(The instruments strike up again: scraping, scratching, grinding, squeaking.)

MAGICIAN *(whispering)*: See how he comes creeping along . . . how he darts back and forth looking for his rat hole . . . what's he afraid of? . . . what? . . . what are you afraid of there . . .

A VOICE *(suddenly firmly, strongly—echoing loudly)*: Pablo— you're free! You must get out of that rope now!

PABLO *(wailing)*: I need more time!

(The squeaking music fades away.)

DIRECTOR: And now, for the finale: Humility!

(The music of the instruments is whining, wavering.)

MAGICIAN *(whispering)*: Look how he kisses the ground . . . how he wrings his hands . . . ah . . . he's completely at home now . . . he licks the very floor out of submission . . . you too . . . you kiss the very floor too . . . our good old stone floor here. . . .

A VOICE *(as before)*: Pablo! You must escape now! You're free!

(The music fades. Applause. Fanfare. Then drum and trumpet begin once more.)

DIRECTOR: Ladies and gentlemen!

TRUMPET: Ladies and gentlemen!

DIRECTOR: While our escape artist gathers all his strength for the finale!

TRUMPET: For the finale!

DIRECTOR: Our worthy shadow duelist!

TRUMPET: Shadow duelist!

DIRECTOR: In a duel with himself!

TRUMPET: With himself!

(*Applause. Loud drumming.*)

DIRECTOR: Observe!

TRUMPET: Observe!

DIRECTOR: Several brand-new passes!

TRUMPET: Passes!

DIRECTOR: Parries!

TRUMPET: Parries!

(*Over the drumroll, powerful clashing sounds.*)

MAGICIAN (*hurriedly, like an announcer again—with the drumming and clashing behind him*): The strugglings of the escape artist continue without pause, he is still heavily bound by the rope, his very flesh is lacerated and torn, the sign of superhuman strain is written on his face; but yet he does not relent, still he strives to force his bonds. Anxiously we wonder how long he can go on enduring this, the veins on his forehead are swollen as if about to burst, he's bathed in sweat, his heart beats wildly. . . .

(*Several whizzing whip-like sword strokes. Fanfare. Applause.*)

DIRECTOR (*dashing out*): Ladies and gentlemen!

TRUMPET: Ladies and gentlemen!

MAGICIAN (*in the background, murmuring low*): An incredible struggle . . .

DIRECTOR: After the triumphal victory of the shadow duelist over himself—

MAGICIAN (*continuing in the background*): Powers of an unsuspected strength have kept him helplessly bound . . .

DIRECTOR: As a final prelude to the unchaining act—

(*Suddenly a confused mixture of carousel music, fanfares, voices singing, bells, car horns, motor rumblings, all burst into the room.*)

MANAGERESS (*screams*): The door—the door is open!

MAGICIAN: The door . . .

PABLO: The world outside . . .

DIRECTOR: Who opened that door?!

A VOICE (*above the flow of sound from outside*): Pablo, you're free!

MANAGERESS: Carlo! Carlo's running out! Carlo!

PABLO: Carlo's free . . .

DIRECTOR: Carlo!

MANAGERESS: Carlo's outside!

DIRECTOR: Stop him!

PABLO: Someone always ends up by breaking out. . . .

MAGICIAN: Someone always ends up coming back again. . . .

A VOICE (*a step above all the other sounds*): You're free, Pablo!

(*The door closes noisily; slams. Silence. Then the drum begins a fresh tattooing:*)

DIRECTOR (*exhausted*): Ladies and gentlemen!

(*The trumpet sounds a single monotonous note.*)

MAGICIAN (*resuming his narration*): He strains himself to the maximum, to the utmost limit of exertion—even now drops of blood are falling around him. . . .

DIRECTOR (*breathlessly*): Now let us proceed to the next number—

(*The trumpet sounds a long extended tone.*)

MAGICIAN (*during the trumpet blast*): Now finally he seems to have realized the uselessness of his efforts. . . .

DIRECTOR (*hardly able to gasp out the words*): The lion tamer in her virtuoso, breathtaking, animal-training number!

(*The trumpet plays a series of monotonous, much-extended tones.*)

(*The Magician murmurs on unintelligibly.*)

(*The trumpet calls like a distress signal; the SOS is submerged, then gradually returns to the surface.*)

(*Sound of the Lion Tamer's whip. Cries of "Hey!" "Let's go!" "On your feet!" "Let's see what you can do!" Humming of voices. Excited calls. Then everything is submerged again, as if beneath a wave. Applause.*)

PABLO (*very near; whispering*): The pier . . . the shore . . . the sea . . . I'm outside . . . I'm in the open air . . . Now I overcome the tower . . . I overcome it now. . . .

MAGICIAN (*his voice heard above the general uproar—he speaks haltingly, gropingly, uncertainly*): To our utter amazement we see that he has managed to stand up. But this must be the last gasp—just a reflex action. In another minute he'll collapse completely. . . . No, no, this isn't the way it's supposed to happen. . . .

(*His voice becomes indistinct. The roaring begins to rise. The whip cracks.*)

PABLO: The whip doesn't even graze me . . . nothing here can touch me anymore . . . I'm free. . . .

MAGICIAN (*on the point of collapse*): The rope around his chest loosens . . . his arms burst free . . . and now . . .

(*The roaring increases. Confused voices. Clock-ticks. Drum-rolls.*)

DIRECTOR (*drowning*): The traditions of the tower . . .

DWARF (*drowning*): Taradition, taradition . . .

MANAGERESS (*drowning*): Pablo . . . Carlo . . . Nelly . . .

MAGICIAN (*drowning*): Now he emerges . . . he rises . . .

PABLO: The tower . . . O where is the tower . . .

(*Once more the great, swelling roar. Then silence.*)

A VOICE (*very slowly, matter-of-factly, cool*): The rope dangles down from him now like an umbilical cord. . . .